THE top10★ OF EVERYTHING 2001

THE top10
OF EVERYTHING
2001

RUSSELL ASH

A Dorling Kindersley Book

Contents

Dorling DK Kindersley

LONDON, NEW YORK, SYDNEY, DELHI,
PARIS, MUNICH, and JOHANNESBURG

Project Editor David Tombesi-Walton
Senior Designer Tracy Hambleton-Miles

DTP Designer Jason Little
Production Silvia La Greca, Elizabeth Cherry
Picture Research Anna Grapes

Managing Editor Stephanie Jackson
Managing Art Editor Nigel Duffield

Produced for Dorling Kindersley by
Cooling Brown, 9–11 High Street,
Hampton, Middlesex TW12 2SA

Editor Alison Bolus
Designers Tish Mills, Elaine Hewson
Creative Director Arthur Brown

Author's Research Manager Aylla Macphail

First American Edition, 2000
00 01 02 03 04 05 10 9 8 7 6 5 4 3 2 1

Published in the United States by Dorling Kindersley Publishing, Inc.,
95 Madison Avenue, New York, New York 10016

Copyright © 2000 Dorling Kindersley Limited
Text copyright © 2000 Russell Ash

DK Publishing offers special discounts for bulk purchases for sales promotions
or premiums. Specific, large-quantity needs can be met with special editions,
including personalized covers, excerpts of existing guides, and corporate imprints.
For more information, contact Special Markets Department, Dorling Kindersley
Publishing Inc., 95 Madison Avenue, New York, NY 10016 Fax: 800-600-9098.

Library of Congress Cataloging-in-Publication Data
Ash, Russell.
    The Top 10 of everything 2001 / Russell Ash. -- 1st American ed.
    p. cm.
    ISBN 0-7894-5960-4 (hardcover). -- ISBN 0-7894-6132-3 (pbk.)
    1. Curiosities and wonders. 2. World records--Miscellanea.
I. Title. II. Title: Top ten of everything 2001.
AG243.A69   2000
031.02--dc21   2000-23292
                                            CIP

Reproduction by Colourpath, London
Printed and bound by Printer Barcelona, Spain

See our complete catalog at
www.dk.com

THE YEAR 2000

Introduction

Looking Back

This is the 12th annual edition of *The Top 10 of Everything* and the first to be published in the new century and the new millennium. We start with a look back at the 20th century in A Century of Change before moving on to chart many of the developments of the 1990s.

Information Overload?

The Internet is a mixed blessing: on the one hand, it gives increased access to information, especially official figures; on the other, we are increasingly overwhelmed by the sheer volume of data. Perhaps today more than ever the value of *The Top 10 of Everything* is that it distills down all this available information to a manageable level, which is why, despite the Internet, books like this still have a place.

Listomania

During the past dozen years, the number of published lists has increased inexorably, and the 20th century ended with a tidal wave of lists of the best movies, books, and recordings of all time. Scarcely a day goes by when I am not inspired with an idea for a new list, such as the top advertising campaigns, leading fat consumers, latest assassinated monarchs, deadliest serial killers, fastest roller coasters, largest mollusks, and champion cowboys, as featured here.

Not Just the Best

The book focuses on superlatives in numerous categories and also contains a variety of "firsts" or "latests," which recognize the pioneers and the most recent achievers in various fields of endeavor. Lists of movies are based on worldwide box-office income, and those on recorded music, videos, and books are based on sales, unless otherwise stated.

History in the Making

The Top 10 of Everything now spans three decades and has become a historical resource. Schools use back numbers when undertaking projects on social changes, while others buy *Top 10* to commemorate births and other family events, as a "time capsule" of the year.

A Never-ending Task

While I endeavor to ensure that all the information is as up to date as possible, certain statistics are slow to be collated and published. At the same time, lists relating to bestsellers and sporting achievements can change almost daily. Even lists that one would not expect to alter do: a revised height for Everest was published while I was at work on this book.

The Research Network

Compiling *The Top 10 of Everything* has been a pleasure and a revelation to me: in the course of my work on it and the associated television series, and through publicity tours in the UK and US, I have discovered numerous interesting facts, increased my library, and, in particular, met many people who have become consultants on the book. My thanks to all of them and to everyone who has contacted me with helpful information.

Keep in touch

If you have any list ideas or comments, please write to me c/o the publishers or email me direct at ash@pavilion.co.uk.

Other Dorling Kindersley books by Russell Ash:
The Factastic Book of Comparisons
The Factastic Book of 1,001 Lists
Factastic Millennium Facts
Great Wonders of the World

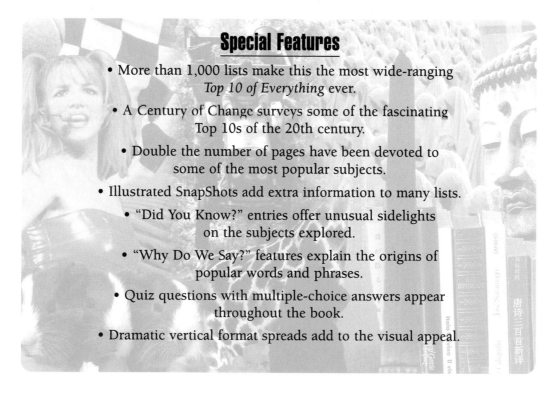

Special Features

- More than 1,000 lists make this the most wide-ranging *Top 10 of Everything* ever.

- A Century of Change surveys some of the fascinating Top 10s of the 20th century.

- Double the number of pages have been devoted to some of the most popular subjects.

- Illustrated SnapShots add extra information to many lists.

- "Did You Know?" entries offer unusual sidelights on the subjects explored.

- "Why Do We Say?" features explain the origins of popular words and phrases.

- Quiz questions with multiple-choice answers appear throughout the book.

- Dramatic vertical format spreads add to the visual appeal.

TOP 10 ★ MOST HIGHLY POPULATED COUNTRIES, 1900–2000

	1900	1950	2000
1	China	China	China
2	India	India	India
3	Russia	USSR	US
4	US	US	Indonesia
5	Germany	Japan	Brazil
6	Austria	Indonesia	Russia
7	Japan	Germany	Pakistan
8	UK	UK	Bangladesh
9	Turkey	Brazil	Japan
10	France	Italy	Nigeria

TEEMING MILLIONS

China began the 20th century with some 400 million inhabitants and ended it with 1.2 billion, about one-fifth of the world's population.

TOP 10 ★ MOST HIGHLY POPULATED CITIES, 1900

	CITY/LOCATION	POPULATION*
1	**London**, UK	6,581,000
2	**New York**, US	3,437,000
3	**Paris**, France	2,714,000
4	**Berlin**, Germany	1,889,000
5	**Chicago**, US	1,699,000
6	**Vienna**, Austria	1,675,000
7	**Wuhan**, China	1,500,000
8	**Tokyo**, Japan	1,440,000
9	**Philadelphia**, US	1,294,000
10	**St. Petersburg**, Russia	1,265,000

* Including adjacent suburban areas

Censuses and population estimates conducted around 1900 indicated that these cities, plus just three others (Constantinople in Turkey, Moscow in Russia, and Xian in China), were the only ones with populations in excess of 1 million. As we enter the 21st century, there are over 400 world cities with million-plus populations.

★ A CENTURY OF SPEED: THE PROGRESSION OF THE LAND SPEED RECORD

DECADE*	DRIVER	COUNTRY	SPEED MPH	SPEED KM/H
1900	Camille Jenatzy	Belgium	65.792	105.882
1910	Barney Oldfield	US	131.275	211.267
1920	Tommy Milton	US	155.343	250.000
1930	Henry Segrave	UK	231.567	372.671
1940	John Cobb	UK	369.741	595.041
1950	John Cobb	UK	393,827	633.803
1960	Mickey Thompson	US	406,600	654.359#
1970	Gary Gabelich	US	630,389	1,014.513
1980	Gary Gabelich	US	630,389	1,014.513
1990	Richard Noble	UK	634.052	1,020.408
2000	Andy Green	UK	763.035	1,227.985

* As of the first year of each decade

 # Based on flying mile; all others over flying km

A CENTURY OF US POPULATION

(Year/population)

1900 75,994,575 **1910** 91,972,266 **1920** 105,710,620
1930 122,775,046 **1940** 131,669,275 **1950** 150,697,361
1960 179,323,175 **1970** 203,302,031 **1980** 226,542,199
1990 248,709,873 **2000*** 274,634,000

* Estimated

The greatest rate of increase in the US population within a decade occurred not in this century but in the first decade of the 19th century, when it expanded by 36.4 percent. The lowest growth rate during the past 200 years was registered in the 1930s, at just 7.2 percent.

A CENTURY OF UK POPULATION

(Year/population)

1901 38,237,000 **1911** 42,082,000 **1921*** 44,027,000
1931* 46,038,000 **1941** 48,216,000 **1951** 50,225,000
1961 52,709,000 **1971** 55,928,000 **1981** 56,352,000
1991 57,808,000, **2001#** 59,994,000

* Figures for Northern Ireland estimated

 # Estimated

Did You Know? United Nations estimates for world population in 2050 predict a 50 percent increase on today's 6 billion, bringing the total to about 9 billion.

TOP 10 ★
MOST EXPENSIVE MOVIES OF THE 20TH CENTURY

	DECADE	MOVIE/YEAR	COST $
1	1900–09	*For the Term of His Natural Life** (1908)	34,000
2	1910–19	*A Daughter of the Gods* (1916)	1,000,000
3	1920–29	*Ben-Hur* (1925)	3,900,000
4	1930–39	*Gone With the Wind* (1939)	4,250,000
5	1940–49	*Joan of Arc* (1948)	8,700,000
6	1950–59	*Ben-Hur* (1959)	15,000,000
7	1960–69	*Cleopatra* (1963)	44,000,000
8	1970–79	*Superman* (1978)	55,000,000
9	1980–89	*Who Framed Roger Rabbit* (1988)	70,000,000
10	1990–99	*Titanic* (1997)	200,000,000

* *Australian; all others US*

FRANKLY, MY DEAR...
Gone With the Wind, *starring Clark Gable and Vivien Leigh, was the most expensive movie ever made, allowing for inflation. It was also the most successful.*

TOP 10 ★
SUCCESSIVE HOLDERS OF THE TITLE "WORLD'S TALLEST HABITABLE BUILDING" IN THE 20TH CENTURY

	BUILDING/LOCATION	YEAR	STORIES	FT	M
1	**City Hall**, Philadelphia	1901	7	511	155
2	**Singer Building***, New York	1908	34	656	200
3	**Metropolitan Life**, New York	1909	50	700	212
4	**Woolworth Building**, New York	1913	59	792	241
5	**40 Wall Street**, New York with spire	1929	71	854 / 927	260 / 282
6	**Chrysler Building**, New York with spire	1930	77	925 / 1,046	282 / 319
7	**Empire State Building**, New York with spire	1931	102	1,250 / 1,472	381 / 449
8	**World Trade Center**, New York with spire	1973	110	1,362 / 1,710	415 / 521
9	**Sears Tower**, Chicago with spires	1974	110	1,454 / 1,707	443 / 520
10	**Petronas Towers**, Kuala Lumpur, Malaysia	1996	96	1,482	452

* *Demolished 1970*

UNBEATEN CITY HALL
Once the world's tallest building, Philadelphia City Hall remains the largest and most expensive municipal building in the US.

The Universe & The Earth

Star Gazing

TOP 10 STARS NEAREST TO THE EARTH*

	STAR	LIGHT YEARS	MILES (MILLIONS)	KM (MILLIONS)
1	Proxima Centauri	4.22	24,792,500	39,923,310
2	Alpha Centauri	4.35	25,556,250	41,153,175
3	Barnard's Star	5.98	35,132,500	56,573,790
4	Wolf 359	7.75	45,531,250	73,318,875
5	Lalande 21185	8.22	48,292,500	77,765,310
6	Luyten 726-8	8.43	49,526,250	79,752,015
7	Sirius	8.65	50,818,750	81,833,325
8	Ross 154	9.45	55,518,750	89,401,725
9	Ross 248	10.40	61,100,000	98,389,200
10	Epsilon Eridani	10.80	63,450,000	102,173,400

* Excluding the Sun

A spaceship traveling at 25,000 mph (40,237 km/h) – which is faster than any human has yet reached in space – would take more than 113,200 years to reach the Earth's closest star, Proxima Centauri. While the nearest stars in this list lie just over four light years away from the Earth, others within the Milky Way lie at a distance of 2,500 light years.

CLOSE TO THE EARTH

The name of Proxima Centauri, a red dwarf star in the constellation of Centaurus, literally means "nearest of Centaurus," and it is indeed the Earth's closest star beyond the Sun.

TOP 10 ★
BODIES FARTHEST FROM THE SUN*

	BODY	AVERAGE DISTANCE FROM THE SUN MILES	KM
1	Pluto	3,675,000,000	5,914,000,000
2	Neptune	2,794,000,000	4,497,000,000
3	Uranus	1,784,000,000	2,871,000,000
4	Chiron	1,740,000,000	2,800,000,000
5	Saturn	887,000,000	1,427,000,000
6	Jupiter	483,600,000	778,300,000
7	Mars	141,600,000	227,900,000
8	Earth	92,900,000	149,600,000
9	Venus	67,200,000	108,200,000
10	Mercury	36,000,000	57,900,000

* In the Solar System, excluding satellites and asteroids

Chiron, a "mystery object" which may be either a comet or an asteroid, was discovered on November 1, 1977, by American astronomer Charles Kowal. It measures 124–186 miles (200–300 km) in diameter.

AMERICAN DISCOVERY

The Solar System's smallest planet, Pluto, found in 1930, is the only planet to have been discovered by an American – Clyde Tombaugh.

TOP 10 ★
BRIGHTEST STARS*

	STAR/CONSTELLATION	APPARENT MAGNITUDE[#]
1	**Sirius**, Canis Major	-1.46
2	**Canopus**, Carina	-0.73
3	**Alpha Centauri**, Centaurus	-0.27
4	**Arcturus**, Boötes	-0.04
5	**Vega**, Lyra	+0.03
6	**Capella**, Auriga	+0.08
7	**Rigel**, Orion	+0.12
8	**Procyon**, Canis Minor	+0.38
9	**Achernar**, Eridanus	+0.46
10	**Beta Centauri**, Centaurus	+0.61

* Excluding the Sun

 # Based on apparent visual magnitude as viewed from the Earth – the lower the number, the brighter the star

At its brightest, the star Betelgeuse is brighter than some of these, but its variability disqualifies it from the Top 10. More distant stars naturally appear fainter. To compensate for this effect, absolute magnitude estimates the brightness of a star at an imaginary fixed distance of 10 parsecs, or 32.6 light years, enabling comparison between the "true" brightness of different stars.

RINGS OF ICE
Saturn's ring system was not discovered until 1656. Composed of ice, the rings are up to 167,770 miles (270,000 km) in diameter.

TOP 10 ★
LARGEST BODIES IN THE SOLAR SYSTEM

	BODY	MAXIMUM DIAMETER MILES	KM
1	**Sun**	865,036	1,392,140
2	**Jupiter**	88,846	142,984
3	**Saturn**	74,898	120,536
4	**Uranus**	31,763	51,118
5	**Neptune**	30,778	49,532
6	**Earth**	7,926	12,756
7	**Venus**	7,520	12,103
8	**Mars**	4,222	6,794
9	**Ganymede**	3,274	5,269
10	**Titan**	3,200	5,150

Most of the planets are visible with the naked eye and have been observed since ancient times. The exceptions are Uranus, discovered on March 13, 1781 by British astronomer Sir William Herschel; Neptune, found by German astronomer Johann Galle on September 23, 1846; and, outside the Top 10, Pluto, located using photographic techniques by American astronomer Clyde Tombaugh. Its discovery was announced on March 13, 1930; its diameter is uncertain but is thought to be about 1,430 miles (2,302 km).

TOP 10 ★
LONGEST DAYS IN THE SOLAR SYSTEM

	BODY	LENGTH OF DAY* DAYS	HOURS	MINS
1	**Venus**	244	0	0
2	**Mercury**	58	14	0
3	**Sun**	25[#]	0	0
4	**Pluto**	6	9	0
5	**Mars**		24	37
6	**Earth**		23	56
7	**Uranus**		17	14
8	**Neptune**		16	7
9	**Saturn**		10	39
10	**Jupiter**		9	55

* Period of rotation, based on 23-hour, 56-minute sidereal day

 # Variable

TOP 10 ★
GALAXIES NEAREST TO THE EARTH

	GALAXY	DISTANCE LIGHT YEARS
1	**Large Cloud of Magellan**	169,000
2	**Small Cloud of Magellan**	190,000
3	**Ursa Minor dwarf**	250,000
4	**Draco dwarf**	260,000
5	**Sculptor dwarf**	280,000
6	**Fornax dwarf**	420,000
7 =	**Leo I dwarf**	750,000
=	**Leo II dwarf**	750,000
9	**Barnard's Galaxy**	1,700,000
10	**Andromeda Spiral**	2,200,000

These and other galaxies are members of the so-called "Local Group," although with vast distances such as these, "local" is a relative term.

TOP 10 ★
MOST MASSIVE BODIES IN THE SOLAR SYSTEM*

	BODY	MASS[#]
1	**Sun**	332,800.000
2	**Jupiter**	317.828
3	**Saturn**	95.161
4	**Neptune**	17.148
5	**Uranus**	14.536
6	**Earth**	1.000
7	**Venus**	0.815
8	**Mars**	0.10745
9	**Mercury**	0.05527
10	**Pluto**	0.0022

* Excluding satellites

 # Compared with the Earth = 1; the mass of the Earth is approximately 80 million trillion tons

When was Halley's Comet last seen? A 1976
see p.14 for the answer B 1986
C 1996

Asteroids, Meteorites & Comets

MOST RECENT OBSERVATIONS
OF HALLEY'S COMET

1 1986
The Japanese Suisei probe passed within 93,827 miles (151,000 km) of its 9-mile (15-km) nucleus on March 8, 1986, revealing a whirling nucleus within a hydrogen cloud emitting 20–50 tons of water per second. The Soviet probes Vega 1 and Vega 2 passed within 5,524 miles (8,890 km) and 4,990 miles (8,030 km) respectively. The European Space Agency's Giotto passed as close as 370 miles (596 km) on March 14 of the same year. All were heavily battered by dust particles, and it was concluded that Halley's comet is composed of dust bonded by water and carbon dioxide ice.

2 1910
Predictions of disaster were widely published, with many people convinced that the world would come to an end. Mark Twain, who had been born at the time of the 1835 appearance and who believed that his fate was linked to that of the comet, died when it reappeared in this year.

3 1835
Widely observed but noticeably dimmer than in 1759.

4 1759
The comet's first return, as predicted by Halley, thus proving his calculations correct.

5 1682
Observed in Africa and China and extensively in Europe, where it was observed on September 5–19 by Edmund Halley, who predicted its return.

6 1607
Seen extensively in China, Japan, Korea, and Europe, described by German astronomer Johannes Kepler and its position accurately measured by amateur Welsh astronomer Thomas Harriot.

7 1531
Observed in China, Japan, Korea, and in Europe on August 13–23 by Peter Appian, German geographer and astronomer, who noted that comets' tails point away from the Sun.

8 1456
Observed in China, Japan, Korea, and by the Turkish army, which was threatening to invade Europe. When the Turks were defeated by Papal forces, it was seen as a portent of the latter's victory.

9 1378
Observed in China, Japan, Korea, and Europe.

10 1301
Seen in Iceland, parts of Europe, China, Japan, and Korea.

Before Edmund Halley (1656–1742) studied and foretold the return of the famous comet that now bears his name, no one had succeeded in proving that comets travel in predictable orbits. The dramatic return in 1759 of the comet Halley had observed in 1682 established the science of cometary observation. There have been about 30 recorded appearances of Halley's comet. The most famous occurred in 1066, when William of Normandy (later known as William the Conqueror) regarded it as a sign of his imminent victory over King Harold at the Battle of Hastings; it is clearly shown in the Bayeux Tapestry.

TOP 10 MOST FREQUENTLY
SEEN COMETS
(Comet/years between appearances)

❶ Encke, 3.302 ❷ Grigg-Skjellerup, 4.908
❸ Honda-Mrkós-Pajdusáková, 5.210 ❹ Tempel 2, 5.259
❺ Neujmin 2, 5.437 ❻ Brorsen, 5.463
❼ Tuttle-Giacobini-Kresák, 5.489 ❽ Tempel-L. Swift, 5.681
❾ Tempel 1, 5.982 ❿ Pons-Winnecke, 6.125

COMETS COMING
CLOSEST TO THE EARTH

	COMET	DATE*	DISTANCE AU#
1	Lexell	July 1, 1770	2.3
2	Tempel-Tuttle	Oct 26, 1366	3.4
3	Halley	Apr 10, 837	5.0
4	Biela	Dec 9, 1805	5.5
5	Grischow	Feb 8, 1743	5.8
6	Pons-Winnecke	June 26, 1927	5.9
7	La Hire	Apr 20, 1702	6.6
8	Schwassmann-Wachmann	May 31, 1930	9.3
9	Cassini	Jan 8, 1760	10.2
10	Schweizer	Apr 29, 1853	12.6

* Of closest approach to the Earth

Astronomical Units: 1 AU = mean distance from the Earth to the Sun (92,955,900 miles/149,598,200 km)

ROCK OF AGES

Visitors are encouraged to touch the 11-ft (3.4-m) Ahnighito, the largest meteorite on public display, and to appreciate that it is as old as the Solar System – some 4.5 billion years.

THE 10 ★
FIRST ASTEROIDS TO BE DISCOVERED

	ASTEROID/DISCOVERER	DISCOVERED
1	**Ceres**, Giuseppe Piazzi	Jan 1, 1801
2	**Pallas**, Heinrich Olbers	Mar 28, 1802
3	**Juno**, Karl Ludwig Harding	Sep 1, 1804
4	**Vesta**, Heinrich Olbers	Mar 29, 1807
5	**Astraea**, Karl Ludwig Hencke	Dec 8, 1845
6	**Hebe**, Karl Ludwig Hencke	July 1, 1847
7	**Iris**, John Russell Hind	Aug 13, 1847
8	**Flora**, John Russell Hind	Oct 18, 1847
9	**Metis**, Andrew Graham	Apr 25, 1848
10	**Hygeia**, Annibale de Gasparis	Apr 12, 1849

Asteroids, sometimes known as "minor planets," are fragments of rock orbiting between Mars and Jupiter. There are perhaps 45,000 of them, but fewer than 10 percent have been named.

ASTEROIDS

Since the discovery of Ceres, the first and largest asteroid, over 6,000 have been found, 26 of them larger than 120 miles (200 km) in diameter. Gaspra, pictured here, measures only 12 x 7 miles (20 x 12 km), but was closely studied by the *Galileo* spacecraft in 1991. The total mass of all the asteroids is less than that of the Moon. It is believed that, on average, one asteroid larger than ¼ mile (0.4 km) strikes the Earth every 50,000 years. As recently as 1994, a small asteroid with the temporary designation 1994XM, measuring a modest 33 ft (18 m) in diameter, came within 69,594 miles (112,600 km) of the Earth – making it the closest recorded near-miss.

SNAP SHOTS

TOP 10 ★
LARGEST METEORITES EVER FOUND

	SITE/LOCATION	ESTIMATED WEIGHT TONS
1	**Hoba West**, Grootfontein, Namibia	over 60.0
2	**Ahnighito ("The Tent")**, Cape York, West Greenland	57.3
3	**Campo del Cielo**, Argentina	41.4
4	**Canyon Diablo***, Arizona	30.0
5	**Sikhote-Alin**, Russia	27.0
6	**Chupaderos**, Mexico	24.3
7	**Bacuberito**, Mexico	22.0
8	**Armanty**, Western Mongolia	20.0
9	**Mundrabilla#**, Western Australia	17.0
10	**Mbosi**, Tanzania	16.0

* *Formed Meteor Crater; fragmented – total in public collections is around 11.5 tons*

\# *In two parts – 11.5 and 6.1 tons*

The Hoba meteorite was found on a farm in 1920. A 9 x 8 ft (2.73 x 2.43 m) slab, it consists of 82 percent iron and 16 percent nickel. In 1989, 36 Malaysian soldiers with the UN Peacekeeping Force attempted to hack pieces off it as souvenirs, causing an outcry. "The Tent," known by its original Inuit name of Ahnighito, was discovered in 1894 by the American Arctic explorer Admiral Robert Peary. Now in the Hayden Planetarium at the New York Museum of Natural History, it is the largest meteorite in the world on exhibition.

TOP 10 ★
LARGEST METEORITES EVER FOUND IN THE US

	SITE/LOCATION	ESTIMATED WEIGHT TONS
1	**Canyon Diablo***, Arizona	30.00
2	**Willamette**, Oregon	15.00
3	**Old Woman**, California	2.75
4	**Brenham**, Kansas	2.40
5	**Navajo**, Arizona	2.18
6	**Quinn Canyon**, Nevada	1.45
7	**Goose Lake**, California	1.17
8	**Norton County**, Kansas	1.00
9	**Tucson**, Arizona	0.97
10	**Sardis#**, Georgia	0.80

* *Formed Meteor Crater; fragmented – total in public collections is around 11.5 tons*

\# *Now badly corroded*

It has been suggested that the weight of a meteorite discovered at Cosby's Creek, Tennessee, was 0.958 tons, but only 95 kg of it has been accounted for. There are approximately 1,200 meteorites known in the US; by comparison, there have been only 17 definite meteorites found in the UK. The number of meteorites falling has been calculated to amount to some 500 a year across the whole globe, although many fall in the ocean and unpopulated areas, where their descent goes unnoticed. There is no record of anyone being killed by a meteorite.

Did You Know? A car damaged by a 22-lb (10-kg) meteorite in Peekskill, New York, in 1992 was sold to the Montana Meteorite Lab for $69,000 – complete with the meteorite.

Space Firsts

THE 10 ★
FIRST BODIES TO HAVE BEEN VISITED BY SPACECRAFT

	BODY	SPACECRAFT	COUNTRY	YEAR
1	Moon	Pioneer 4	US	1959
2	Venus	Mariner 2	US	1962
3	Mars	Mariner 4	US	1965
4	Sun	Pioneer 5	US	1966
5	Jupiter	Pioneer 10	US	1973
6	Mercury	Mariner 10	US	1974
7	Saturn	Pioneer 11	US	1979
8	Comet Giacobini-Zinner	International Sun–Earth Explorer 3 (International Cometary Explorer)	Europe/US	1985
9	Uranus	Voyager 2	US	1986
10	Halley's Comet	Giotto	Europe	1986

THE 10 ★
FIRST ANIMALS IN SPACE

	NAME/ANIMAL	COUNTRY	DATE
1	Laika, dog	USSR	Nov 3, 1957
2 =	Laska and Benjy, mice	US	Dec 13, 1958
4 =	Able and Baker, female rhesus monkey and female squirrel monkey	US	May 28, 1959
6 =	Otvazhnaya, female Samoyed husky, and an unnamed rabbit	USSR	July 2, 1959
8	Sam, male rhesus monkey	US	Dec 4, 1959
9	Miss Sam, female rhesus monkey	US	Jan 21, 1960
10 =	Belka and Strelka, female Samoyed huskies	USSR	Aug 19, 1960

TOP 10 ★
FIRST WOMEN IN SPACE

	NAME/SPACECRAFT	DATE
1	Valentina V. Tereshkova, Vostok 6	June 16–19, 1963
2	Svetlana Savitskaya, Soyuz T7	Aug 19, 1982
3	Sally K. Ride, Challenger STS-7	June 18–24, 1983
4	Judith A. Resnik, Discovery STS-41-D	Aug 30–Sep 5, 1984
5	Kathryn D. Sullivan, Discovery STS-41-G	Oct 5–13, 1984
6	Anna L. Fisher, Discovery STS-51-A	Nov 8–16, 1984
7	Margaret R. Seddon, Discovery STS-51-D	Apr 12–19, 1985
8	Shannon W. Lucid, Discovery STS-41-G	June 17–24, 1985
9	Bonnie J. Dunbar, Discovery STS-61-A	Oct 30–Nov 6, 1985
10	Mary L. Cleave, Discovery STS-61-B	Nov 26–Dec 3, 1985

On May 18, 1991, Helen Sharman, a 27-year-old chemist, became Britain's first astronaut and the 15th woman in space when she went on a seven-day mission on Soyuz TM12 to the Mir space station.

TOP 10 ★
FIRST MOONWALKERS

	ASTRONAUT/SPACECRAFT	TOTAL EVA* HR:MIN	MISSION DATES
1	Neil A. Armstrong, Apollo 11	2:32	July 16–24, 1969
2	Edwin E. ("Buzz") Aldrin, Apollo 11	2:15	July 16–24, 1969
3	Charles Conrad, Jr., Apollo 12	7:45	Nov 14–24, 1969
4	Alan L. Bean, Apollo 12	7:45	Nov 14–24, 1969
5	Alan B. Shepard, Apollo 14	9:23	Jan 31–Feb 9, 1971
6	Edgar D. Mitchell, Apollo 14	9:23	Jan 31–Feb 9, 1971
7	David R. Scott, Apollo 15	19:08	July 26–Aug 7, 1971
8	James B. Irwin, Apollo 15	18:35	July 26 –Aug 7, 1971
9	John W. Young, Apollo 16	20:14	Apr 16–27, 1972
10	Charles M. Duke, Apollo 16	20:14	Apr 16–27, 1972

* Extra Vehicular Activity (i.e. time spent out of the lunar module on the Moon's surface)

MOON ROCKET

Apollo 11 blasts off from Cape Canaveral on July 16, 1969. Aboard are Americans Neil Armstrong and "Buzz" Aldrin, destined to be the first men to walk on the Moon.

TOP 10 ★
FIRST PEOPLE TO ORBIT THE EARTH

	NAME/SPACECRAFT	COUNTRY OF ORIGIN	DATE
1	**Yuri A. Gagarin**, *Vostok I*	USSR	Apr 12, 1961
2	**Gherman S. Titov**, *Vostok II*	USSR	Aug 6–7, 1961
3	**John H. Glenn**, *Friendship 7*	US	Feb 20, 1962
4	**M. Scott Carpenter**, *Aurora 7*	US	May 24, 1962
5	**Andrian G. Nikolayev**, *Vostok III*	USSR	Aug 11–15, 1962
6	**Pavel R. Popovich**, *Vostok IV*	USSR	Aug 12–15, 1962
7	**Walter M. Schirra**, *Sigma 7*	US	Oct 3, 1962
8	**L. Gordon Cooper**, *Faith 7*	US	May 15–16, 1963
9	**Valeri F. Bykovsky**, *Vostok V*	USSR	June 14–19, 1963
10	**Valentina V. Tereshkova**, *Vostok VI*	USSR	June 16–19, 1963

Yuri Gagarin, at the age of 27, orbited the Earth once, taking 1 hour 48 minutes. Titov, the youngest-ever astronaut at 25 years 329 days, performed 17 orbits during 25 hours. The first American to orbit the Earth, John Glenn, is the oldest on this list at 40; he has since gone on to become the oldest astronaut of all time.

THE 10 ★
FIRST COUNTRIES TO HAVE ASTRONAUTS OR COSMONAUTS IN ORBIT

	COUNTRY/ASTRONAUT OR COSMONAUT	DATE*
1	**USSR**, Yuri A. Gagarin	Apr 12, 1961
2	**US**, John H. Glenn	Feb 20, 1962
3	**Czechoslovakia**, Vladimir Remek	Mar 2, 1978
4	**Poland**, Miroslaw Hermaszewski	June 27, 1978
5	**East Germany**, Sigmund Jahn	Aug 26, 1978
6	**Bulgaria**, Georgi I. Ivanov	Apr 10, 1979
7	**Hungary**, Bertalan Farkas	May 26, 1980
8	**Vietnam**, Pham Tuan	July 23, 1980
9	**Cuba**, Arnaldo T. Mendez	Sep 18, 1980
10	**Mongolia**, Jugderdemidiyn Gurragcha	Mar 22, 1981

* *Of first space entry of a national of that country*

THE 10 ★
FIRST SPACEWALKERS

	ASTRONAUT	SPACECRAFT	EVA* HR:MIN	EVA DATE
1	**Alexei Leonov**	*Voskhod 2*	0:23	Mar 18, 1965
2	**Edward H. White**	*Gemini 4*	0:36	June 3, 1965
3	**Eugene A. Cernan**	*Gemini 9*	2:07	June 3, 1966
4	**Michael Collins**	*Gemini 10*	0:50	July 19, 1966
5	**Richard F. Gordon**	*Gemini 11*	0:33	Sep 13, 1966
6	**Edwin E. ("Buzz") Aldrin**	*Gemini 12*	2:29	Nov 12, 1966
7 =	**Alexei Yeleseyev**	*Soyuz 5*	0:37	Jan 16, 1969
=	**Yevgeny Khrunov**	*Soyuz 5*	0:37	Jan 16, 1969
9 =	**Russell L. Schweickart**	*Apollo 9*	0:46	Mar 6, 1969
=	**David R. Scott**	*Apollo 9*	0:46	Mar 6, 1969

* *Extravehicular Activity*

Leonov's first spacewalk almost ended in disaster when his spacesuit "ballooned" and he was unable to return through the air-lock into the capsule until he had reduced the pressure in his suit to a dangerously low level. Edward H. White was killed in the Apollo spacecraft fire of January 27, 1967.

FIRST IN SPACE

In 1961, Soviet cosmonaut Yuri Gagarin became the first human to enter space and orbit the Earth. His flight aboard Vostok 1 lasted just 108 minutes. After receiving his country's highest honors, Gagarin was killed in a MiG-15 plane crash in 1968.

Space Explorers

In 1995, the US's 100th crewed flight, Atlantis STS-71, linked up with Russian space station Mir for the first time, exchanging astronauts and cosmonauts between the two spacecraft.

TOP 10 ★
MOST EXPERIENCED SPACEMEN*

	SPACEMAN	MISSIONS	TOTAL DURATION OF MISSIONS			
			DAYS	HOURS	MINS	SECS
1	Sergei V. Avdeyev	3	747	14	22	47
2	Valeri V. Polyakov	2	678	16	33	18
3	Anatoli Y. Solovyov	5	651	0	11	25
4	Viktor M. Afanasyev	3	545	2	34	41
5	Musa K. Manarov	2	541	0	29	38
6	Alexander S. Viktorenko	4	489	1	35	17
7	Sergei K. Krikalyov	4#	483	9	37	26
8	Yuri V. Romanenko	3	430	18	21	30
9	Alexander A. Volkov	3	391	11	52	14
10	Vladimir G. Titov	5#	387	0	51	03

* To January 1, 2000

\# Including flights aboard US space shuttles

All the missions listed were undertaken by the USSR (and, latterly, Russia). In recent years, a number of US astronauts have added to their space logs by spending time on board the Russian *Mir* space station, but none has matched the records set by Russian cosmonauts. While Valeri Polyakov holds the record for the longest continuous space flight, Sergei Avdeyev exceeded Polyakov's cumulative record on June 20, 1999, by spending his 679th day in space.

TOP 10 ★
MOST EXPERIENCED SPACEWOMEN*

	SPACEWOMAN#	MISSIONS	TOTAL DURATION OF MISSIONS			
			DAYS	HOURS	MINS	SECS
1	Shannon W. Lucid	5	223	2	52	26
2	Yelena V. Kondakova	2	178	10	41	31
3	Tamara E. Jernigan	5	63	1	25	40
4	Bonnie J. Dunbar	5	50	8	24	44
5	Marsha S. Ivins	4	43	0	27	43
6	Kathryn C. Thornton	4	40	15	15	18
7	Janice E. Voss	4	37	21	10	18
8	Wendy B. Lawrence	3	37	5	23	20
9	Susan J. Helms	3	33	20	16	31
10	Nancy J. Currie	3	30	17	23	46

* To January 1, 2000

\# All US except 2 (Russian)

Shannon Lucid became both America's most experienced astronaut and the world's most experienced female astronaut in 1996. She took off in US space shuttle *Atlantis STS-76* on March 22, and transferred to the Russian *Mir* Space Station, returning on board *Atlantis STS-79* on September 26 after traveling 75.2 million miles (121 million km) in 188 days, 4 hours, 0 minutes, 14 seconds – also a record duration for a single mission by a US astronaut.

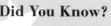

Did You Know? The greatest number of people in space at the same time was 13, when, on March 14, 1995, a space shuttle, a Russian spacecraft, and the *Mir* space station orbited simultaneously.

TOP 10 ★
OLDEST US ASTRONAUTS*

	ASTRONAUT	LAST FLIGHT	AGE#
1	John H. Glenn	Nov 6, 1998	77
2	F. Story Musgrave	Dec 7, 1996	61
3	Vance D. Brand	Dec 11, 1990	59
4	Karl G. Henize	Aug 6, 1985	58
5	Roger K. Crouch	July 17, 1997	56
6	William E. Thornton	May 6, 1985	56
7	Don L. Lind	May 6, 1985	54
8	Henry W. Hartsfield	Nov 6, 1988	54
9	John E. Blaha	Dec 7, 1996	54
10	William G. Gregory	Mar 18, 1995	54

* *Including payload specialists, etc., to January 1, 2000*

\# *Those of apparently identical age have been ranked according to their precise age in days at the time of their last flight.*

At 53, Shannon Lucid (born January 14, 1943, last flight March 31, 1996) holds the record as the oldest woman in space.

TOP 10 ★
YOUNGEST US ASTRONAUTS*

	ASTRONAUT	FIRST FLIGHT	AGE#
1	Kenneth D. Bowersox	June 25, 1984	28
2	Sally K. Ride	June 18, 1983	32
3	Tamara E. Jernigan	June 5, 1991	32
4	Eugene A. Cernan	June 3, 1966	32
5	Koichi Wakata	Jan 11, 1996	32
6	Steven A. Hawley	Aug 30, 1984	32
7	Mary E. Weber	July 13, 1995	32
8	Kathryn D. Sullivan	Oct 5, 1984	33
9	Ronald E. McNair+	Feb 3, 1984	33
10	George D. Nelson	Apr 6, 1984	33

* *To January 1, 2000*

\# *Those of apparently identical age have been ranked according to their precise age in days at the time of their first flight.*

+ *Killed in Challenger disaster, January 28, 1986*

TOP 10 ★
LONGEST SPACE MISSIONS*

	NAME/MISSION DATES	DAYS
1	Valeri V. Polyakov Jan 8, 1994–Mar 22, 1995	437.7
2	Sergei V. Avdeyev Aug 13, 1998–Aug 28, 1999	379.6
3 =	Musa K. Manarov Dec 21, 1987–Dec 21, 1988	365.9
=	Vladimir G. Titov Dec 21, 1987–Dec 21, 1988	365.9
5	Yuri V. Romanenko Feb 5–Dec 5, 1987	326.5
6	Sergei K. Krikalyov May 18, 1991–Mar 25, 1992	311.8
7	Valeri V. Polyakov Aug 31, 1988–Apr 27, 1989	240.9
8 =	Oleg Y. Atkov Feb 8–Oct 2, 1984	237.0
=	Leonid D. Kizim Feb 8–Oct 2, 1984	237.0
=	Anatoli Y. Solovyov Feb 8–Oct 2, 1984	237.0

* *To January 1, 2000*

Space medicine specialist Valeri V. Polyakov (born April 27, 1942) spent his 52nd birthday in space during his record-breaking mission aboard the *Mir* space station.

"ASTRONAUT"

In a pioneering science-fiction novel, *Across the Zodiac*, published in 1880, British writer Percy Greg (1836–89) presented the first fictional account of interplanetary travel by space ship, calling his vessel *Astronaut* (from the Greek for "star sailor"). By the late 1920s, the word had become used to mean a space *traveler*, rather than his ship, and, once the space age began, it was this sense that became established in the West, with cosmonaut as the Russian equivalent. **WHY DO WE SAY?**

SPACE-AGE WOMAN

With three further missions since her first flight aboard Space Shuttle Endeavor STS-57 in 1993, NASA astronaut Janice Voss has earned a place among the world's most experienced spacewomen.

Waterworld

DEEPEST OCEANS AND SEAS

OCEAN OR SEA	GREATEST DEPTH FT	M	AVERAGE DEPTH FT	M
1 Pacific Ocean	35,837	10,924	13,215	4,028
2 Indian Ocean	24,460	7,455	13,002	3,963
3 Atlantic Ocean	30,246	9,219	12,880	3,926
4 Caribbean Sea	22,788	6,946	8,685	2,647
5 South China Sea	16,456	5,016	5,419	1,652
6 Bering Sea	15,659	4,773	5,075	1,547
7 Gulf of Mexico	12,425	3,787	4,874	1,486
8 Mediterranean Sea	15,197	4,632	4,688	1,429
9 Japan Sea	12,276	3,742	4,429	1,350
10 Arctic Ocean	18,456	5,625	3,953	1,205

The deepest point in the deepest ocean is the Marianas Trench in the Pacific at a depth of 35,837 ft (10,924 m). The Pacific is so vast that it contains more water than all the world's other seas and oceans put together.

LONGEST RIVERS

RIVER	LOCATION	LENGTH MIILES	KM
1 Nile	Tanzania/Uganda/Sudan/Egypt	4,145	6,670
2 Amazon	Peru/Brazil	4,007	6,448
3 Yangtze–Kiang	China	3,915	6,300
4 Mississippi–Missouri–Red Rock	US	3,710	5,971
5 Yenisey–Angara–Selenga	Mongolia/Russia	3,442	5,540
6 Huang Ho (Yellow River)	China	3,395	5,464
7 Ob'-Irtysh	Mongolia/Kazakhstan/Russia	3,362	5,410
8 Congo	Angola/Dem. Rep. of Congo	2,920	4,700
9 Lena–Kirenga	Russia	2,734	4,400
10 Mekong	Tibet/China/Myanmar (Burma)/ Laos/Cambodia/Vietnam	2,703	4,350

LONGEST GLACIERS

GLACIER	LOCATION	LENGTH MILES	KM
1 Lambert-Fisher	Antarctica	320	515
2 Novaya Zemlya	Russia	260	418
3 Arctic Institute	Antarctica	225	362
4 Nimrod-Lennox-King	Antarctica	180	290
5 Denman	Antarctica	150	241
6 =Beardmore	Antarctica	140	225
=Recovery	Antarctica	140	225
8 Petermanns	Greenland	124	200
9 Unnamed	Antarctica	120	193
10 Slessor	Antarctica	115	185

LARGEST FRESHWATER LAKES IN THE US*

LAKE	LOCATION	APPROX. AREA SQ MILES	SQ KM
1 Michigan	Illinois/Indiana/ Michigan/Wisconsin	22,400	58,016
2 Iliamna	Alaska	1,000	2,590
3 Okeechobee	Florida	700	1,813
4 Becharof	Alaska	458	1,186
5 Red	Minnesota	451	1,168
6 Teshepuk	Alaska	315	816
7 Naknek	Alaska	242	627
8 Winnebago	Wisconsin	215	557
9 Mille Lacs	Minnesota	207	536
10 Flathead	Montana	197	510

* Excluding those partly in Canada

TOP 10 DEEPEST DEEP-SEA TRENCHES

(Trench/ocean/deepest point in ft/m)

❶ **Marianas**, Pacific, 35,837/10,924 ❷ **Tonga***, Pacific, 35,430/10,800 ❸ **Philippine**, Pacific, 34,436/10,497 ❹ **Kermadec***, Pacific, 32,960/10,047 ❺ **Bonin**, Pacific, 32,786/9,994 ❻ **New Britain**, Pacific, 32,609/9,940 ❼ **Kuril**, Pacific, 31,985/9,750 ❽ **Izu**, Pacific, 31,805/9,695 ❾ **Puerto Rico**, Atlantic, 28,229/8,605 ❿ **Yap**, Pacific, 27,973/8,527

* Some authorities consider these parts of one feature

JUNGLE FEEDER

It was not until 1953 that the source of the Amazon was identifed as a stream called Huarco, flowing from the Misuie glacier in the Peruvian Andes mountains. It joins the Amazon's main tributary at Ucayali, Peru.

TOP 10 ★
COUNTRIES WITH THE GREATEST AREAS OF INLAND WATER

	COUNTRY	PERCENTAGE OF TOTAL AREA	WATER AREA SQ MILES	SQ KM
1	Canada	7.60	291,573	755,170
2	India	9.56	121,391	314,400
3	China	2.82	104,460	270,550
4	US	2.20	79,541	206,010
5	Ethiopia	9.89	46,680	120,900
6	Colombia	8.80	38,691	100,210
7	Indonesia	4.88	35,908	93,000
8	Russia	0.47	30,657	79,400
9	Australia	0.90	26,610	68,920
10	Tanzania	6.25	22,799	59,050

Large areas of some countries are occupied by major rivers and lakes. Lake Victoria, for example, raises the water area of Uganda to 15.39 percent of its total. In Europe, three Scandinavian countries have considerable percentages of water: Sweden 8.68 percent, Finland 9.36 percent, and Norway 5.05 percent.

TOP 10 ★
HIGHEST WATERFALLS

	WATERFALL	LOCATION	TOTAL DROP FT	M
1	Angel	Venezuela	3,212	979*
2	Tugela	South Africa	3,107	947
3	Utigård	Norway	2,625	800
4	Mongefossen	Norway	2,540	774
5	Yosemite	California	2,425	739
6	Østre Mardøla Foss	Norway	2,152	656
7	Tyssestrengane	Norway	2,120	646
8	Cuquenán	Venezuela	2,000	610
9	Sutherland	New Zealand	1,904	580
10	Kjellfossen	Norway	1,841	561

* Longest single drop 2,648 ft (807 m)

FALL AND ANGEL

Angel Falls in Venezuela were discovered in 1933 by American adventurer James Angel, after whom they are named. Their overall height is equivalent to two-and-a-half Empire State Buildings.

TOP 10 ★
DEEPEST FRESHWATER LAKES

	LAKE	LOCATION	GREATEST DEPTH FT	M
1	Baikal	Russia	5,371	1,637
2	Tanganyika	Burundi/Tanzania/Dem. Rep. of Congo/Zambia	4,825	1,471
3	Malawi	Malawi/Mozambique/Tanzania	2,316	706
4	Great Slave	Canada	2,015	614
5	Matana	Celebes, Indonesia	1,936	590
6	Crater	Oregon, US	1,932	589
7	Toba	Sumatra, Indonesia	1,736	529
8	Hornindals	Norway	1,686	514
9	Sarez	Tajikistan	1,657	505
10	Tahoe	California/Nevada, US	1,645	501

TOP 10 ★
LARGEST LAKES

	LAKE	LOCATION	APPROX. AREA SQ MILES	SQ KM
1	Caspian Sea	Azerbaijan/Iran/Kazakhstan/Russia/Turkmenistan	143,205	371,000
2	Superior	Canada/US	31,820	82,413
3	Victoria	Kenya/Tanzania/Uganda	26,570	68,800
4	Huron	Canada/US	23,010	59,596
5	Michigan	US	22,400	58,016
6	Aral Sea	Kazakhstan/Uzbekistan	15,444	40,000
7	Tanganyika	Burundi/Tanzania/Dem. Rep. of Congo/Zambia	13,860	32,900
8	Great Bear	Canada	12,030	31,150
9	Baikal	Russia	11,775	30,500
10	Great Slave	Canada	11,030	28,570

TOP 10 ★
LARGEST LAKES IN NORTH AMERICA

	LAKE	LOCATION	APPROX. AREA SQ MILES	SQ KM
1	Superior	Canada/US	31,820	82,413
2	Huron	Canada/US	23,010	59,596
3	Michigan	US	22,400	58,016
4	Great Bear	Canada	12,030	31,150
5	Great Slave	Canada	11,030	28,570
6	Erie	Canada/US	9,930	25,719
7	Winnipeg	Canada	9,094	24,553
8	Ontario	Canada/US	7,520	19,477
9	Athabasca	Canada	3,058	7,920
10	Reindeer	Canada	2,444	6,330

The Great Lakes together form the largest area of freshwater on the Earth. They comprise Superior, Huron, Michigan, Erie, and Ontario, which together have an area of 94,616 sq miles (245,055 sq km).

Where in the Solar System does a day last 244 Earth days?
see p.13 for the answer

A Pluto
B Neptune
C Venus

Islands of the World

TOP 10 LARGEST VOLCANIC ISLANDS

	ISLAND/LOCATION	STATUS	APPROX. AREA SQ MILES	SQ KM
1	**Sumatra**, Indonesia	Active volcanic	171,068.7	443,065.8
2	**Honshu**, Japan	Volcanic	87.182.0	225,800.3
3	**Java**, Indonesia	Volcanic	53.588.5	138,793.6
4	**North Island**, New Zealand	Volcanic	43.082.4	111,582.8
5	**Luzon**, Philippines	Active volcanic	42.457.7	109,964.9
6	**Iceland**, Indonesia	Active volcanic	39,315.2	101,826.0
7	**Mindanao**, Philippines	Active volcanic	37,656.5	97,530.0
8	**Hokkaido**, Japan	Active volcanic	30,394.7	78,719.4
9	**New Britain**, Papua New Guinea	Volcanic	13,569.4	35,144.6
10	**Halmahera**, Indonesia	Active volcanic	6,965.1	18,039.6

Source: *United Nations*

TOP 10 ★ LARGEST ISLANDS

	ISLAND/LOCATION	APPROX. AREA* SQ MILES	SQ KM
1	**Greenland**	840,070	2,175,600
2	**New Guinea**, Papua New Guinea/Indonesia	309,000	800,000
3	**Borneo**, Indonesia/Malaysia/Brunei	287,300	744,100
4	**Madagascar**	226,657	587,041
5	**Baffin Island**, Canada	195,875	507,450
6	**Sumatra**, Indonesia	164,000	424,760
7	**Honshu**, Japan	89,176	230,966
8	**Great Britain**	88,787	229,957
9	**Victoria Island**, Canada	83,896	217,206
10	**Ellesmere Island**, Canada	75,767	196,160

* *Mainlands, including areas of inland water, but excluding offshore islands*

Australia is regarded as a continental land mass rather than an island: otherwise it would rank first at 2,941,517 sq miles (7,618,493 sq km), or 35 times the size of Great Britain. The largest US island is Hawaii, which measures 4,037 sq miles (10,456 sq km), and the largest off mainland US is Kodiak, Alaska, at 3,672 sq miles (9,510 sq km).

TOP 10 ★ LARGEST ISLANDS IN EUROPE

	ISLAND/LOCATION	AREA SQ MILES	SQ KM
1	**Great Britain**, North Atlantic	88,787	229,957
2	**Iceland**, North Atlantic	39,769	103,000
3	**Ireland**, North Atlantic	32,342	83,766
4	**West Spitsbergen**, Arctic Ocean	15,200	39,368
5	**Sicily**, Mediterranean Sea	9,807	25,400
6	**Sardinia**, Mediterranean Sea	9,189	23,800
7	**North East Land**, Barents Sea	5,792	15,000
8	**Cyprus**, Mediterranean Sea	3,572	9,251
9	**Corsica**, Mediterranean Sea	3,367	8,720
10	**Crete**, Mediterranean Sea	3,189	8,260

Great Britain became an island only after the end of the last ice age, some 8,000 years ago, when the land bridge that had previously existed was inundated and the North Sea became connected with the English Channel. Until then the Dogger Bank, now a notable fishing ground, was land, and the Thames River was a tributary of the Rhine.

TOP 10 ★ LARGEST ISLANDS IN THE US

	ISLAND/LOCATION	AREA SQ MILES	SQ KM
1	**Hawaii**, Hawaii	4,037	10,456
2	**Kodiak**, Alaska	3,672	9,510
3	**Prince of Wales**, Alaska	2,587	6,700
4	**Chicagof**, Alaska	2,085	5,400
5	**Saint Lawrence**, Alaska	1,710	4,430
6	**Admiralty**, Alaska	1,649	4,270
7	**Baranof**, Alaska	1,636	4,237
8	**Nunivak**, Alaska	1,625	4,210
9	**Unimak**, Alaska	1,606	4,160
10	**Long Island**, New York	1,401	3,269

Did You Know? The volcanic island of Surtsey emerged from the sea to the south of Iceland in 1963. It was named after the Norse god Surtur.

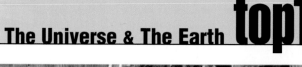

UNDER THE VOLCANO

Volcanic Sumatra's tallest peak, Gunung Kerinici, is a 12,484-ft (3,805-m) active volcano that was first climbed in 1877. Southeast Asia has more active volcanoes than any other part of the world.

TOP 10 HIGHEST ISLANDS

(Island/location/highest elevation in ft/m)

1 New Guinea, Papua New Guinea/Indonesia, 16,503/5,030
2 Akutan, Alaska, 14,026/4,275 **3 Borneo**, Indonesia/Malaysia/Brunei, 13,698/4,175 **4 Hawaii**, 13,678/4,169 **5 Formosa**, China, 13,114/3,997 **6 Sumatra**, Indonesia, 12,480/3,804 **7 Ross**, Antarctica, 12,448/3,794 **8 Honshu**, Japan, 12,388/3,776 **9 South Island**, New Zealand, 12,349/3,764 **10 Lombok**, Lesser Sunda Islands, Indonesia, 12,224/3,726

Source: *United Nations*

TOP 10 ★
LARGEST LAKE ISLANDS

ISLAND	LAKE/LOCATION	AREA SQ MILES	SQ KM
1 Manitoulin	Huron, Ontario, Canada	1,068	2,766
2 Vozrozhdeniya	Aral Sea, Uzbekistan/Kazakhstan	888	2,300
3 René-Lavasseur	Manicouagan Reservoir, Quebec, Canada	780	2,020
4 Olkhon	Baykal, Russia	282	730
5 Samosir	Toba, Sumatra, Indonesia	243	630
6 Isle Royale	Superior, Michigan	209	541
7 Ukerewe	Victoria, Tanzania	205	530
8 St. Joseph	Huron, Ontario, Canada	141	365
9 Drummond	Huron, Michigan	134	347
10 Idjwi	Kivu, Dem. Rep. of Congo	110	285

Not all islands are surrounded by sea: many sizeable islands are situated in lakes. The second largest in this list, Vozrozhdeniya, is growing as the Aral Sea contracts, and is set to link up with the surrounding land as a peninsula.

TOP 10 LARGEST ISLANDS IN THE UK

(Island/location/area in sq miles/sq km)

1 Lewis and Harris, Outer Hebrides, 859/2,225
2 Skye, Inner Hebrides, 643/1,666 **3 Mainland**, Shetland, 373/967
4 Mull, Inner Hebrides, 347/899 **5 Anglesey**, Wales, 276/714
6 Islay, Inner Hebrides, 247/639 **7 Isle of Man**, England, 221/572
8 Mainland, Orkney, 207/536 **9 Arran**, Inner Hebrides, 168/435
10 Isle of Wight, England, 147/381

MALTESE SQUEEZE

Close-packed high-rise housing in the capital, Valetta, exemplifies Malta's status as the world's most densely populated island country. Over 383,000 people are packed into just 122 sq miles (316 sq km).

TOP 10 ★
MOST DENSELY POPULATED ISLAND COUNTRIES

ISLAND	AREA SQ MILES	SQ KM	POPULATION*	POPULATION PER SQ MILE	SQ KM
1 Malta	122	316	383,285	3,142	1,213
2 Bermuda	21	53	62,912	2,996	1,187
3 Maldives	115	298	310,425	2,699	1,042
4 Bahrain	268	694	641,539	2,394	924
5 Mauritius	720	1,865	1,196,172	1,661	642
6 Taiwan	13,800	35,742	22,319,222	1,617	624
7 Barbados	166	430	259,248	1,562	603
8 Tuvalu	10	25	10,730	1,073	429
9 Marshall Islands	70	181	68,088	973	376
10 Japan	143,939	372,801	126,434,470	878	339

* *Estimated for the year 2000*   Source: *United Nations*

The Face of the Earth

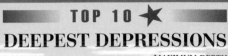

DEEPEST DEPRESSIONS

	DEPRESSION/LOCATION	MAXIMUM DEPTH BELOW SEA LEVEL FT	M
1	**Dead Sea**, Israel/Jordan	1,312	400
2	**Turfan Depression**, China	505	154
3	**Qattâra Depression**, Egypt	436	133
4	**Poluostrov Mangyshlak**, Kazakhstan	433	132
5	**Danakil Depression**, Ethiopia	383	117
6	**Death Valley**, US	282	86
7	**Salton Sink**, US	235	72
8	**Zapadny Chink Ustyurta**, Kazakhstan	230	70
9	**Prikaspiyskaya Nizmennost'**, Kazakhstan/Russia	220	67
10	**Ozera Sarykamysh**, Turkmenistan/Uzbekistan	148	45

LYING LOW

The shore of the Dead Sea is the lowest exposed ground below sea level, but the bed of the sea actually reaches 2,388 ft (728 m) below sea level. Much of Antarctica is also below sea level.

HIGHEST ACTIVE VOLCANOES

	VOLCANO	LOCATION	LATEST ACTIVITY	HEIGHT FT	M
1	Guallatiri	Chile	1987	19,882	6,060
2	Lááscar	Chile	1991	19,652	5,990
3	Cotopaxi	Ecuador	1975	19,347	5,897
4	Tupungatito	Chile	1986	18,504	5,640
5	Popocatépetl	Mexico	1995	17,887	5,452
6	Ruiz	Colombia	1992	17,716	5,400
7	Sangay	Ecuador	1988	17,159	5,230
8	Guagua Pichincha	Ecuador	1988	15,696	4,784
9	Purace	Colombia	1977	15,601	4,755
10	Kliuchevskoi	Russia	1995	15,584	4,750

This list includes all volcanoes that have been active at some time during the 20th century. The tallest currently active volcano in Europe is Mt. Etna.

LARGEST DESERTS

	DESERT	LOCATION	APPROX. AREA SQ MILES	SQ KM
1	Sahara	North Africa	3,500,000	9,000,000
2	Australian	Australia	1,470,000	3,800,000
3	Arabian	Southwest Asia	502,000	1,300,000
4	Gobi	Central Asia	400,000	1,036,000
5	Kalahari	Southern Africa	201,000	520,000
6	Turkestan	Central Asia	174,000	450,000
7	Takla Makan	China	125,000	327,000
8 =Namib	Southwest Africa		120,000	310,000
=Sonoran	US/Mexico		120,000	310,000
10 =Somali	Somalia		100,000	260,000
=Thar	Northwest India/Pakistan		100,000	260,000

Did You Know? Analysis of the latest data concerning Everest indicates that the mountain is growing higher and moving north-east at a rate of 2.4 in (6 cm) per year.

TOP 10 ★
LONGEST CAVES

CAVE/LOCATION	TOTAL KNOWN LENGTH MILES	KM
1 Mammoth cave system, Kentucky	352	567
2 Optimisticeskaja, Ukraine	125	201
3 Jewel Cave, South Dakota	108	174
4 Hölloch, Switzerland	103	166
5 Lechuguilla Cave, New Mexico	100	161
6 Siebenhengsteholen-system, Switzerland	87	140
7 =Fisher Ridge cave system, Kentucky	78	126
=Wind Cave, South Dakota	78	126
9 Ozernay, Ukraine	69	111
10 Gua Air Jernih, Malaysia	68	109

Source: Tony Waltham, BCRA, 1999

TOP 10 ★
DEEPEST CAVES

CAVE SYSTEM/LOCATION	TOTAL KNOWN DEPTH FT	M
1 Lampreuchtsofen, Austria	5,354	1,632
2 Gouffre Mirolda, France	5,282	1,610
3 Réseau Jean Bernard, France	5,256	1,602
4 Shakta Pantjukhina, Georgia	4,948	1,508
5 Sistema Huautla, Mexico	4,839	1,475
6 Sistema del Trave, Spain	4,737	1,444
7 Boj Bulok, Uzbekistan	4,642	1,415
8 Puerto di Illamina, Spain	4,619	1,408
9 Lukina Jama, Croatia	4,567	1,392
10 Sistema Cheve, Mexico	4,547	1,386

Source: Tony Waltham, BCRA, 1999

TOP 10 ★
HIGHEST MOUNTAINS

MOUNTAIN/LOCATION	HEIGHT* FT	M
1 Everest, Nepal/Tibet	29,022	8,846
2 K2, Kashmir/China	28,250	8,611
3 Kangchenjunga, Nepal/Sikkim	28,208	8,598
4 Lhotse, Nepal/Tibet	27,890	8,501
5 Makalu I, Nepal/Tibet	27,790	8,470
6 Dhaulagiri I, Nepal	26,810	8,172
7 Manaslu I, Nepal	26,760	8,156
8 Cho Oyu, Nepal	26,750	8,153
9 Nanga Parbat, Kashmir	26,660	8,126
10 Annapurna I, Nepal	26,504	8,078

Height of principal peak; lower peaks of the same mountain are excluded

In November 1999 it was announced that an analysis of data beamed from sensors on Everest's summit to GPS satellites had claimed a new height of 29,035 ft (8,850 m). This height has been accepted by the National Geographic Society but awaits confirmation as the official figure.

TOP 10 ★
COUNTRIES WITH THE HIGHEST ELEVATIONS*

COUNTRY/PEAK	HEIGHT FT	M
1 Nepal#, Everest	29,022	8,846
2 Pakistan, K2	28,250	8,611
3 India, Kangchenjunga	28,208	8,598
4 Bhutan, Khula Kangri	24,784	7,554
5 Tajikistan, Mt. Garmo (formerly Kommunizma)	24,590	7,495
6 Afghanistan, Noshaq	24,581	7,490
7 Kyrgystan, Pik Pobedy	24,406	7,439
8 Kazakhstan, Khan Tengri	22,949	6,995
9 Argentina, Cerro Aconcagua	22,834	6,960
10 Chile, Ojos del Salado	22,588	6,885

* Based on the tallest peak in each country

Everest straddles Nepal and Tibet, which, now known as Xizang, is a province of China

TOP 10 LARGEST METEORITE CRATERS
(Crater/location/diameter in miles/km)

1 = **Sudbury**, Ontario, Canada, 87/140; = **Vredefort**, South Africa, 87/140; **3** **Manicouagan**, Quebec, Canada, 62/100; = **Popigai**, Russia, 62/100 **5** **Puchezh-Katunki**, Russia, 50/80 **6** **Kara**, Russia, 37/60 **7** **Siljan**, Sweden, 32/52 **8** **Charlevoix**, Quebec, Canada, 29/46 **9** **Araguainha Dome**, Brazil, 25/40 **10** **Carswell**, Saskatchewan, Canada, 23/37

METEORITE CRATERS

Unlike on the Solar System's other planets and moons, many astroblemes (collision sites) on the Earth have been weathered over time. Geologists are thus unsure whether or not certain craterlike structures are of meteoric origin or are the remnants of extinct volcanoes. The Vredefort Ring, for example, was thought to be volcanic but has since been claimed as a definite meteor crater. Barringer Crater in Arizona (0.79 miles/1.265 km) is, however, the largest that all scientists agree is an astrobleme. The original diameter of many craters, such as Manicouagan (seen from a space shuttle), has been reduced by erosion.

 **SNAP SHOTS**

World Weather

COLDEST PLACES IN THE US

WEATHER STATION/STATE	MEAN TEMPERATURE °F	°C
1 **International Falls**, Minnesota	36.8	2.67
2 **Duluth**, Minnesota	38.5	3.61
3 **Caribou**, Maine	38.8	3.78
4 **Marquette**, Michigan	39.1	3.94
5 **Sault St. Marie**, Michigan	39.7	4.28
6 **Fargo**, North Dakota	41.0	5.00
7 **Alamosa**, Colorado	41.1	5.05
8 =**Saint Cloud**, Minnesota	41.5	5.28
=**Williston**, Maryland	41.5	5.28
10 **Bismark**, North Dakota	41.6	5.33

Source: National Climatic Data Center

TOP 10 ★

HOTTEST CITIES IN THE US

CITY/STATE	AVERAGE ANNUAL TEMPERATURE °F	°C
1 **Key West**, Florida	77.8	25.4
2 **Miami**, Florida	75.9	24.2
3 **West Palm Beach**, Florida	74.7	23.7
4 =**Fort Myers**, Florida	74.4	23.3
=**Yuma**, Arizona	74.4	23.3
6 **Brownsville**, Texas	73.8	23.1
7 =**Tampa**, Florida	72.4	22.4
=**Vero Beach**, Florida	72.4	22.4
9 **Corpus Christi**, Texas	71.6	22.3
10 **Daytona Beach**, Florida	70.4	21.3

Source: National Climatic Data Center

TOP 10 ★

WETTEST CITIES IN THE US

CITY/STATE	MEAN ANNUAL PRECIPICATION IN	MM
1 **Quillayute**, Washington	105.18	2,672
2 **Astoria**, Oregon	66.40	1,687
3 **Tallahassee**, Florida	65.71	1,669
4 **Mobile**, Alabama	63.96	1,625
5 **Pensacola**, Florida	62.25	1,581
6 **New Orleans**, Louisiana	61.88	1,572
7 **Baton Rouge**, Louisiana	60.89	1,547
8 **West Palm Beach**, Florida	60.75	1,543
9 **Meridian**, Mississippi	56.71	1,440
10 **Tupelo**, Mississippi	55.87	1,419

Source: National Climatic Data Center

TOP 10 ★

COLDEST INHABITED PLACES

WEATHER STATION/LOCATION	AVERAGE TEMPERATURE °F	°C
1 **Norilsk**, Russia	12.4	−10.9
2 **Yakutsk**, Russia	13.8	−10.1
3 **Yellowknife**, Canada	22.3	−5.4
4 **Ulan-Bator**, Mongolia	23.9	−4.5
5 **Fairbanks**, Alaska	25.9	−3.4
6 **Surgut**, Russia	26.4	−3.1
7 **Chita**, Russia	27.1	−2.7
8 **Nizhnevartovsk**, Russia	27.3	−2.6
9 **Hailar**, Mongolia	27.7	−2.4
10 **Bratsk**, Russia	28.0	−2.2

COLD COMFORT

Yakutsk, Siberia, a port with a population of 200,000, experiences some of the world's coldest winters, but receives surprisingly little precipitation – just 8.39 in (213 mm) a year.

TOP 10 DRIEST CITIES IN THE US

(City/state/mean annual precipitation in in/mm)

1 **Yuma**, Arizona, 3.17/80.5 **2** **Las Vegas**, Nevada, 4.13/104.9 **3** **Bishop**, California, 5.37/136.4 **4** **Bakersfield**, California, 5.72/145.3 **5** **Reno**, Nevada, 7.53/191.3 **6** **Alamosa**, Colorado, 7.57/192.3 **7** **Phoenix**, Arizona, 7.66/194.6 **8** **Yakima**, Washington, 7.97/202.4 **9** **Winslow**, Arizona, 8.04/204.2 **10** **Winnemucca**, Nevada, 8.23/209.0

Source: National Climatic Data Center

TOP 10 ★
HOTTEST INHABITED PLACES

WEATHER STATION/LOCATION	AVERAGE TEMPERATURE °F	°C
1 Djibouti, Djibouti	86.0	30.0
2 =Timbuktu, Mali	84.7	29.3
=Tirunelevi, India	84.7	29.3
=Tuticorin, India	84.7	29.3
5 =Nellore, India	84.6	29.2
=Santa Marta, Colombia	84.6	29.2
7 =Aden, South Yemen	84.0	28.9
=Madurai, India	84.0	28.9
=Niamey, Niger	84.0	28.9
10 =Hudaydah, North Yemen	83.8	28.8
=Ouagadougou, Burkina Faso	83.8	28.8
=Thanjavur, India	83.8	28.8
=Tiruchirapalli, India	83.8	28.8

HOT SPOT

A small town at the end of a Saharan caravan route, Timbuktu in Mali is one of the world's hottest places, coming second only to Djibouti.

TOP 10 ★
WETTEST INHABITED PLACES

WEATHER STATION/LOCATION	AVERAGE ANNUAL RAINFALL IN	MM
1 Buenaventura, Colombia	265.47	6,743
2 Monrovia, Liberia	202.01	5,131
3 Pago Pago, American Samoa	196.46	4,990
4 Moulmein, Myanmar	191.02	4,852
5 Lae, Papua New Guinea	182.87	4,645
6 Baguio, Luzon Island, Philippines	180.04	4,573
7 Sylhet, Bangladesh	175.47	4,457
8 Conakry, Guinea	170.91	4,341
9 =Padang, Sumatra Island, Indonesia	166.34	4,225
=Bogor, Java, Indonesia	166.34	4,225

The total annual rainfall of the Top 10 wettest locations is equivalent to over 26 6-ft (1.83-m) adults standing on top of each other. The greatest rainfall in a 12-month period was 1,041.75 in (26,461 mm) at Cherrapunji, India.

TOP 10 ★
DRIEST INHABITED PLACES

WEATHER STATION/LOCATION	AVERAGE ANNUAL RAINFALL IN	MM
1 Aswan, Egypt	0.02	0.5
2 Luxor, Egypt	0.03	0.7
3 Arica, Chile	0.04	1.1
4 Ica, Peru	0.09	2.3
5 Antofagasta, Chile	0.19	4.9
6 Minya, Egypt	0.20	5.1
7 Asyut, Egypt	0.21	5.2
8 Callao, Peru	0.47	12.0
9 Trujilo, Peru	0.54	14.0
10 Fayyum, Egypt	0.75	19.0

The total annual rainfall of the Top 10 driest inhabited places, as recorded over long periods, is just 2½ in (64.8 mm) – the average length of an adult little finger. The Atacama Desert often receives virtually no rain for years on end.

Did You Know? The highest temperatures recorded in the US and Europe are 118°F (47.8°C) (Phoenix, Arizona) and 117°F (47.2°C) (Seville, Spain).

Out of This World

HEAVIEST ELEMENTS

ELEMENT	DISCOVERER/COUNTRY	YEAR DISCOVERED	DENSITY*
1 Osmium	S. Tennant, UK	1804	22.59
2 Iridium	S. Tennant	1804	22.56
3 Platinum	J. C. Scaliger#, Italy/France	1557	21.45
4 Rhenium	W. Noddack et al., Germany	1925	21.01
5 Neptunium	Edwin M. McMillan/ Philip H. Abelson, US	1940	20.47
6 Plutonium	G. T. Seaborg et al., US	1940	20.26
7 Gold	—	Prehistoric	19.29
8 Tungsten	J. J. and F. Elhuijar, Spain	1783	19.26
9 Uranium	M. J. Klaproth, Germany	1789	19.05
10 Tantalum	A. G. Ekeberg, Sweden	1802	16.67

* Grams per cu cm at 20°C
\# Earliest reference to this element

LIGHTEST ELEMENTS*

ELEMENT	DISCOVERER/COUNTRY	YEAR DISCOVERED	DENSITY#
1 Lithium	J. A. Arfvedson, Sweden	1817	0.533
2 Potassium	Sir Humphry Davy, UK	1807	0.859
3 Sodium	Sir Humphry Davy	1807	0.969
4 Calcium	Sir Humphry Davy	1808	1.526
5 Rubidium	R. W. Bunsen/G. Kirchoff, Germany	1861	1.534
6 Magnesium	Sir Humphry Davy	1808+	1.737
7 Phosphorus	Hennig Brandt, Germany	1669	1.825
8 Beryllium	F. Wöhler, Germany/ A. A. B. Bussy, France	1828★	1.846
9 Cesium	R. W. Bunsen/G. Kirchoff	1860	1.896
10 Sulfur	—	Prehistoric	2.070

* Solids only   \# Grams per cu cm at 20°C   + Recognized by Joseph Black, 1755, but not isolated   ★ Recognized by Nicholas Vauquelin, 1797, but not isolated

TOP 10 MOST EXTRACTED METALLIC ELEMENTS

(Element/estimated annual extraction in tons)

1 Iron, 789,247,000 **2** Aluminum, 16,535,000 **3** Copper, 7,209,000 **4** Manganese, 6,856,000 **5** Zinc, 5,534,000 **6** Lead, 3,086,000 **7** Nickel, 562,000 **8** Magnesium, 358,000 **9** Sodium, 220,000 **10** Tin, 182,000

Certain metallic minerals are extracted in relatively small quantities, while compounds containing these elements are major industries: contrasting with 220,500 tons of metallic sodium, 185 million tons of salt are extracted annually; metallic calcium is represented by about 2,210 tons, contrasting with some 123 million tons of lime (calcium carbonate); and 220 tons of the metal potassium contrast with 56 million tons of potassium salts.

METALLIC ELEMENTS WITH THE GREATEST RESERVES

ELEMENT	ESTIMATED GLOBAL RESERVES (TONS)
1 Iron	121,254,200,000
2 Magnesium	22,046,200,000
3 Potassium	11,023,100,000
4 Aluminum	6,613,800,000
5 Manganese	3,698,300,000
6 Zirconium	over 1,102,300,000
7 Chromium	1,102,300,000
8 Barium	496,000,000
9 Titanium	485,000,000
10 Copper	341,700,000

This list includes accessible reserves of commercially mined metallic elements, but excludes two, calcium and sodium, that exist in such vast quantities that their reserves are considered "unlimited" and unquantifiable.

COPPER TO SPARE

Copper is among the world's most extracted elements. Bingham Copper Mine, Utah, is the largest manmade excavation in the world.

TOP 10 ★
MOST COMMON ELEMENTS IN THE EARTH'S CRUST

ELEMENT	PARTS PER MILLION*
1 Oxygen	474,000
2 Silicon	277,100
3 Aluminum	82,000
4 =Iron	41,000
=Calcium	11,000
6 =Magnesium	23,000
=Sodium	23,000
8 Potassium	21,000
9 Titanium	5,600
10 Hydrogen	1,520

* mg per kg

TOP 10 ★
MOST COMMON ELEMENTS IN THE UNIVERSE

ELEMENT	PARTS PER MILLION
1 Hydrogen	739,000
2 Helium	240,000
3 Oxygen	10,700
4 Carbon	4,600
5 Neon	1,340
6 Iron	1,090
7 Nitrogen	970
8 Silicon	650
9 Magnesium	580
10 Sulfur	440

TOP 10 PRINCIPAL COMPONENTS OF AIR
(Component/volume percent)

❶ **Nitrogen**, 78.110 ❷ **Oxygen**, 20.953 ❸ **Argon**, 0.934 ❹ **Carbon dioxide**, 0.01–0.10 ❺ **Neon**, 0.001818 ❻ **Helium**, 0.000524 ❼ **Methane**, 0.0002 ❽ **Krypton**, 0.000114 ❾ = **Hydrogen**, 0.00005; = **Nitrous oxide**, 0.00005

THE 10 DEGREES OF HARDNESS*
(Substance)

❶ Talc ❷ Gypsum ❸ Calcite ❹ Fluorite ❺ Apatite ❻ Orthoclase ❼ Quartz ❽ Topaz ❾ Corundum ❿ Diamond

* According to the Mohs Scale, in which No. 1 is the softest mineral and No. 10 is the hardest

IT'S ELEMENTARY
The gas hydrogen is the simplest and most abundant element. This computer-generated image shows a hydrogen atom with a nucleus and orbiting electron.

TOP 10 ★
MOST EXTRACTED NONMETALLIC ELEMENTS

ELEMENT	ESTIMATED ANNUAL EXTRACTION (TONS)
1 Hydrogen	386,000,000,000
2 Carbon*	18,000,000,000
3 Chlorine	185,000,000
4 Phosphorus	168,000,000
5 Oxygen	110,000,000
6 Sulfur	59,000,000
7 Nitrogen	48,000,000
8 Silicon#	4,282,000
9 Boron	1,102,000
10 Argon	777,000

* Carbon, natural gas, oil, and coal

Various forms

CRYSTAL BOMB
Known since ancient times, sulfur is extracted in large quantities for use in many industrial and chemical processes, including making explosives.

THE GOLD RUSH
In August 1896, 35-year-old George Washington Carmack struck gold while panning the Rabbit (later Bonanza) Creek, south of the Yukon at Klondike near the Canadian/Alaskan border. When news of his discovery reached the outside world, it sparked the world's biggest gold rush since the California stampede of 1849. More than 100,000 prospectors traveled to the inhospitable region to seek their fortunes, and in the first year alone some $22 million worth of Klondike gold was shipped out. Most of the gold-seekers failed, however, with many dying from the freezing winter conditions or else returning home empty-handed. In 1976 much of the area was designated as the Klondike Gold Rush Historical Park.

SNAP SHOTS

Which is the world's highest island?
see p.23 for the answer
A Sumatra
B Hawaii
C New Guinea

Natural Disasters

WORST EARTHQUAKES OF THE 20TH CENTURY

	LOCATION	DATE	ESTIMATED NO. KILLED
1	**Tang-shan**, China	July 28, 1976	242,419
2	**Nan-Shan**, China	May 22, 1927	200,000
3	**Kansu**, China	Dec 16, 1920	180,000
4	**Messina**, Italy	Dec 28, 1908	160,000
5	**Tokyo/Yokohama**, Japan	Sep 1, 1923	142,807
6	**Kansu**, China	Dec 25, 1932	70,000
7	**Yungay**, Peru	May 31, 1970	66,800
8	**Quetta**, India*	May 30, 1935	50–60,000
9	**Armenia**	Dec 7, 1988	over 55,000
10	**Iran**	June 21, 1990	over 40,000

* Now Pakistan

Reaching 7.2 on the Richter scale, the earthquake that struck Kobe, Japan, on January 17, 1995 was exceptionally precisely monitored by the rescue authorities. It left a total of 3,842 dead and 14,679 injured.

WORST AVALANCHES AND LANDSLIDES OF THE 20TH CENTURY*

	LOCATION	INCIDENT	DATE	ESTIMATED NO. KILLED
1	**Yungay**, Peru	Landslide	May 31, 1970	17,500
2	**Italian Alps**	Avalanche	Dec 13, 1916	10,000
3	**Huarás**, Peru	Avalanche	Dec 13, 1941	5,000
4	**Nevada Huascaran**, Peru	Avalanche	Jan 10, 1962	3,500
5	**Medellin**, Colombia	Landslide	Sep 27, 1987	683
6	**Chungar**, Peru	Avalanche	Mar 19, 1971	600
7	**Rio de Janeiro**, Brazil	Landslide	Jan 11, 1966	550
8	**=Northern Assam**, India	Landslide	Feb 15, 1949	500
	=Grand Rivière du Nord, Haiti	Landslide	Nov 13/14, 1963	500
10	**Blons**, Austria	Avalanche	Jan 11, 1954	411

* Excluding those where most deaths resulted from flooding, earthquakes, etc., associated with landslides

The worst incident of all, the destruction of Yungay, Peru, in May 1970, was only part of a much larger cataclysm that left a total of up to 70,000 dead. Following an earthquake and flooding, the town was wiped out by an avalanche that left just 2,500 survivors out of a population of 20,000. Among the most tragic landslide disasters of this century occurred at Aberfan, Wales, on October 20, 1966. Weakened by the presence of a spring, a huge volume of slurry from a 800-ft (244-m) high heap of coal-mine waste suddenly flowed down and engulfed the local school, killing 144 people.

TURKISH EARTHQUAKE

The earthquake that occurred in Turkey on August 17, 1999 was the second worst of the decade, resulting in a death toll unofficially estimated at between 30,000 and 40,000. It lasted only 45 seconds but measured 7.4 on the Richter scale. Its epicenter was 7 miles (11 km) southeast of Izmit, an industrial area 50 miles (90 km) east of Istanbul, where many multistory concrete apartment buildings collapsed into rubble. Most had been poorly constructed with inferior materials and little regard for the area's known vulnerability to earthquakes. In this and the surrounding area, some 20,000 structures were destroyed or damaged, while the country's industrial infrastructure was severely damaged. The Tüpras oil refinery in Korfez was set ablaze, Turkey's electricity supply cut, and water and road networks disrupted.

SNAP SHOTS ★

THE 10 ★ COSTLIEST HURRICANES TO STRIKE THE US

HURRICANE	YEAR	DAMAGE ($)*
1 Andrew	1992	30,475,000,000
2 Hugo	1989	8,491,561,181
3 Agnes	1972	7,500,000,000
4 Betsy	1965	7,425,340,909
5 Camille	1969	6,096,287,313
6 Diane	1955	4,830,580,808
7 Frederic	1979	4,328,968,903
8 New England	1938	4,140,000,000
9 Fran	1996	3,200,000,000
10 Opal	1995	3,069,395,018

Adjusted to 1996 dollars

Source: *The National Hurricane Center*

THE 10 WORST EPIDEMICS OF ALL TIME

	EPIDEMIC	LOCATION	DATE	ESTIMATED NO. KILLED
1	Black Death	Europe/Asia	1347–51	75,000,000
2	Influenza	Worldwide	1918–20	21,640,000
3	Plague	India	1896–1948	12,000,000
4	AIDS	Worldwide	1981–	11,700,000
5	Typhus	Eastern Europe	1914–15	3,000,000
6 =	"Plague of Justinian"	Europe/Asia	541–90	millions*
=	Cholera	Worldwide	1846–60	millions*
=	Cholera	Europe	1826–37	millions*
=	Cholera	Worldwide	1893–94	millions*
10	Smallpox	Mexico	1530–45	>1,000,000

No precise figures available

THE 10 ★ WORST VOLCANIC ERUPTIONS OF ALL TIME

LOCATION/DATE/INCIDENT	EST. NO. KILLED

1 Tambora, Indonesia, Apr 5–12, 1815 — 92,000
The eruption on the island of Sumbawa killed about 10,000 islanders immediately, with a further 82,000 dying subsequently from disease and famine resulting from crops being destroyed. An estimated 1,700,000 tons of ash was hurled into the atmosphere, blocking out the sunlight.

2 Miyi-Yama, Java, 1793 — 53,000
The volcano dominating the island of Kiousiou erupted, engulfing all the local villages in mudslides and killing most of the rural population.

3 Mont Pelée, Martinique, May 8, 1902 — 40,000
After lying dormant for centuries, Mont Pelée began to erupt in April 1902.

4 Krakatoa, Sumatra/Java, Aug 26–27, 1883 — 36,380
Krakatoa exploded with what may have been the biggest bang ever heard by humans, audible up to 3,000 miles (4,800 km) away.

5 Nevado del Ruiz, Colombia, Nov 13, 1985 — 22,940
The hot steam, rocks, and ash ejected from Nevado del Ruiz melted its icecap, resulting in a mudslide that completely engulfed the town of Armero.

6 Mount Etna, Sicily, Mar 11, 1669 — over 20,000
Europe's largest volcano has erupted frequently, but the worst instance occurred in 1669, when the lava flow engulfed the town of Catania.

7 Laki, Iceland, Jan–June 1703 — 20,000
An eruption on the Laki volcanic ridge culminated on June 11, with the largest ever recorded lava flow. It engulfed many villages in a river of lava up to 50 miles (80 km) long and 100 ft (30 m) deep, releasing poisonous gases that killed those who escaped.

8 Vesuvius, Italy, Aug 24, 79 — 16–20,000
The Roman city of Herculaneum was engulfed by a mud flow, while Pompeii was buried under a vast and preserving layer of pumice and volcanic ash.

9 Vesuvius, Italy, Dec 16–17, 1631 — up to 18,000
The next major cataclysm was almost as disastrous, when lava and mudflows gushed down onto the surrounding towns, including Naples.

10 Mount Etna, Sicily, 1169 — over 15,000
Large numbers died in Catania cathedral, where they believed they would be safe, and more were killed when a tidal wave caused by the eruption hit the port of Messina.

THE 10 ★ WORST FLOODS AND STORMS OF THE 20TH CENTURY

	LOCATION	DATE	ESTIMATED NO. KILLED
1	Huang He River, China	Aug 1931	3,700,000
2	Bangladesh	13 Nov 1970	300–500,000
3	Henan, China	Sep 1939	over 200,000
4	Bangladesh	30 Apr 1991	131,000
5	Chang Jiang River, China	Sep 1911	100,000
6	Bengal, India	15–16 Nov 1942	40,000
7	Bangladesh	1–2 June 1965	30,000
8	Bangladesh	28–29 May 1963	22,000
9	Bangladesh	11–12 May 1965	17,000
10	Morvi, India	11 Aug 1979	5–15,000

No. 4 was omitted previously because the total number of fatalities combines the effects of storm, flood and tidal wave, and it is impossible to isolate the figures for just those deaths attributable to the storm and flood aspects of the disaster. On balance, I think it deserves to be recorded.

Background image: **INFLUENZA VIRUSES**

Where is the world's highest waterfall?
see p.21 for the answer
A Venezuela
B India
C China

Life on Earth

COME INTO MY PARLOR ...

Listed as "vulnerable" by the International Union for the Conservation of Nature, the distinctive Dolomedes Great raft or Fishing spider can sit on water as it awaits its prey.

THE 10 ★
MOST ENDANGERED BIG CATS*

1	Amur leopard
2	Anatolian leopard
3	Asiatic cheetah
4	Eastern puma
5	Florida cougar
6	North African leopard
7	Siberian tiger
8	South Arabian leopard
9	South China tiger
10	Sumatran tiger

* In alphabetical order

Source: *International Union for the Conservation of Nature*

All 10 of these big cats are classed by the International Union for Conservation of Nature as being "critically endangered," that is, facing an extremely high risk of extinction in the wild in the immediate future.

THE 10 ★
MOST ENDANGERED SPIDERS

	SPIDER	COUNTRY
1	Kauai cave wolf spider	US
2	Doloff cave spider	US
3	Empire cave pseudoscorpion	US
4	Glacier Bay wolf spider	US
5	Great raft spider	Europe
6	Kocevje subterranean spider (*Troglohyphantes gracilis*)	Slovenia
7	Kocevje subterranean spider (*Troglohyphantes similis*)	Slovenia
8	Kocevje subterranean spider (*Troglohyphantes spinipes*)	Slovenia
9	Lake Placid funnel wolf spider	US
10	Melones cave harvestman	US

Source: *International Union for the Conservation of Nature*

The first spider on this list is considered by the IUCN as "endangered" (facing a very high risk of extinction in the wild in the near future), and the others as "vulnerable" (facing a high risk of extinction in the wild in the medium-term future). Some exist exclusively in one habitat, making them especially susceptible to environmental threats.

THE 10 ★
COUNTRIES WITH THE MOST ASIAN ELEPHANTS

	COUNTRY	NUMBER*
1	India	24,000
2	Myanmar	6,000
3	Indonesia	4,500
4	Laos	4,000
5	Sri Lanka	3,000
6 =	Thailand	2,000
=	Cambodia	2,000
9 =	Borneo	1,000
=	Malaysia	1,000
10	Vietnam	400

* Based on maximum estimates

The total numbers of Asian elephants is put at anything from a minimum of 37,860 to a maximum 48,740. Estimates of populations of Asian elephants are notoriously unreliable as this species is exclusively a forest animal and its numbers cannot be sampled using aerial survey techniques.

Source: *International Union for the Conservation of Nature*

THE 10 ★
MOST RECENTLY EXTINCT ANIMAL SPECIES

1	Partula Tree Snails from Hawaii
2	Palos Verde Blue Butterfly
3	Canary Islands Blackfly
4	Lord Howe Islands Phasmid Fly
5	Dusky Seaside Sparrow
6	Colombian Grebe and Atitlan Grebe
7	Glaucous Macaw
8	Hawaiian Honey Creeper
9	Pohmpei (Caroline Island bird)
10	Bali Tiger

The saddest thing about this list is that by the time you read it, it will be out of date because yet another species will have become extinct, usually as a direct result of human intervention.

Did You Know? Once thought extinct but later rediscovered, the Kakapo parrot cannot fly, but instead climbs trees and glides down to the ground.

"AS DEAD AS A DODO'

When Portuguese sailors first encountered a large, flightless bird on the island of Mauritius, they were struck by its ludicrous clumsy appearance and the ease with which they were able to catch it; so they christened it the "doudo," the Portuguese word for "stupid." Even its Latin name emphasizes its silliness – *Didus ineptus*. As doudos, or dodos, tasted delicious, they were hunted down; and by 1681, when the last was seen by English naturalist Benjamin Harry, they were completely extinct – hence the expression, "as dead as a dodo."

WHY DO WE SAY?

THE 10 ★
MOST ENDANGERED MAMMALS

MAMMAL	ESTIMATED NO.
1 =Tasmanian wolf	?
=Halcon fruit bat	?
=Ghana fat mouse	?
4 Javan rhinoceros	50
5 Iriomote cat	60
6 Black lion tamarin	130
7 Pygmy hog	150
8 Kouprey	100–200
9 Tamaraw	200
10 Indus dolphin	400

The first three mammals on the list have not been seen for many years and may well be extinct.

THE 10 ★
COUNTRIES WITH THE MOST THREATENED SPECIES

	COUNTRY	MAMMALS	BIRDS	REPTILES	AMPHIBIANS	FISH	INVERTEBRATES	TOTAL
1	US	35	50	28	24	123	594	854
2	Australia	58	45	37	25	37	281	483
3	Indonesia	128	104	19	0	60	29	340
4	Mexico	64	36	18	3	86	40	247
5	Brazil	71	103	15	5	12	34	240
6	China	75	90	15	1	28	4	213
7	South Africa	33	16	19	9	27	101	205
8	Philippines	49	86	7	2	26	18	188
9	India	75	73	16	3	4	22	193
10 =Japan	29	33	8	10	7	45	132
=Tanzania	33	30	4	0	19	46	132

TOP 10 COUNTRIES WITH THE MOST AFRICAN ELEPHANTS
(Country/elephants)

1 Tanzania, 73,459* **2** Dem. Rep. of Congo, 65,974# **3** Botswana, 62,998*
4 Gabon, 61,794+ **5** Zimbabwe, 56,297* **6** Congo, 32,563# **7** Zambia, 19,701*
8 Kenya, 13,834* **9** South Africa, 9,990* **10** Cameroon, 8,824#

*Definite #Possible +Probable
Source: International Union for the Conservation of Nature

LONE WOLF

Although officially declared extinct in 1936, the marsupial Thylacine, or Tasmanian wolf, remains the subject of frequent alleged sightings.

Land Animals 1

TOP 10 ★
HEAVIEST TERRESTRIAL MAMMALS

	MAMMAL	LENGTH* FT	LENGTH* M	WEIGHT LB	WEIGHT KG
1	African elephant	24	7.3	14,432	7,000
2	White rhinoceros	14	4.2	7,937	3,600
3	Hippopotamus	13	4.0	5,512	2,500
4	Giraffe	19	5.8	3,527	1,600
5	American bison	13	3.9	2,205	1,000
6	Arabian camel (dromedary)	12	3.5	1,521	690
7	Polar bear	8	2.6	1,323	600
8	Moose	10	3.0	1,213	550
9	Siberian tiger	11	3.3	661	300
10	Gorilla	7	2.0	485	220

* From head to toe or head to tail

The list excludes domesticated cattle and horses. It also avoids comparing close kin, such as the African and Indian elephants.

TOP 10 ★
SLEEPIEST ANIMALS*

	ANIMAL	AVERAGE HOURS OF SLEEP PER DAY
1	Koala	22
2	Sloth	20
3 =	Armadillo	19
=	Opossum	19
5	Lemur	16
6 =	Hamster	14
=	Squirrel	14
8 =	Cat	13
=	Pig	13
10	Spiny anteater	12

* Excluding periods of hibernation

SLEEPYHEAD

The eastern Australian koala (which is actually a marsupial, not a bear), sleeps almost constantly to conserve the little energy it has.

TOP 10 ★
HEAVIEST PRIMATES

	PRIMATE	LENGTH* IN	LENGTH* CM	WEIGHT LB	WEIGHT KG
1	Gorilla	79	200	485	220
2	Man	70	177	170	77
3	Orangutan	54	137	165	75
4	Chimpanzee	36	92	110	50
5 =	Baboon	39	100	99	45
=	Mandrill	37	95	99	45
7	Gelada baboon	30	75	55	25
8	Proboscis monkey	30	76	53	24
9	Hanuman langur	42	107	44	20
10	Siamung gibbon	35	90	29	13

* Excluding tail

The longer, leaner, and lighter forms of the langurs, gibbons, and monkeys – evolved for serious monkeying around in trees – contrast sharply with their heavier great ape cousins.

GENTLE GIANT

The largest of all primates, the gorilla has a menacing appearance that has been exploited in such films as King Kong. In fact, gorillas are usually docile.

TOP 10 ★
HEAVIEST CARNIVORES

CARNIVORE	LENGTH		WEIGHT	
	FT	M	LB	KG
1 Southern elephant seal	21	6.5	7,716	3,500
2 Walrus	12	3.8	2,646	1,200
3 Steller sea lion	9	3.0	2,425	1,100
4 Grizzly bear	9	3.0	1,720	780
5 Polar bear	8	2.6	1,323	600
6 Tiger	9	2.8	661	300
7 Lion	6	1.9	551	250
8 American black bear	6	1.8	500	227
9 Giant panda	5	1.5	353	160
10 Spectacled bear	6	1.8	309	140

Of the 273 mammal species in the order *Carnivora*, or meat-eaters, many (including its largest representatives on land, the bears) are in fact omnivorous, and around 40 specialize in eating fish or insects. All, however, share a common ancestry indicated by the butcher's-knife form of their canine teeth. As the Top 10 would otherwise consist exclusively of seals and related marine carnivores, only three have been included in order to enable the terrestrial heavyweight division to make an appearance. The polar bear is probably the largest land carnivore if shoulder height (when the animal is on all fours) is taken into account: it tops an awesome 5.3 ft (1.6 m), compared with the 4 ft (1.2 m) of its nearest rival, the grizzly.

TOP BEAR

Although among the heaviest carnivores, many records of giant grizzlies have been exaggerated by hunters and showmen for prestige.

"GORILLA"

"Gorilla" was adopted in 1847 as part of the original scientific name for the large ape, *Troglodytes gorilla*. The word was coined by Dr. Thomas Staughton Savage, an American missionary in Africa, who had heard of the Gorillai, a mythical African tribe of hairy women, imaginatively described in a 5th- or 6th-century BC Greek account of the voyages of Hanno the Carthaginian.

WHY DO WE SAY?

Did You Know? Giant pandas spend up to 15 hours a day eating, consuming as much as 99 lb (45 kg) of bamboo shoots a day.

"WHITE ELEPHANT"

The rare albino or white elephant was considered sacred to the people of Siam (now Thailand). Legend has it that the king would sometimes present such an elephant to an unpopular courtier. Decorum would have meant that the courtier could not refuse the gift, but the immense cost of looking after the beast would have ruined him financially. A "white elephant" thus became a synonym for a burdensome gift that one could not dispose of.

WHY DO WE SAY?

TOP 10 MOST INTELLIGENT MAMMALS

1 Human **2** Chimpanzee **3** Gorilla
4 Orangutan **5** Baboon **6** Gibbon
7 Monkey **8** Smaller-toothed whale **9** Dolphin **10** Elephant

This list is based on research conducted by Edward O. Wilson, Professor of Zoology at Harvard University, who defined intelligence as speed and extent of learning performance over a wide range of tasks, also taking account of the ratio of the animal's brain size to its body bulk.

TOP 10 ★ MOST PROLIFIC WILD MAMMALS

	ANIMAL	AVERAGE LITTER
1	Malagasy tenrec	25.0
2	Virginian opossum	22.0
3	Golden hamster	11.0
4	Ermine	10.0
5	Prairie vole	9.0
6	Coypu	8.5
7 =	European hedgehog	7.0
=	African hunting dog	7.0
9 =	Meadow vole	6.5
=	Wild boar	6.5

The prairie vole probably holds the world record for most offspring produced in a season. It has up to 17 litters in rapid succession, bringing up to 150 young into the world.

DEADLY CHARM

Traditionally used by Indian snake charmers, the menacingly hooded Indian cobra's venom is sufficiently powerful to kill an elephant.

TOP 10 ★ MOST VENOMOUS CREATURES

	CREATURE*	TOXIN	FATAL AMOUNT MG#
1	Indian cobra	Peak V	0.009
2	Mamba	Toxin 1	0.02
3	Brown snake	Texilotoxin	0.05
4 =	Inland taipan	Paradotoxin	0.10
=	Mamba	Dendrotoxin	0.10
6	Taipan	Taipoxin	0.11
7 =	Indian cobra	Peak X	0.12
=	Poison arrow frog	Batrachotoxin	0.12
9	Indian cobra	Peak 1X	0.17
10	Krait	Bungarotoxin	0.50

* Excluding bacteria
# Quantity required to kill one average-sized human adult

The venom of these creatures is almost unbelievably powerful: 1 milligram of Mamba Toxin 1 would be sufficient to kill 50 people. Such creatures as scorpions (0.5 mg) and black widow spiders (1.0 mg) fall just outside the Top 10.

PENSIVE PRIMATE

Numbered among the most intelligent mammals, and noted for its use of tools, the forest-dwelling orangutan's name derives from the Malay words for "man of the woods."

TOP 10 ★
LONGEST LAND ANIMALS

ANIMAL*	LENGTH#	
	FT	M
1 Royal python	35	10.7
2 Tapeworm	33	10.0
3 African elephant	24	7.3
4 Estuarine crocodile	19	5.9
5 Giraffe	19	5.8
6 White rhinoceros	14	4.2
7 Hippopotamus	13	4.0
8 American bison	13	3.9
9 Arabian camel (dromedary)	12	3.5
10 Siberian tiger	11	3.3

* Longest representative of each species

\# Head to toe or head to tail

GROWING FAST

The giraffe is the tallest of all living animals. In 1937 a calf giraffe that measured 5 ft 2 in (1.58 m) at birth was found to be growing at an astonishing 0.5 in (1.3 cm) per hour.

TOP 10 ★
FASTEST MAMMALS

MAMMAL	MAXIMUM RECORDED SPEED	
	MPH	KM/H
1 Cheetah	65	105
2 Pronghorn antelope	55	89
3 =Mongolian gazelle	50	80
=Springbok	50	80
5 =Grant's gazelle	47	76
=Thomson's gazelle	47	76
7 Brown hare	45	72
8 Horse	43	69
9 =Greyhound	42	68
=Red deer	42	68

QUICK OFF THE MARK

The speedy cheetah can accelerate to 60 mph (96 km/h) in just three seconds.

TOP 10 ★
DEADLIEST SNAKES

SNAKE	MAXIMUM DEATHS PER BITE	MORTALITY RATE RANGE (PERCENT)
1 Black mamba	200	75–100
2 Forest cobra	50	70–95
3 Russell's viper	150	40–92
4 Taipan	26	10–90
5 Common krait	60	70–80
6 Jararacussa	100	60–80
7 Terciopelo	40	Not known
8 Egyptian cobra	35	50
9 Indian cobra	40	30–35
10 Jararaca	30	25–35

What is special about Kitti's hognosed bat?
see p.42 for the answer
A It is the rarest
B It is the lightest
C It is the fastest

Marine Animals

TOP 10 HEAVIEST MARINE MAMMALS

MAMMAL	LENGTH FT	M	WEIGHT TONS
1 Blue whale	110.0	33.5	143.3
2 Fin whale	82.0	25.0	49.6
3 Right whale	57.4	17.5	44.1
4 Sperm whale	59.0	18.0	39.7
5 Gray whale	46.0	14.0	36.0
6 Humpback whale	49.2	15.0	29.2
7 Baird's whale	18.0	5.5	12.1
8 Southern elephant seal	21.3	6.5	4.0
9 Northern elephant seal	19.0	5.8	3.7
10 Pilot whale	21.0	6.4	3.2

Probably the largest animal that ever lived, the blue whale dwarfs the other whales listed here, all but one of which far outweigh the biggest land animal, the elephant.

TOP 10 ★ HEAVIEST SHARKS

SHARK	WEIGHT LB	KG
1 Whale shark	46,297	21,000
2 Basking shark	32,000	14,515
3 Great white shark	7,300	3,314
4 Greenland shark	2,250	1,020
5 Tiger shark	2,070	939
6 Great hammerhead shark	1,860	844
7 Six-gill shark	1,300	590
8 Gray nurse shark	1,225	556
9 Mako shark	1,200	544
10 Thresher shark	1,100	500

As well as specimens that have been caught, estimates have been made of beached examples, but such is the notoriety of sharks that many accounts of their size are exaggerated, and this list should be taken as an approximate ranking based on the best available evidence.

MARINE MONSTER

There are several species of right whale, with exceptional specimens reputedly exceeding 70 tons.

TOP 10 FISHING COUNTRIES

(Country/annual catch in tons)

1 China, 36,549,637 2 Peru, 10,493,199
3 Chile, 8,365,223 4 Japan, 7,448,229
5 US, 6,187,216 6 India, 5,796,982
7 Indonesia, 4,850,937 8 Russia, 4,819,957 9 Thailand, 4,019,985
10 Norway, 3,093,291

TOP 10 ★ HEAVIEST TURTLES

TURTLE	WEIGHT LB	KG
1 Pacific leatherback turtle	1,908	865
2 Atlantic leatherback turtle	1,000	454
3 Green sea turtle	900	408
4 Loggerhead turtle	850	386
5 Alligator snapping turtle	403	183
6 Black sea turtle	278	126
7 Flatback turtle	185	84
8 Hawksbill turtle	150	68
9= Kemps ridley turtle	110	50
= Olive ridley turtle	110	50

Background image: **SCHOOL OF MACKEREL**

TOP 10 ⭐
HEAVIEST SPECIES
OF FRESHWATER FISH CAUGHT

SPECIES	ANGLER/LOCATION/DATE	LB	OZ	KG
			WEIGHT	
1 White sturgeon	Joey Pallotta III, Benicia, California, July 9, 1983	468	0	212.28
2 Alligator gar	Bill Valverde, Rio Grande, Texas, Dec 2, 1951	279	0	126.55
3 Beluga sturgeon	Merete Lehne, Guryev, Kazakhstan, May 3, 1993	224	1	101.97
4 Nile perch	Adrian Brayshaw, Lake Nasser, Egypt, Dec 18, 1997	213	0	96.62
5 Flathead catfish	Ken Paulie, Withlacoochee River, Florida, May 14, 1998	123	9	56.05
6 Blue catfish	William P. McKinley, Wheeler Reservoir, Tennessee, July 5, 1996	111	0	50.35
7 Chinook salmon	Les Anderson, Kenai River, Alaska, May 17, 1985	97	4	44.11
8 Giant tigerfish	Raymond Houtmans, Zaire River, Zaire, July 9, 1988	97	0	44.00
9 Smallmouth buffalo	Randy Collins, Athens Lake, Arkansas, June 6, 1993	82	3	37.28
10 Atlantic salmon	Henrik Henrikson, Tana River, Norway (date unknown) 1928	79	2	35.89

Source: *International Game Fish Association*

TOP 10 ⭐
HEAVIEST SPECIES
OF SALTWATER FISH CAUGHT

SPECIES	ANGLER/LOCATION/DATE	LB	OZ	KG
			WEIGHT	
1 Great white shark	Alfred Dean, Ceduna, South Australia, Apr 21, 1959	2,664	0	1,208.39
2 Tiger shark	Walter Maxwell, Cherry Grove, California, June 14, 1964	1,780	0	807.4
3 Greenland shark	Terje Nordtvedt, Trondheims-fjord, Norway, Oct 18, 1987	1,708	9	775.00
4 Black marlin	A. C. Glassell, Jr., Cabo Blanco, Peru, Aug 4, 1953	1,560	0	707.62
5 Bluefin tuna	Ken Fraser, Aulds Cove, Nova Scotia, Canada, Oct 26, 1979	1,496	0	678.59
6 Atlantic blue marlin	Paulo Amorim, Vitoria, Brazil, Feb 29, 1992	1,402	2	635.99
7 Pacific blue marlin	Jay W. de Beaubien, Kaaiwi Point, Kona, May 31, 1982	1,376	0	624.15
8 Swordfish	L. Marron, Iquique, Chile, May 7, 1953	1,182	0	536.16
9 Mako shark	Patrick Guillanton, Black River, Mauritius, Nov 16, 1988	1,115	0	505.76
10 Hammerhead shark	Allen Ogle, Sarasota, Florida, May 20, 1982	991	0	449.52

Source: *International Game Fish Association*

TOP 10 ⭐
SPECIES OF FISH
MOST CAUGHT

SPECIES	TONS CAUGHT PER ANNUM
1 Anchoveta	13,110,282
2 Alaska pollock	4,737,078
3 Chilean jack mackerel	4,688,601
4 Silver carp	2,571,703
5 Atlantic herring	2,078,487
6 Grass carp	2,007,409
7 South American pilchard	1,976,354
8 Common carp	1,793,172
9 Chubb mackerel	1,661,261
10 Skipjack tuna	1,611,825

Some 3 million tons of shrimps and prawns, and a similar amount of squid, cuttlefish, and octopuses, are caught annually.

SPEEDY SWIMMER

The highly streamlined sailfish is acknowledged as the fastest over short distances, with anglers reporting them capable of unreeling 300 ft (91 m) of line in three seconds.

TOP 10 FASTEST FISH

(Fish/recorded speed in mph/km/h)

1 Sailfish, 68/110 2 Marlin, 50/80 3 Bluefin tuna, 46/74 4 Yellowfin tuna, 44/70 5 Blue shark, 43/69 6 Wahoo, 41/66 7 = Bonefish, 40/64; = Swordfish, 40/64 9 Tarpon, 35/56 10 Tiger shark, 33/53

Flying fish have a top speed in the water of only 23 mph (37 km/h), but airborne they can reach 35 mph (56 km/h). Many sharks qualify for the list; only two are listed here to prevent the list becoming overly shark-infested.

From which play does the phrase "in the doghouse" come?
see p.45 for the answer

A *Peter Pan*
B *A Midsummer Night's Dream*
C *The Importance of Being Earnest*

TOP 10 ISLANDS WITH THE MOST ENDEMIC BIRD SPECIES*

(Island/species)

❶ New Guinea, 195 ❷ Jamaica, 26 ❸ Cuba, 23 ❹ New Caledonia, 20 ❺ Rennell Solomon Islands, 15 ❻ São Tomé, 14 ❼ = Aldabra, Seychelles, 13; = Grand Cayman, Cayman Islands, 13 ❾ Puerto Rico, 12 ❿ New Britain, Papua New Guinea, 11

* Birds that are found uniquely on these islands.
Source: *United Nations*

TOP 10 MOST COMMON NORTH AMERICAN GARDEN BIRDS

(Bird/percentage of feeders visited)

❶ Dark-eyed junco, 83 ❷ House finch, 70 ❸ = American goldfinch, 69; = Downy woodpecker, 69 ❺ Blue jay, 67 ❻ Mourning dove, 65 ❼ Black-capped chickadee, 60 ❽ House sparrow, 59 ❾ Northern cardinal, 56 ❿ European starling, 52

Source: *Project FeederWatch/ Cornell Lab of Ornithology*
These are the birds that watchers are most likely to see at their feeders in North America.

TINSELTOWN BIRD

One of the most common garden birds, finches were spread from the western American states in the 1940s by dealers who sold them as "Hollywood Finches."

TOP 10 ★ LIGHTEST BATS

BAT/HABITAT	LENGTH		WEIGHT	
	IN	CM	OZ	G
1 Kitti's hognosed bat (*Craseonycteris thonglongyai*), Thailand	1.10	2.9	0.07	2.0
2 Proboscis bat (*Rhynchonycteris naso*), Central and South America	1.50	3.8	0.09	2.5
3 =Banana bat (*Pipistrellus nanus*), Africa	1.50	3.8	0.11	3.0
=Smoky bat (*Furiptera horrens*), Central and South America	1.50	3.8	0.11	3.0
5 =Little yellow bat (*Rhogeessa mira*), Central America	1.57	4.0	0.12	3.5
=Lesser bamboo bat (*Tylonycteris pachypus*), Southeast Asia	1.57	4.0	0.12	3.5
7 Disc-winged bat (*Thyroptera tricolor*), Central and South America	1.42	3.6	0.14	4.0
8 =Lesser horseshoe bat (*Rhynolophus hipposideros*), Europe and Western Asia	1.46	3.7	0.18	5.0
=California myotis (*Myotis californienses*), North America	1.69	4.3	0.18	5.0
10 Northern blossom bat (*Macroglossus minimus*), Southeast Asia to Australia	2.52	6.4	0.53	15.0

This list focuses on the smallest example of 10 different bat families. The weights shown are typical, rather than extreme – and since a bat can eat more than half its own weight, the weights of individual examples may vary considerably. The smallest of all weighs less than a table-tennis ball, and even the heaviest listed here weighs less than an empty aluminum drink can. Length is of head and body only, since tail lengths vary from zero (as in Kitti's hognosed bat and the Northern blossom bat) to long (as in the Proboscis bat and Lesser horseshoe bat).

TOP 10 ★ FASTEST BIRDS

BIRD	RECORDED SPEED	
	MPH	KM/H
1 Spine-tailed swift	106	171
2 Frigate bird	95	153
3 Spur-winged goose	88	142
4 Red-breasted merganser	80	129
5 White-rumped swift	77	124
6 Canvasback duck	72	116
7 Eider duck	70	113
8 Teal	68	109
9 =Mallard	65	105
= Pintail	65	105

This list picks out star performers among the medium- to large-sized birds that can hit their top speed without help from wind or gravity. Fastest among swimming birds is the gentoo penguin at 22.3 mph (35 km/h), while the speediest of flightless birds is the ostrich at 45 mph (72 km/h).

TOP 10 ★ RAREST BIRDS

BIRD/COUNTRY	ESTIMATED NO.*
1 = Spix's macaw, Brazil	1
=Cebu flower pecker, Philippines	1
3 Hawaiian crow, Hawaii	5
4 Black stilt, New Zealand	12
5 Echo parakeet, Mauritius	13
6 Imperial Amazon parrot, Dominica	15
7 Magpie robin, Seychelles	20
8 Kakapo, New Zealand	24
9 Pink pigeon, Mauritius	70
10 Mauritius kestrel, Mauritius	100

* Of breeding pairs reported since 1986

Several rare bird species are known from old records or from only one specimen, but must be assumed to be extinct in the absence of recent sightings or records of breeding pairs. Rare birds come under most pressure on islands like Mauritius, where the dodo met its fate.

What is an Australian trumpet?
see p.49 for the answer
A A swan
B A marine snail
C A venomous spider

OCEAN FLYER

Featuring in Coleridge's poem The Rime of the Ancient Mariner, *the albatross has a massive wingspan and can soar over the oceans for days at a time.*

TOP 10 BIRDS WITH THE LARGEST WINGSPANS

(Bird/wingspan in ft/m)

1 Marabou stork, 13/4.0 **2** Albatross, 12/3.7 **3** Trumpeter swan, 11/3.4
4 = Mute swan, 10/3.1; = Whooper swan, 10/3.1; = Grey pelican, 10/3.1;
= California condor, 10/3.1; = Black vulture, 10/3.1
9 = Great bustard, 9/2.7; = Kori bustard, 9/2.7

TOP 10 ★
HEAVIEST FLIGHTED BIRDS

BIRD	WINGSPAN		WEIGHT		
	FT	M	LB	OZ	KG
1 Great bustard	9	2.7	46	1	20.9
2 Trumpeter swan	11	3.4	37	1	16.8
3 Mute swan	10	3.1	35	15	16.3
4 =Albatross	12	3.7	34	13	15.8
=Whooper swan	10	3.1	34	13	15.8
6 Manchurian crane	7	2.1	32	14	14.9
7 Kori bustard	9	2.7	30	0	13.6
8 Grey pelican	10	3.1	28	11	13.0
9 Black vulture	10	3.1	27	8	12.5
10 Griffon vulture	7	2.1	26	7	12.0

Wing size does not necessarily correspond to weight in flighted birds. The 13-ft (4-m) wingspan of the marabou stork beats all the birds listed here, yet its body weight is normally no heavier than any of these. When laden with a meal of carrion, however, the marabou can double its weight and may fail to take off.

"A LITTLE BIRD TOLD ME"

This phrase is often used to announce that one has information but may not be willing to reveal the source of it. Birds as messengers are legendary, but this expression, like so many others, has its origin in the Bible. In the Book of Ecclesiastes (9:20), the writer warns those who complain against kings and the rich and powerful that "a bird of the air shall carry the voice, and that which hath wings shall tell the matter."

TOP 10 ★
MOST COMMON BIRDS IN THE US

BIRD

1 Red-winged blackbird
2 European starling
3 American robin
4 Mourning dove
5 Common grackle
6 American crow
7 Western meadowlark
8 House sparrow
9 Northern cardinal
10 Cliff sparrow

Source: *US Fish and Wildlife Service*

SWANNING AROUND

A heavyweight among flighted birds, exceptional specimens of the mute swan may top 49 lb 10 oz (22.5 kg) and have wingspans of up to 12 ft (3.7 m).

Cats, Dogs & Pets

MOVIES STARRING DOGS

	MOVIE	YEAR
1	*101 Dalmatians*	1996
2	*One Hundred and One Dalmatians**	1961
3	*Lady and the Tramp**	1955
4	*Oliver & Company**	1988
5	*Turner & Hooch*	1989
6	*The Fox and the Hound**	1981
7	*Beethoven*	1992
8	*Homeward Bound II: Lost in San Francisco*	1996
9	*Beethoven's 2nd*	1993
10	*K-9*	1991

* Animated

Man's best friend has been stealing scenes since the earliest years of moviemaking, with the 1905 low-budget *Rescued by Rover* standing as one of the most successful productions of the pioneer period. The numerous silent era movies starring Rin Tin Tin, an ex-German army dog who emigrated to the US, and his successor, Lassie, whose long series of feature and TV movies date from the 1940s onward, are among the most enduring in cinematic history.

TOP 10 DOGS' NAMES IN THE US

1 Max 2 Buddy 3 Molly 4 Maggie
5 Bailey 6 Jake 7 Lucy 8 Sam
9 Bear 10 Shadow

Based on a database of 117,000 I.D. tag records.
Source: American Pet Classics

TOP DOGS

Labrador retrievers are the most popular pedigree dogs in both the US and the UK, where they were first bred as gundogs in the 19th century.

DOG BREEDS IN THE US

	BREED	NO. REGISTERED*
1	Labrador retriever	154,897
2	Golden retriever	62,652
3	German shepherd	57,256
4	Dachsund	50,772
5	Beagle	49,080
6	Poodle	45,852
7	Chihuahua	42,013
8	Rottweiler	41,776
9	Yorkshire terrier	40,684
10	Boxer	34,998

* By American Kennel Club, Inc., 1999
Source: *The American Kennel Club*

The Labrador retriever tops the list for the eighth consecutive year. This breed is also No. 1 in the UK. New to this year's Top 10 is the boxer, while the rottweiler drops from fourth place in 1998 down to No. 8 in 1999.

CAT BREEDS IN THE US

	BREED	NO. REGISTERED*
1	Persian	30,656
2	Maine coon	4,642
3	Siamese	2,389
4	Exotic	2,188
5	Abyssinian	1,962
6	Oriental	1,210
7	Birman	1,017
8	Scottish fold	1,007
9	American shorthair	986
10	Burmese	923

* Year ending December 31, 1999
Source: *Cat Fanciers' Association*

Some people consider that the Maine coon is so called because it resulted from crossbreeding a cat and a racoon.

MOST INTELLIGENT DOG BREEDS

1	Border collie
2	Poodle
3	German shepherd (Alsatian)
4	Golden retriever
5	Doberman pinscher
6	Shetland sheepdog
7	Labrador retriever
8	Papillon
9	Rottweiler
10	Australian cattle dog

Source: *Stanley Coren, The Intelligence of Dogs*

Background image: GUINEA PIGS

TOP 10 CATS' NAMES IN THE US

1 Tiger **2** Max **3** Tigger **4** Sam **5** Kitty
6 Sammy **7** Smokey **8** Shadow
9 Misty **10** Fluffy

Based on a database of
117,000 I.D. tag records.
Source: American Pet Classics

WHAT'S NEW, PUSSYCAT?

*Although their role as household mouse
exterminators is less significant today, cats maintain
their place among the world's favorite
animals.*

TOP 10 ★
PETS IN THE US

PET	ESTIMATED NO.*
1 Cat	66,150,000
2 Dog	58,200,000
3 Small animal pet#	12,740,000
4 Parakeet	11,000,000
5 Freshwater fish	10,800,000
6 Reptile	7,540,000
7 Finch	7,350,000
8 Cockatiel	6,320,000
9 Canary	2,580,000
10 Parrot	1,550,000

Source: *Pet Industry Joint Advisory Council*

* *Number of households owning, rather than
individual specimens*

*Includes small rodents: rabbits, ferrets,
hamsters, guinea pigs, and gerbils*

"IN THE DOGHOUSE"

In J. M. Barrie's famous children's play *Peter
Pan* (1904), irascible Mr. Darling mistreats
the dog-nursemaid, Nana, as a result of which
the Darling children – Wendy, John, and
Michael – leave home. As a penance, Mr.
Darling lives in the doghouse until the
children return. Mr. Darling was based on
Arthur Llewelyn Davies, the real-life father of
the boys on whom
Barrie based the story,
and Nana was Barrie's
own dog, Luath.

**WHY DO
WE SAY ?**

TOP 10 RABBITS' NAMES
IN THE US

1 Thumper **2** Flopsy **3** Charlie **4** Fudge
5 Rosie **6** Smokey **7** Snowy
8 Daisy **9** George **10** Molly

FURRY FAVORITES

*Although Flopsy is second choice,
Beatrix Potter's more famous creations of
Peter and Benjamin are surprisingly absent
from the Top 10 rabbits' names.*

Creepy Crawlies 1

TOP 10 ★
FASTEST FLYING INSECTS

SPECIES	MPH	KM/H
1 Hawkmoth (*Sphingidaei*)	33.3	53.6
2 =West Indian butterfly (*Nymphalidae prepona*)	30.0	48.0
=Deer bot fly (*Cephenemyia pratti*)	30.0	48.0
4 Deer bot fly (*Chrysops*)	25.0	40.0
5 West Indian butterfly (*Hesperiidae sp.*)	18.6	30.0
6 Dragonfly (*Anax parthenope*)	17.8	28.6
7 Hornet (*Vespa crabro*)	13.3	21.4
8 Bumblebee (*Bombus lapidarius*)	11.1	17.9
9 Horsefly (*Tabanus bovinus*)	8.9	14.3
10 Honeybee (*Apis millefera*)	7.2	11.6

Few accurate assessments of these speeds have been attempted, and this list reflects only the results of those scientific studies recognized by entomologists.

BEETLE BEATS ALL

This red-spotted longhorn beetle is one of about 400,000 beetles identified so far. This makes the beetle the most common known species of insect.

TOP 10 ★
LARGEST MOTHS

MOTH	WINGSPAN IN	MM
1 Atlas moth (*Attacus atlas*)	11.8	300
2 Owlet moth (*Thysania agrippina*)*	11.4	290
3 *Haematopis grataria*	10.2	260
4 Hercules emperor moth (*Coscinocera hercules*)	8.3	210
5 Malagasy silk moth (*Argema mitraei*)	7.1	180
6 *Eacles imperialis*	6.9	175
7 =Common emperor moth (*Bunaea alcinoe*)	6.3	160
=Giant peacock moth (*Saturnia pyri*)	6.3	160
9 Gray moth (*Brahmaea wallichii*)	6.1	155
10 =Black witch (*Ascalapha odorata*)	5.9	150
=Regal moth (*Citheronia regalis*)	5.9	150
=Polyphemus moth (*Antheraea polyphemus*)	5.9	150

* *Exceptional specimen measured at 12¼ in (308 mm)*

TOP 10 ★
MOST COMMON INSECTS*

SPECIES	APPROXIMATE NO. OF KNOWN SPECIES
1 Beetles (*Coleoptera*)	400,000
2 Butterflies and moths (*Lepidoptera*)	165,000
3 Ants, bees, and wasps (*Hymenoptera*)	140,000
4 True flies (*Diptera*)	120,000
5 Bugs (*Hemiptera*)	90,000
6 Crickets, grasshoppers, and locusts (*Orthoptera*)	20,000
7 Caddisflies (*Trichoptera*)	10,000
8 Lice (*Phthiraptera/Psocoptera*)	7,000
9 Dragonflies and damselflies (*Odonata*)	5,500
10 Lacewings (*Neuroptera*)	4,700

* *By number of known species*

This list includes only species that have been discovered and named: it is surmised that many thousands of species still await discovery.

Did You Know? The heaviest of all insects is the Goliath beetle, which can weigh up to 3½ oz (100 g), or more than twice the weight of a golf ball.

TOP 10 ★

CREATURES WITH THE MOST LEGS

	CREATURE	AVERAGE NO. OF LEGS
1	Millipede *Illacme plenipes*	750
2	Centipede *Himantarum gabrielis*	354
3	Centipede *Haplophilus subterraneus*	178
4	Millipedes*	30
5	Symphylans	24
6	Caterpillars*	16
7	Woodlice	14
8	Crabs, shrimps	10
9	Spiders	8
10	Insects	6

* Most species

LEGGING IT TO THE TOP

The Haplophilus subterraneus *centipede measures up to 2¾ in (70 mm) and has 89 pairs of legs. It is interesting to note that all centipedes always have an odd number of body segments (although the number of legs is, of course, always even!).*

Because "centipede" means 100 feet and "millipede" 1,000 feet, many people believe that centipedes have 100 legs and millipedes 1,000. However, despite their names and depending on their species, centipedes have anything from 28 to 354 legs and millipedes up to 400, with the record standing at more than 700. The other principal difference between them is that each body segment of a centipede has two legs, while that of a millipede has four.

BIG WING

Male African giant swallowtails, Papilio antimachus, *are Africa's largest butterflies, with wingspans of up to an impressive 9⅛ in (230 mm).*

TOP 10 ★
LARGEST BUTTERFLIES

	BUTTERFLY	WINGSPAN IN	MM
1	Queen Alexandra's birdwing	11.0	280
2	African giant swallowtail	9.1	230
3	Goliath birdwing	8.3	210
4=	*Trogonoptera trojana*	7.9	200
=	Buru opalescent birdwing	7.9	200
=	*Troides hypolitus*	7.9	200
7=	*Ornithoptera lydius*	7.5	190
=	Chimaera birdwing	7.5	190
=	*Troides magellanus*	7.5	190
=	*Troides miranda*	7.5	190

Creepy Crawlies 2

TOP 10 LARGEST SNAILS

(Species/length in in/mm)

1 **Australian trumpet** (*Syrinx aruanus*), 30¼/770 **2** **Horse conch**
(*Pleuroploc filamentosa*), 22¼/580 **3** = **Baler shell** (*Voluta amphora*), 18¾/480;
= **Triton's trumpet** (*Charonia tritonis*), 18¾/480 **5** **Beck's volute** (*Voluta becki*), 18½/470
6 **Umbilicate volute** (*Voluta umbilicalis*), 16½/420 **7** **Madagascar helmet**
(*Cassis madagascariensis*), 16/409 **8** **Spider conch** (*Lambis truncata*), 15¾/400
9 **Knobbly trumpet** (*Charonia nodifera*), 15¼/390 **10** **Goliath conch**
(*Strombus goliath*), 15/380

TOP 10 ★
DEADLIEST SPIDERS

	SPIDER/LOCATION
1	**Banana spider** (*Phonenutria nigriventer*), Central and South America
2	**Sydney funnel web** (*Atrax robustus*), Australia
3	**Wolf spider** (*Lycosa raptoria/erythrognatha*), Central and South America
4	**Black widow** (Latrodectus species), worldwide
5	**Violin spider/Recluse spider**, worldwide
6	**Sac spider**, Southern Europe
7	**Tarantula** (*Eurypelma rubropilosum*), Neotropics
8	**Tarantula** (*Acanthoscurria atrox*), Neotropics
9	**Tarantula** (*Lasiodora klugi*), Neotropics
10	**Tarantula** (*Pamphobeteus* species), Neotropics

This list ranks spiders according to their "lethal potential" – their
venom yield divided by their venom potency. The Banana spider, for
example, yields 6 mg of venom, with 1 mg the estimated lethal dose in
man. However, few spiders are capable of killing humans – there were
just 14 recorded deaths caused by black widows in the US in the
whole of the 19th century.

READY TO STRIKE
*Found only in New South Wales, male
Sydney funnel web spiders are, unusually,
more dangerous than the females.*

TOP 10 ★
MOST POPULAR US STATE INSECTS

INSECT/STATES	NO.
1 **Honeybee**, Arkansas, Georgia, Kansas, Louisiana, Maine, Mississippi, Missouri, Nebraska, New Hampshire, New Jersey, North Carolina, South Dakota, Utah, Vermont, Wisconsin	15
2 **Swallowtail butterfly**, Florida (giant/zebra longwing), Georgia (tiger), Mississippi (spicebush), Ohio (tiger), Oklahoma (black), Oregon (Oregon), Virginia (tiger), Wyoming (western)	8
3 **Ladybird beetle/ladybug**, Delaware (convergent), Iowa, Massachusetts, New York (nine-spotted), New Hampshire (two-spotted), Ohio, Tennessee (ladybug)	7
4 **Monarch butterfly**, Alabama, Idaho, Illinois, Texas, Vermont	5
5 **Firefly**, Pennsylvania, Tennessee	2
6 = **Baltimore checkerspot butterfly**, Maryland	1
= **California dogface butterfly**, California	1
= **Carolina mantis**, South Carolina	1
= **Colorado hairstreak butterfly**, Colorado	1
= **European praying mantis**, Connecticut	1
= **Four-spotted skimmer dragonfly**, Alaska	1
= **Green darner dragonfly**, Texas	1
= **Karner blue butterfly**, New Hampshire	1
= **Tarantula hawk wasp**, New Mexico	1
= **Viceroy butterfly**, Kentucky	1

SNAIL'S PACE

Although exceeded by marine species, the Giant African snail is the largest terrestrial mollusk. Exceptional specimens may reach almost 15.5 in (400 mm) in length and weigh 2 lb (900 g).

THE 10 COUNTRIES WITH THE MOST THREATENED INVERTEBRATES

(Country/threatened invertebrate species)

1 US, 594   **2** Australia, 281   **3** South Africa, 101   **4** Portugal, 67   **5** France, 61   **6** Spain, 57   **7** Tanzania, 46   **8** = Japan, 45; = Dem. Rep. of Congo, 45   **10** = Austria, 41; = Italy, 41

Source: *International Union for the Conservation of Nature*

TOP 10 ★
LARGEST MOLLUSKS*

	SPECIES	CLASS	LENGTH IN	LENGTH MM
1	**Giant squid** (*Architeuthis sp.*)	Cephalopod	660	16,764#
2	**Giant clam** (*Tridacna gigas*)	Marine bivalve	51	1,300
3	**Australian trumpet**	Marine snail	30	770
4	***Hexabranchus sanguineus***	Sea slug	20	520
5	***Carinaria cristata***	Heteropod	19	500
6	**Steller's coat of mail shell** (*Cryptochiton stelleri*)	Chiton	18	470
7	**Freshwater mussel** (*Cristaria plicata*)	Freshwater bivalve	11	300
8	**Giant African snail** (*Achatina achatina*)	Land snail	7	200
9	**Tusk shell** (*Dentalium vernedi*)	Scaphopod	5	138
10	**Apple snail** (*Pila werneri*)	Freshwater snail	4	125

* *Largest species within each class*

\# *Estimated; actual length unknown*

Which breed of dog is regarded as the most intelligent?
see p.44 for the answer
A   Border collie
B   Saint Bernard
C   Afghan hound

TOP 10 TALLEST TREES IN THE US*

	TREE	LOCATION	HEIGHT FT	M
1	Coast Douglas fir	Coos County, Oregon	329	100.3
2	Coast redwood	Prairie Creek Redwoods State Park, California	313	95.4
3	General Sherman, giant sequoia	Sequoia National Park, California	275	83.8
4	Noble fir	Mount St. Helens National Monument, Washington	272	82.9
5	Grand fir	Redwood National Park, California	257	78.3
6	Western hemlock	Olympic National Park, Washington	241	73.5
7	Sugar pine	Dorrington, California	232	70.7
8	Ponderosa pine	Plumas National Forest, California	223	68.0
9	Port-Orford cedar	Siskiyou National Forest, Oregon	219	66.8
10	Pacific silver fir	Forks, Washington	217	66.1

By species (i.e., the tallest known example of each of the 10 tallest species)
Source: American Forests

ON TAP

In the 20th century, annual world demand for natural rubber, especially from the automotive industry, increased from under 50,000 to over 6 million tons.

TOP 10 ★ RUBBER-PRODUCING COUNTRIES

	COUNTRY	1998 PRODUCTION TONS
1	Thailand	2,382,976
2	Indonesia	1,723,885
3	Malaysia	1,192,804
4	India	597,284
5	China	495,900
6	Philippines	220,400
7	Vietnam	199,131
8	Côte d'Ivoire	127,466
9	Sri Lanka	116,572
10	Nigeria	99,180
	World total	7,471,658

Source: Food and Agriculture Organization of the United Nations

TOP 10 ★ TIMBER-PRODUCING COUNTRIES

	COUNTRY	1998 PRODUCTION CU FT	CU M
1	US	17,478,536,826	494,937,000
2	China	11,054,092,059	313,017,000
3	India	10,822,357,195	306,455,000
4	Brazil	7,780,280,892	220,313,000
5	Indonesia	7,168,471,891	202,988,500
6	Canada	6,751,387,981	191,178,000
7	Nigeria	4,145,483,167	117,387,000
8	Russia	2,965,302,211	83,968,000
9	Sweden	2,126,790,686	60,224,000
10	Ethiopia	1,847,310,388	52,310,000
	World total	119,562,158,989	3,385,623,000

Source: Food and Agriculture Organization of the United Nations

TREE TOPS

The US leads the world in timber production, supplying the requirements of industries such as construction and paper manufacture.

TOP 10 ★
MOST COMMON TREES IN THE US

	TREE
1	Silver maple
2	Black cherry
3	Boxelder
4	Eastern cottonwood
5	Black willow
6	Northern red oak
7	Flowering dogwood
8	Black oak
9	Ponderosa pine
10	Coast douglas fir

Source: *American Forests*

TOP 10 ★
COUNTRIES WITH THE LARGEST AREAS OF FOREST

	COUNTRY	AREA SQ MILES	AREA SQ KM
1	Russia	2,957,203	7,659,120
2	Canada	1,907,345	4,940,000
3	Brazil	1,884,179	4,880,000
4	US	1,142,824	2,959,900
5	Dem. Rep. of Congo	671,046	1,738,000
6	Australia	559,848	1,450,000
7	China	503,848	1,304,960
8	Indonesia	431,562	1,117,740
9	Peru	327,415	848,000
10	India	264,480	685,000
	World total	15,976,944	41,380,090

The world's forests occupy some 28 percent of the total land area of the planet. Almost 45 percent of the area of Russia is forested, representing a total area that is almost the size of Australia.

NATURAL BEAUTY

The largest National Forest in the US, the Tongass in Alaska, is a magnificent wilderness that encompasses mountains, rivers, glaciers, and islands. This vast forest is over three times the size of the next forest in the Top 10.

TOP 10 ★
LARGEST NATIONAL FORESTS IN THE US

	FOREST	LOCATION	AREA SQ MILES	AREA SQ KM
1	Tongass National Forest	Sitka, Alaska	25,937	67,177
2	Chugach National Forest	Anchorage, Alaska	8,281	21,448
3	Toiyabe National Forest	Sparks, Nevada	5,000	12,950
4	Tonto National Forest	Phoenix, Arizona	4,531	11,735
5 =	Boise National Forest	Boise, Idaho	4,218	10,925
=	Gila National Forest	Silver City, New Mexico	4,218	10,925
7 =	Humboldt National Forest	Elko, Nevada	3,906	10,116
=	Challis National Forest	Challis, Idaho	3,906	10,116
9 =	Shoshone National Forest	Cody, Wyoming	3,750	9,712
=	Flathead National Forest	Kalispell, Montana	3,750	9,712

Source: *Land Areas of the National Forest System*

Did You Know? A vast area of the Tunguska Forest of Siberia was flattened in an instant on June 30, 1908, when a meteorite – or perhaps part of Encke's comet – exploded in the sky above it.

THE WINNING LEG

The second longest bone, the tibia is named after the Latin word for a flute, which it resembles in shape and length. The three longest bones are all in the leg.

COUNTRIES THAT SPEND THE MOST ON HEALTH CARE

	COUNTRY	HEALTH SPENDING PER CAPITA ($)
1	US	4,093
2	Switzerland	3,603
3	Germany	2,677
4	Norway	2,622
5	Japan	2,442
6	Denmark	2,388
7	France	2,349
8	Sweden	2,222
9	Austria	2,012
10	Netherlands	1,978

Source: *World Bank*, World Development Indicators 1999

MOST COMMON REASONS FOR VISITS TO A PHYSICIAN

	REASON FOR VISIT	VISITS, 1997
1	General medical examination	59,796,000
2	Progress visit, not otherwise specified	28,583,000
3	Cough	25,735,000
4	Routine prenatal examination	22,979,000
5	Postoperative visit	18,861,000
6	Symptoms referable to throat	17,151,000
7	Well baby examination	15,526,000
8	Vision dysfunctions	13,443,000
9	Earache or ear infection	13,359,000
10	Back symptoms	12,863,000

Source: *National Ambulatory Medical Care Survey/ Center for Disease Control/National Center for Health Statistics*

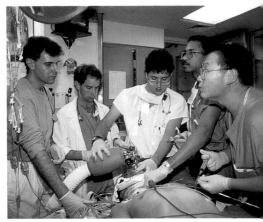

ER, US

The world's hospital emergency rooms have to be equipped to treat victims of everything from minor injuries to major traumas.

LONGEST BONES IN THE HUMAN BODY

	BONE	AVERAGE LENGTH IN	CM
1	Femur (thighbone)	19.88	50.50
2	Tibia (shinbone)	16.94	43.03
3	Fibula (outer lower leg)	15.94	40.50
4	Humerus (upper arm)	14.35	36.46
5	Ulna (inner lower arm)	11.10	28.20
6	Radius (outer lower arm)	10.40	26.42
7	7th rib	9.45	24.00
8	8th rib	9.06	23.00
9	Innominate bone (hipbone)	7.28	18.50
10	Sternum (breastbone)	6.69	17.00

THE 10 MOST COMMON HOSPITAL ER CASES

(Reason for visit/visits, 1997)

❶ **Stomach and abdominal pain,** 5,527,000 ❷ **Chest pain and related symptoms,** 5,315,000 ❸ **Fever,** 4,212,000 ❹ **Headache,** 2,518,000 ❺ **Injury – upper extremity,** 2,383,000 ❻ **Shortness of breath,** 2,242,000 ❼ **Cough,** 2,220,000 ❽ **Back symptoms,** 2,073,000 ❾ **Pain, nonspecific site,** 2,040,000 ❿ **Symptoms referable to throat,** 1,953,000

Source: *Center for Disease Control/ National Center for Health Statistics*

MOST COMMON TYPES OF ILLNESS

	TYPE	NEW CASES ANNUALLY
1	Diarrhea (including dysentery)	4,002,000,000
2	Malaria	up to 500,000,000
3	Acute lower respiratory infections	395,000,000
4	Occupational injuries	350,000,000
5	Occupational diseases	217,000,000
6	Trichomoniasis	170,000,000
7	Mood (affective) disorders	122,865,000
8	Chlamydial infections	89,000,000
9	Alcohol dependence syndrome	75,000,000
10	Gonococcal (bacterial) infections	62,000,000

Source: *World Health Organization*

MOST COMMON PHOBIAS

	OBJECT OF PHOBIA	MEDICAL TERM
1	Spiders	Arachnephobia or arachnophobia
2	People and social situations	Anthropophobia or sociophobia
3	Flying	Aerophobia or aviatophobia
4	Open spaces	Agoraphobia, cenophobia or kenophobia
5	Confined spaces	Claustrophobia, cleisiophobia, cleithrophobia, or clithrophobia
6 =	Vomiting	Emetophobia or emitophobia
=	Heights	Acrophobia, altophobia, hypsophobia, or hypsiphobia
8	Cancer	Carcinomaphobia, carcinophobia, carcinomatophobia, cancerphobia, or cancerophobia
9	Thunderstorms	Brontophobia or keraunophobia
10 =	Death	Necrophobia or thanatophobia
=	Heart disease	Cardiophobia

MOST COMMON ELEMENTS IN THE HUMAN BODY

	ELEMENT	AVERAGE WEIGHT* OZ	G
1	Oxygen	1,608	45,500
2	Carbon	445	12,600
3	Hydrogen	247	7,000
4	Nitrogen	74	2,100
5	Calcium	37	1,050
6	Phosphorus	25	700
7	Sulfur	6	175
8	Potassium	5	140
9 =	Chlorine	4	105
=	Sodium	4	105

* Average in 154 lb (70 kg) person

The Top 10 elements account for more than 99 percent of the total, with the balance comprising minute quantities of metallic elements including iron, zinc, tin, and aluminum. Each has one or more specific functions: oxygen is essential for energy production, carbon and hydrogen are major cell components, while nitrogen is vital for DNA and most body functions.

WEIGHTY MATTER

The modern technique of Magnetic Resonance Imaging (MRI) enables us to view the human brain, the human body's third-largest organ.

LARGEST HUMAN ORGANS

	ORGAN		AVERAGE WEIGHT OZ	G
1	Skin		384.0	10,886
2	Liver		1,560	55.0
3	Brain	male	49.7	1,408
		female	44.6	1,263
4	Lungs	right	20.5	580
		left	18.0	510
		total	38.5	1,090
5	Heart	male	11.1	315
		female	9.3	265
6	Kidneys	right	4.9	140
		left	5.3	150
		total	10.2	290
7	Spleen		6.0	170
8	Pancreas		3.5	98
9	Thyroid		1.2	35
10	Prostate (male only)		0.7	20

This list is based on average immediate post-mortem weights, as recorded by St. Bartholomew's Hospital, London, and other sources during a 10-year period. Various instances of organs far in excess of the average have been recorded, including male brains of over 70.6 oz (2,000 g). The Victorians believed that the heavier the brain, the greater the intelligence, and were impressed by the recorded weights of 58 oz (1,650 g) for author William Makepeace Thackeray.

Did You Know? Among the least-common phobias are geniophobia (fear of eggshells,) barophobia (gravity), apeirophobia (infinity), and linonophobia (string).

Human Achievements

THE 10 ★
NORTH POLE FIRSTS

1 First to reach the Pole?
American adventurer Frederick Albert Cook claimed that he had reached the Pole, accompanied by two Inuits, on April 21, 1908, but his claim is disputed. It is more likely that Robert Edwin Peary, Matthew Alexander Henson (both Americans), and four Inuits were first at the Pole on April 6, 1909.

2 First to fly over the Pole in an airship
A team of 16, led by Roald Amundsen, the Norwegian explorer who first reached the South Pole in 1911, flew across the North Pole on May 12, 1926 in the Italian-built airship Norge.

3 First to land at the Pole in an aircraft
Soviets Pavel Afanaseyevich Geordiyenko, Mikhail Yemel'yenovich Ostrekin, Pavel Kononovich Sen'ko, and Mikhail Mikhaylovich Somov arrived at and departed from the Pole by air on April 23, 1948.

4 First solo flight over the Pole in a single-engined aircraft
Capt. Charles Francis Blair, Jr. of the US flew a single-engined Mustang fighter, Excalibur III, on May 29, 1951, crossing from Bardufoss, Norway, to Fairbanks, Alaska.

5 First submarine to surface at the Pole
USS Skate surfaced at the Pole on March 17, 1959.

6 First confirmed overland journey to the Pole
American Ralph S. Plaisted, with companions Walter Pederson, Gerald Pitzel, and Jean Luc Bombardier, reached the Pole on April 18, 1968, using snowmobiles.

7 First solo overland journey to the Pole
Japanese explorer Naomi Uemura reached the Pole on May 1, 1978, traveling by dog sled, and was then picked up by an airplane.

8 First to reach the Pole on skis
A team of seven, led by Dimitry Shparo (USSR), was the first to reach the North Pole on May 31, 1979.

9 First crossing on a Pole-to-Pole expedition
Sir Ranulph Fiennes and Charles Burton walked over the North Pole on April 10, 1982, having crossed the South Pole on December 15, 1980.

10 First woman to walk to the Pole
Along with five male companions, American physical education teacher Ann Bancroft reached the Pole on May 1, 1986.

Lt.-Cdr. Richard Byrd and Floyd Bennett claimed to have traversed the Pole on May 9, 1926 in an aircraft, but recent analysis of Byrd's diary indicates that they turned back some 150 miles (241 km) short of the Pole, thereby disqualifying their entry.

POLE TO POLE
The 1979–82 Transglobe Expedition led by Sir Ranulph Fiennes, here at Scott Base, South Pole, was the first to traverse both Poles.

THE 10 ★
CIRCUMNAVIGATION FIRSTS

CIRCUMNAVIGATION/CRAFT	VOYAGER(S)	RETURN DATE
1 First, *Vittoria*	Juan Sebastian de Elcano*	Sep 6, 1522
2 First in less than 80 days, *various*	"Nellie Bly"#	Jan 25, 1890
3 First solo, *Spray*	Capt. Joshua Slocum	July 3, 1898
4 First by air, *Chicago, New Orleans*	Lt. Lowell Smith, Lt. Leslie P. Arnold	Sep 28, 1924
5 First nonstop by air, *Lucky Lady II*	Capt. James Gallagher	Mar 2, 1949
6 First underwater, *Triton*	Capt. Edward L. Beach	Apr 25, 1960
7 First nonstop solo, *Suhaili*	Robin Knox-Johnston	Apr 22, 1969
8 First helicopter, *Spirit of Texas*	H. Ross Perot, Jr. and Jay Coburn	Sep 30, 1982
9 First air without refueling, *Voyager*	Richard Rutan and Jeana Yeager	Dec 23, 1986
10 First by balloon, *Breitling Orbiter 3*	Brian Jones and Bertrand Piccard	Mar 21, 1999

* The expedition was led by Ferdinand Magellan, but he did not survive the voyage.

Real name Elizabeth Cochrane. This US journalist set out to beat the fictitious "record" established in Jules Verne's novel Around the World in 80 Days.

THE 10 FIRST MOUNTAINEERS TO CLIMB EVEREST
(Mountaineer/nationality/date)

1 Edmund Hillary, New Zealander, May 29, 1953　**2 Tenzing Norgay**, Nepalese, May 29, 1953　**3 Jürg Marmet**, Swiss, May 23, 1956　**4 Ernst Schmied**, Swiss, May 23, 1956　**5 Hans-Rudolf von Gunten**, Swiss, May 24, 1956　**6 Adolf Reist**, Swiss, May 24, 1956　**7 Wang Fu-chou**, Chinese, May 25, 1960　**8 Chu Ying-hua**, Chinese, May 25, 1960　**9 Konbu**, Tibetan, May 25, 1960　**10 = Nawang Gombu**, Indian, May 1, 1963; = **James Whittaker**, American, May 1, 1963

Nawang Gombu and James Whittaker are 10th equally because they ascended the last feet to the summit side by side.

 The citizens of which country have won the most Nobel Prizes for Literature?
see p.69 for the answer

A　US
B　UK
C　France

THE 10 ★
FIRST SUCCESSFUL HUMAN DESCENTS OVER NIAGARA FALLS

	NAME/METHOD	DATE
1	**Annie Edson Taylor**, Wooden barrel	Oct 24, 1901
2	**Bobby Leach**, Steel barrel	July 25, 1911
3	**Jean Lussier**, Steel and rubber ball fitted with oxygen cylinders	July 4, 1928
4	**William Fitzgerald** (a.k.a. Nathan Boya), Steel and rubber ball fitted with oxygen cylinders	July 15, 1961
5	**Karel Soucek**, Barrel	July 3, 1984
6	**Steven Trotter**, Barrel	Aug 18, 1985
7	**Dave Mundy**, Barrel	Oct 5, 1985
8=	**Peter deBernardi**, Metal container	Sep 28, 1989
=	**Jeffrey Petkovich**, Metal container	Sep 28, 1989
10	**Dave Mundy**, Diving bell	Sep 26, 1993

Source: *Niagara Falls Museum*

TOP 10 ★
FASTEST CROSS-CHANNEL SWIMMERS

	SWIMMER/NATIONALITY	YEAR	TIME HRS:MINS
1	**Chad Hundeby**, American	1994	7:17
2	**Penny Lee Dean**, American	1978	7:40
3	**Tamara Bruce**, Australian	1994	7:53
4	**Philip Rush**, New Zealander	1987	7:55
5	**Hans van Goor**, Dutch	1995	8:02
6	**Richard Davey**, British	1988	8:05
7	**Irene van der Laan**, Dutch	1982	8:06
8	**Paul Asmuth**, American	1985	8:12
9	**Anita Sood**, Indian	1987	8:15
10	**John van Wisse**, Australian	1994	8:17

Source: *Channel Swimming Association*

The first person to swim the Channel was Matthew Webb (British), who on August 24–25, 1875 made the crossing in what now seems the rather leisurely time of 21 hours 45 minutes.

NIAGARA FALLS

Annie Edson Taylor, a Michigan schoolteacher, celebrated her 43rd birthday in 1901 by being the first to plunge over Niagara Falls and survive. She was followed in 1911 by 69-year-old Bobby Leach (who later died when he slipped on a piece of orange peel!). On July 4, 1928, watched by an excited crowd of 100,000, Jean Lussier (seen here), a circus acrobat from Springfield, Massachusetts, traveled over the Falls in a 758-lb (344-kg) steel-reinforced rubber sphere. In 1920, barber Charles Stephens became one of many killed in the attempt. Other failed efforts include those of George Stathakis (1930) and William Hill, Jr. (1951).

SNAP SHOTS ★

THE 10 LATEST WINNERS OF *TIME* MAGAZINE'S "PERSON OF THE YEAR" AWARD
(Year/recipient)

1 1999, **Jeffrey T. Bezos**, founder of Amazon.com **2** 1998, **Bill Clinton**, US President/**Kenneth Starr**, Independent Counsel **3** 1997, **Andrew S. Grove**, CEO of Intel, microchip company **4** 1996, **David Ho**, AIDS researcher **5** 1995, **Newt Gingrich**, US politician **6** 1994, **Pope John Paul II** **7** 1993, **Yasser Arafat**, **F. W. de Klerk**, **Nelson Mandela**, **Yitzhak Rabin**, "peacemakers" **8** 1992, **Bill Clinton**, US President **9** 1991, **George Bush**, US President **10** 1990, **Ted Turner**, US businessman

CHANNEL NO. 3
In 1994, 17-year-old Australian Tamara Bruce achieved the third-fastest Channel swim of all time, becoming the 487th person to swim from England to France.

Murder File

MOST COMMON MURDER WEAPONS AND METHODS IN ENGLAND AND WALES

	WEAPON OR METHOD	VICTIMS (1998/99)
1	Sharp instrument	207
2	Hitting and kicking	101
3	Strangulation and asphyxiation	81
4	Blunt instrument	68
5	Poison or drugs	56
6	Shooting	47
7	Burning	30
8	Motor vehicle	15
9	Drowning	7
10	Explosion	2

MOST COMMON MURDER WEAPONS AND METHODS IN THE US

	WEAPON OR METHOD	VICTIMS (1998)
1	Handguns	7,361
2	Knives or cutting instruments	1,877
3	Firearms (type not stated)	609
4	"Personal weapons" (hands, feet, fists, etc.)	949
5	Blunt objects (hammers, clubs, etc.)	741
6	Shotguns	619
7	Rifles	538
8	Strangulation	211
9	Fire	130
10	Asphyxiation	99

Source: FBI Uniform Crime Reports

RELATIONSHIPS OF MURDER VICTIMS TO PRINCIPAL SUSPECTS IN THE US

	RELATIONSHIP	VICTIMS (1998)
1	Acquaintance	3,773
2	Stranger	1,839
3	Wife	649
4	Girlfriend	429
5	Friend	418
6	Son	259
7	Daughter	210
8	Husband	190
9	Boyfriend	182
10=	Father	120
=	Neighbor	120

Source: FBI Uniform Crime Reports

Nearly 27 percent of the 14,088 murders committed in the US in 1998 were committed by acquaintances, and another 13 percent by strangers. FBI statistics also recorded 5,393 murders where the victim's relationship to the suspect was unknown, 265 "other family members" (those not specified elsewhere), 88 brothers, 99 mothers, and 25 sisters.

MOST PROLIFIC SERIAL KILLERS OF THE 20TH CENTURY

	NAME/COUNTRY/CRIMES AND PUNISHMENT	VICTIMS*
1	**Pedro Alonso López**, Colombia	300

Captured in 1980, López, nicknamed the "Monster of the Andes," led police to 53 graves, but probably murdered at least 300 in Colombia, Ecuador, and Peru. He was sentenced to life.

2	**Henry Lee Lucas**, US	200

Lucas admitted in 1983 to 360 murders. He remains on Death Row in Huntsville Prison, Texas.

3	**Luis Alfredo Gavarito**, Colombia	140

Gavarito confessed in 1999 to a spate of murders, which are still the subject of investigation.

4	**Dr. Harold Shipman**, UK	131

In January 2000, Manchester doctor Shipman was found guilty of the murder of 15 women patients, but police believe his total number of victims to be at least 131, and perhaps over 150.

5=	**Donald Henry "Pee Wee" Gaskins**, US	100

Gaskins was executed in 1991 for a series of murders that may have reached 200.

=	**Javed Iqbal**, Pakistan	100

Iqbal and two accomplices were found guilty in March 2000 of murdering boys in Lahore. He was sentenced to be publicly strangled, dismembered, and his body dissolved in acid.

7	**Delfina and Maria de Jesús Gonzales**, Mexico	91

In 1964 the Gonzales sisters were sentenced to 40 years' imprisonment for killing 80 women and 11 men.

8	**Bruno Lüdke**, Germany	86

Lüdke confessed to murdering 86 women in 1928–43. He died in a hospital after a lethal injection.

9	**Daniel Camargo Barbosa**, Ecuador	71

Barbosa was sentenced to just 16 years in prison for a catalog of crimes.

10	**Kampatimar Shankariya**, India	70

Caught after a two-year killing spree, Shankariya was hanged in Jaipur, India, in 1979.

* *Estimated minimum; includes individual and partnership murderers; excludes mercy killings by doctors, murders by bandits and by groups, such as political and military atrocities, and gangland slayings.*

WORST CITIES FOR MURDER IN THE US

	CITY	MURDERS (1998)*
1	Chicago	703
2	New York	633
3	Detroit	430
4	Los Angeles	426
5	Philadelphia	338
6	Baltimore	312
7	Washington, D.C.	260
8	Houston	254
9	Dallas	252
10	New Orleans	230

* *Murders and non-negligent manslaughter*

Source: FBI Uniform Crime Reports

THE 10 ⭐
COUNTRIES WITH THE HIGHEST MURDER RATES

	COUNTRY	ANNUAL MURDERS PER 100,000 POPULATION
1	Swaziland	88.1
2	Colombia	81.9
3	Namibia	72.4
4	South Africa	56.9
5	Lesotho	33.9
6	Belize	33.2
7	Philippines	30.1
8	Jamaica	27.6
9	Guatemala	27.4
10	French Guiana	27.2
	US	7.3

TOP 10 ⭐
COUNTRIES WITH THE LOWEST MURDER RATES

	COUNTRY	ANNUAL MURDERS PER 100,000 POPULATION
1=	Argentina	0.1
=	Brunei	0.1
3=	Burkina Faso	0.2
=	Niger	0.2
5=	Guinea	0.5
=	Guinea-Bissau	0.5
=	Iran	0.5
8=	Finland	0.6
=	Saudi Arabia	0.6
10=	Cameroon	0.7
=	Ireland	0.7
=	Mongolia	0.7

Among countries that report to international monitoring organizations, some 18 record murder rates of fewer than one per 100,000. It should be borne in mind, however, that some countries do not report, and there are a number of places that, having had no murders in recent years, could claim a murder rate of zero.

FIREPOWER
While handguns are the most common murder weapons in the US and certain other countries, restrictions on their use elsewhere relegates them to a less significant position.

TOP 10 ⭐
CIRCUMSTANCES FOR MURDER IN THE US

	REASON	MURDERS (1998)
1	**Argument** (unspecified)	4,080
2	**Robbery**	1,232
3	**Narcotic drug laws violation**	679
4	**Juvenile gang killing**	627
5	**Felony** (unspecified)	268
6	**Argument over money or property**	240
7	**Brawl due to influence of alcohol**	206
8	**Romantic triangle**	184
9	**Brawl due to influence of narcotics**	116
10	**Suspected felony**	104

Source: FBI Uniform Crime Reports

A total of 14,088 murders were reported in 1998, including 1,560 without a specified reason, and 4,358 for which the reasons were unknown.

THE 10 ⭐
WORST STATES FOR MURDER IN THE US

	STATE	FIREARMS USED	TOTAL MURDERS (1998)
1	California	1,469	2,171
2	Texas	899	1,346
3	New York	521	898
4	Illinois*	537	701
5	Michigan	439	684
6	Pennsylvania	424	611
7	North Carolina	373	607
8	Louisiana	415	540
9	Georgia	329	519
10	Maryland	331	405

* Provisional figures

Source: FBI Uniform Crime Reports

Of the 8,482 murders committed in the Top 10 states in 1998, 5,737 (or 67 percent) involved firearms. New Hampshire had just four murders.

What was Richard Bong's claim to fame?
see p.77 for the answer

A He won the Nobel Prize for Physics
B He was the leading US air ace of World War II
C He held the Olympic long-jump record

Military Matters

CHINESE ARMED FORCES
Members of the Chinese army, the largest military force in the world, parade in the now infamous Tiananmen Square, Beijing.

"BAZOOKA"

American radio comedian Bob Burns (1893–1956) invented a bizarre trombone-like musical instrument to which he gave the name "bazooka." Bazoo was a slang word for the mouth, and Burns added the *ka* suffix to make it sound like an instrument, such as a harmonica. When the antitank rocket-launcher was demonstrated during World War II, a soldier commented that it "looks just like Bob Burns' bazooka."

WHY DO WE SAY?

THE 10 YEARS WITH THE MOST NUCLEAR EXPLOSIONS
(Year/explosions)

1 1962, 178 **2** 1958, 116 **3** 1968, 79
4 1966, 76 **5** 1961, 71 **6** 1969, 67
7 1978, 66 **8** = 1967, 64; = 1970, 64
10 1964, 60

TOP 10 ★

COUNTRIES WITH THE LARGEST DEFENSE BUDGETS

	COUNTRY	BUDGET ($ MILLION)
1	US	270,200
2	Japan	41,100
3	UK	34,600
4	Russia	31,000
5	France	29,500
6	Germany	24,700
7	Saudi Arabia	18,400
8	Italy	16,200
9	China	12,600
10	South Korea	11,600

The so-called "peace dividend" – the savings made as a consequence of the end of the Cold War between the West and the former Soviet Union – means that both the numbers of personnel and the defense budgets of many countries have been cut.

TOP 10 LARGEST ARMED FORCES

	COUNTRY	ARMY	NAVY	AIR	TOTAL
		ESTIMATED ACTIVE FORCES			
1	China	1,830,000	230,000	420,000	2,480,000
2	US	469,300	369,800	361,400	1,371,500*
3	India	980,000	53,000	140,000	1,173,000
4	North Korea	950,000	46,000	86,000	1,082,000
4	Russia	348,000	171,500	184,600	1,004,100#
6	South Korea	560,000	60,000	52,000	672,000
7	Turkey	525,000	51,000	63,000	639,000
8	Pakistan	520,000	22,000	45,000	587,000
9	Iran	350,000	20,600	50,000	545,600+
10	Vietnam	412,000	42,000	30,000★	484,000

* Includes 171,000 Marine Corps personnel
# Includes Strategic Deterrent Forces, Paramilitary, National Guard, etc.
+ Includes 125,000 Revolutionary Guards
★ 15,000 air force/15,000 air defense

TOP 10 SMALLEST ARMED FORCES*
(Country/estimated total active forces)

1 Antigua and Barbuda, 150 **2** Seychelles, 450 **3** Barbados, 610
4 Luxembourg, 768 **5** The Gambia, 800 **6** Bahamas, 860 **7** Belize, 1,050
8 Cape Verde, 1,100 **9** Equatorial Guinea, 1,320 **10** Guyana, 1,600

* Excluding countries not declaring a defense budget

TOP 10 ★
COUNTRIES WITH THE MOST SUBMARINES

COUNTRY	SUBMARINES
1 US	76
2 China	71
3 Russia (and associated states)	over 70
4 North Korea	26
5 South Korea	19
6 =India	16
=Japan	16
8 =Turkey	15
=UK	15
10 Germany	14

TOP 10 ★
COUNTRIES WITH THE LARGEST NAVIES

COUNTRY	MANPOWER (1999)*
1 US	369,800
2 China	230,000
3 Russia	171,500
4 Taiwan	68,000
5 France	62,600
6 South Korea	60,000
7 India	53,000
8 Turkey	51,000
9 Indonesia	47,000
10 North Korea	46,000

* Including naval air forces and marines

CRUISE SHIP
The US Navy is the world's largest. Here, the destroyer USS Merrill launches a Tomahawk cruise missile.

THE 10 ★
20TH-CENTURY WARS WITH THE MOST MILITARY FATALITIES

WAR	YEARS	MILITARY FATALITIES
1 World War II	1939–45	15,843,000
2 World War I	1914–18	8,545,800
3 Korean War	1950–53	1,893,100
4 =Sino-Japanese War	1937–41	1,000,000
=Biafra–Nigeria Civil War	1967–70	1,000,000
6 Spanish Civil War	1936–39	611,000
7 Vietnam War	1961–73	546,000
8 =India–Pakistan War	1947	200,000
=USSR invasion of Afghanistan	1979–89	200,000
=Iran–Iraq War	1980–88	200,000

The statistics of warfare have always been an imperfect science. Not only are battle deaths seldom recorded accurately, but figures are often deliberately inflated by both sides in a conflict. These figures thus represent military historians' "best guesses" – and fail to take into account civilian deaths.

TOP 10 COUNTRIES WITH THE MOST CONSCRIPTED PERSONNEL
(Country/conscripts)

1 China, 1,275,000 **2** Turkey, 528,000 **3** Russia, 330,000
4 Egypt, 320,000 **5** Iran, 250,000 **6** South Korea, 159,000
7 Germany, 142,000 **8** Poland, 141,600
9 Italy, 126,000 **10** Israel, 107,500

Most countries have abolished the peacetime draft (the UK did so in 1960 and the US in 1973), and now recruit their forces entirely on a voluntary basis.

TOP 10 COUNTRIES WITH THE HIGHEST MILITARY/CIVILIAN RATIO
(Country/ratio in 1999)*

1 North Korea, 503 **2** Israel, 289
3 United Arab Emirates, 243 **4** Singapore, 228
5 Jordan, 207 **6** Syria, 193 **7** Iraq, 180 **8** Bahrain, 176
9 = Taiwan, 173; = Qatar, 173
US, 50

* Military personnel per 10,000 population

Did You Know? The first submarine attack to destroy a warship took place on February 17, 1864, when the Confederate submarine *H.L. Hunley* sunk the Union sloop *Housatonic* off Charleston, South Carolina.

World Religions

LARGEST JEWISH POPULATIONS

	COUNTRY	TOTAL JEWISH POPULATION
1	US	6,122,462
2	Israel	4,354,900
3	France	640,156
4	Russia	460,266
5	Ukraine	424,136
6	UK	345,054
7	Canada	342,096
8	Argentina	253,666
9	Brazil	107,692
10	Belarus	107,350
	World total	15,050,000

The Diaspora – the scattering of the Jewish people – has been in progress for nearly 2,000 years, and Jewish communities are found in virtually every country in the world. In 1939 the total world Jewish population was around 17 million. Some 6 million fell victim to Nazi persecution, but numbers have now topped 15 million.

JEWISH PRAYERS

The Wailing Wall, Jerusalem, was part of the temple erected by King Herod. Jews traditionally pray here, lamenting the destruction of the temple in AD 70.

LARGEST CHRISTIAN DENOMINATIONS

	DENOMINATION	MEMBERS
1	Roman Catholic	912,636,000
2	Orthodox	139,544,000
3	Pentecostal	105,756,000
4	Lutheran	84,521,000
5	Baptist	67,146,000
6	Anglican	53,217,000
7	Presbyterian	47,972,000
8	Methodist	25,599,000
9	Seventh Day Adventist	10,650,000
10	Churches of Christ	6,400,000

Source: *Christian Research*

Although Christian communities are found in almost every country in the world, it is difficult to put a precise figure on nominal membership (a declared religious persuasion) rather than active participation (regular attendance at a place of worship). In the US, Roman Catholicism is the largest single denomination in a total of 36 states, and the Southern Baptist Convention in 10 states. However, the latter has the most churches nationwide: a total of 37,893.

LARGEST HINDU POPULATIONS

	COUNTRY	TOTAL HINDU POPULATION
1	India	814,632,942
2	Nepal	21,136,118
3	Bangladesh	14,802,899
4	Indonesia	3,974,895
5	Sri Lanka	2,713,900
6	Pakistan	2,112,071
7	Malaysia	1,043,500
8	US	798,582
9	South Africa	649,980
10	Mauritius	587,884
	World total	865,000,000

More than 99 percent of the world's Hindu population lives in Asia, with 94 percent in India.

RELIGIOUS BELIEFS

	RELIGION	MEMBERS*
1	Christianity	2,015,743,000
2	Islam	1,215,693,000
3	Hinduism	865,000,000
4	Non-religions	774,693,000
5	Buddhism	362,245,000
6	Tribal religions	255,950,000
7	Atheism	151,430,000
8	New religions	102,174,000
9	Sikhism	23,102,000
10	Judaism	15,050,000

* Estimated total projections to mid-1998

Outside the Top 10, several other religions have members numbering in millions, among them some 7 million Baha'is, 6 million Confucians, 4 million Jains, and 3 million Shintoists.

LARGEST CHRISTIAN POPULATIONS

	COUNTRY	TOTAL CHRISTIAN POPULATION
1	US	182,674,000
2	Brazil	157,973,000
3	Mexico	88,380,000
4	China	73,300,000
5	Philippines	65,217,000
6	Germany	63,332,000
7	Italy	47,403,000
8	France	45,624,000
9	Nigeria	38,969,000
10	Dem. Rep. of Congo	37,922,000
	World total	2,015,743,000

Source: *Christian Research*

Did You Know? A Holocaust Memorial Museum in Washington, D.C. honors the millions of Jews killed during the Holocaust.

LARGEST MUSLIM POPULATIONS

	COUNTRY	TOTAL MUSLIM POPULATION
1	Pakistan	157,349,290
2	Indonesia	156,213,374
3	Bangladesh	133,873,621
4	India	130,316,250
5	Iran	74,087,700
6	Turkey	66,462,107
7	Russia	64,624,770
8	Egypt	57,624,098
9	Nigeria	46,384,120
10	Morocco	33,542,780
	World total	1,215,693,000

Historically, Islam spread as a result of conquest, missionary activity, and through contacts with Muslim traders. In such countries as Indonesia, its appeal lay in part in its opposition to Western colonial influences, which, along with the concept of Islamic community and other tenets, has attracted followers worldwide.

BOWING TO MECCA

Islam places many strictures on its female members but is nonetheless the world's fastest-growing religion. Here, hundreds of Muslim women unite in prayer.

TOP 10 ★

LARGEST BUDDHIST POPULATIONS

	COUNTRY	TOTAL BUDDHIST POPULATION
1	China	104,000,000
2	Japan	90,510,000
3	Thailand	57,450,000
4	Vietnam	50,080,000
5	Myanmar (Burma)	41,880,000
6	Sri Lanka	12,540,000
7	South Korea	11,110,000
8	Cambodia	9,870,000
9	India	7,000,000
10	Malaysia	3,770,000
	World total	362,245,000

HEAD OF THE FAITH

Although India now features in ninth place among countries with high Buddhist populations, the religion originated there in the 6th century BC.

World Cities

TOP 10 ★
MOST DENSELY POPULATED CITIES*

	CITY/COUNTRY	POPULATION PER SQ MILE	POPULATION PER SQ KM
1	**Hong Kong**, China	253,957	98,053
2	**Lagos**, Nigeria	174,982	67,561
3	**Dhaka**, Bangladesh	165,500	63,900
4	**Jakarta**, Indonesia	146,724	56,650
5	**Bombay**, India	142,442	54,997
6	**Ahmadabad**, India	131,250	50,676
7	**Ho Chi Minh City** (Saigon), Vietnam	131,097	50,617
8	**Shenyang**, China	114,282	44,125
9	**Bangalore**, India	112,880	43,583
10	**Cairo**, Egypt	107,260	41,413

* Includes only cities with populations of over 2 million

Source: *US Bureau of the Census*

RUSH HOUR – NIGERIAN STYLE

Nigeria's former capital and still its most important city, Lagos, is also one of the world's densest and fastest-growing cities, as a result of which it suffers from traffic congestion, overcrowding, and slum dwellings.

TOP 10 ★
FASTEST-GROWING CITIES

	CITY/COUNTRY	EST. INCREASE, 1995–2010 (%)*
1	**Hangzhou**, China	171.1
2	**Addis Ababa**, Ethiopia	170.7
3	**Kabul**, Afghanistan	156.3
4	**Handan**, China	141.6
5	**Isfahan**, Iran	141.3
6	**Maputo**, Mozambique	139.9
7	**Lagos**, Nigeria	139.5
8	**Luanda**, Angola	138.8
9	**Nairobi**, Kenya	133.6
10	**Qingdao**, China	132.4

* Urban agglomerations of over 1 million population only

Source: *United Nations*

TOP 10 ★
LARGEST CITIES IN NORTH AMERICA

	CITY/STATE/COUNTRY	EST. POPULATION, 2015*
1	**Mexico City**, Mexico	19,200,000
2	**New York**, US	17,600,000
3	**Los Angeles**, US	14,200,000
4	**Chicago**, US	7,500,000
5	**Toronto**, Canada	5,200,000
6	**Philadelphia**, US	4,800,000
7	**Santo Domingo**, Dominican Republic	4,700,000
8=	**Guadalajara**, Mexico	4,500,000
=	**San Francisco**, US	4,500,000
10=	**Dallas**, US	4,400,000
=	**Washington, DC**, US	4,400,000

* Of urban agglomeration

Source: *United Nations*

TOP 10 ★
HIGHEST CITIES

	CITY/COUNTRY	HEIGHT FT	HEIGHT M
1	**Wenchuan**, China	16,730	5,099
2	**Potosí**, Bolivia	13,045	3,976
3	**Oruro**, Bolivia	12,146	3,702
4	**Lhasa**, Tibet	12,087	3,684
5	**La Paz**, Bolivia	11,916	3,632
6	**Cuzco**, Peru	11,152	3,399
7	**Huancayo**, Peru	10,660	3,249
8	**Sucre**, Bolivia	9,301	2,835
9	**Tunja**, Colombia	9,252	2,820
10	**Quito**, Ecuador	9,249	2,819

Lhasa was formerly the highest capital city in the world, a role now occupied by La Paz, capital of Bolivia. Wenchuan is situated at more than half the elevation of Everest, and even the cities at the foot of this list are more than one-third as high.

Did You Know? Ein Bokek, beside the Dead Sea, is the world's lowest inhabited place at 1,291 ft (393.5 m) below sea level.

TOP 10 ★
LARGEST CITIES

	CITY/COUNTRY	EST. POPULATION, 2015*
1	**Tokyo**, Japan	28,900,000
2	**Bombay**, India	26,200,000
3	**Lagos**, Nigeria	24,600,000
4	**São Paulo**, Brazil	20,300,000
5	**Dhaka**, Bangladesh	19,500,000
6	**Karachi**, Pakistan	19,400,000
7	**Mexico City**, Mexico	19,200,000
8	**Shanghai**, China	18,000,000
9	**New York**, USA	17,600,000
10	**Calcutta**, India	17,300,000

* Of urban agglomeration

Source: United Nations

The definition taken in the above and other city lists is the United Nations definition of "urban agglomeration", which comprises the city or town proper and also the suburban fringe or thickly settled territory lying outside of, but adjacent to, the city boundaries.

TOP 10 ★
LARGEST CITIES IN THE US*

	CITY/STATE	POPULATION
1	**New York**, New York	7,420,166
2	**Los Angeles**, California	3,597,556
3	**Chicago**, Illinois	2,802,079
4	**Houston**, Texas	1,786,691
5	**Philadelphia**, Pennsylvania	1,436,287
6	**San Diego**, California	1,220,666
7	**Phoenix**, Arizona	1,198,064
8	**San Antonio**, Texas	1,114,130
9	**Dallas**, Texas	1,075,894
10	**Detroit**, Michigan	970,196

* Estimated figures up to July 1, 1999

Source: US Bureau of the Census

These are estimates for central city areas only, not for the total metropolitan areas that surround them, which may be several times as large.

TOP 10 ★
LARGEST CITIES IN EUROPE

	CITY/COUNTRY	EST. POPULATION, 2015*
1	**Paris**, France	9,700,000
2	**Moscow**, Russia	9,300,000
3	**London**, UK	7,600,000
4	**Essen**, Germany	6,600,000
5	**St. Petersburg**, Russia	5,100,000
6	**Milan**, Italy	4,300,000
7	**Madrid**, Spain	4,100,000
8 =	**Frankfurt**, Germany	3,700,000
=	**Katowice**, Poland	3,700,000
10	**Dusseldorf**, Germany	3,400,000

* Of urban agglomeration

Source: United Nations

PARISIAN GRANDEUR

A population of 9.5 million, a central location, and cultural and other attractions have led to the inexorable growth of Paris to its present rank as Europe's largest city.

TOP 10 ★
LARGEST NONCAPITAL CITIES

	CITY/COUNTRY/CAPITAL CITY	POPULATION
1	**Shanghai**, China *Beijing*	13,584,000 *11,299,000*
2	**Bombay**, India *New Delhi*	15,138,000 *8,419,000*
3	**Calcutta***, India *New Delhi*	11,923,000 *8,419,000*
4	**Lagos**, Nigeria *Abuja*	10,287,000 *378,671*
5	**São Paulo**, Brazil *Brasília*	10,017,821 *1,864,000*
6	**Karachi***, Pakistan *Islamabad*	9,733,000 *350,000*
7	**Tianjin**, China *Beijing*	9,415,000 *11,299,000*
8	**Istanbul***, Turkey *Ankara*	8,274,921 *2,937,524*
9	**New York**, USA *Washington, DC*	7,420,166 *523,124*
10	**Madras**, India *New Delhi*	6,002,000 *8,419,000*

* Former capital

TOP 10 ★
MOST POPULATED FORMER CAPITAL CITIES

	CITY/COUNTRY	CEASED TO BE CAPITAL	POPULATION*
1	**Calcutta**, India	1912	11,021,918
2	**Istanbul**, Turkey	1923	7,774,169
3	**Karachi**, Pakistan	1968	7,183,000
4	**Rio de Janeiro**, Brazil	1960	5,547,033
5	**St. Petersburg**, Russia	1980	4,273,001
6	**Berlin**, Germany	1949	3,472,009
7	**Alexandria**, Egypt	c.641	3,380,000
8	**Melbourne**, Australia	1927	3,189,200
9	**Nanjiang**, China	1949	2,610,594
10	**Philadelphia**, US	1800	1,524,249

* Within administrative boundaries

Place Names

TOP 10 ★
LONGEST PLACE NAMES IN THE US*

	NAME/LOCATION	LETTERS
1	Chargoggagoggmanchauggagoggchaubunagungamaugg (see Top 10 Longest Place Names)	45
2	Nunathloogagamiutbingoi, Dunes, Alaska	23
3	Winchester-on-the-Severn, Maryland	21
4	Scraper-Moechereville, Illinois	20
5	Linstead-on-the-Severn, Maryland	19
6 =	Kentwood-in-the-Pines, California	18
=	Lauderdale-by-the-Sea, Florida	18
=	Vermilion-on-the-Lake, Ohio	18
9 =	Chippewa-on-the-Lake, Ohio	17
=	Fairhaven-on-the-Bay, Maryland	17
=	Highland-on-the-Lake, New York	17
=	Kleinfeltersville, Pennsylvania	17
=	Mooselookmeguntic, Maine	17
=	Palermo-by-the-Lakes, Ohio	17
=	Saybrook-on-the-Lake, Ohio	17

Single and hyphenated names only   Source: *US Geological Survey*

TOP 10 ★
COUNTRIES WITH THE LONGEST OFFICIAL NAMES

	OFFICIAL NAME*	COMMON ENGLISH NAME	LETTERS
1	al-Jamāhīrīyah al-Arabīya al-Lībīyah ash-Sha bīyah al-Ishtirākīyah	Libya	56
2	al-Jumhūrīyah al-Jazā'irīyah ad-Dīmuqrāṭīyah ash-Sha bīyah	Algeria	49
3	United Kingdom of Great Britain and Northern Ireland	United Kingdom	45
4	Sri Lankā Prajathanthrika Samajavadi Janarajaya	Sri Lanka	43
5	Jumhurīyat al-Qumur al-Ittihādīyah al-Islāmīyah	The Comoros	41
6 =	al-Jumhūrīyah al-Islāmīyah al-Mūrītānīyah	Mauritania	36
=	The Federation of St. Christopher and Nevis	St. Kitts and Nevis	36
8	Jamhuuriyadda Dimuqraadiga Soomaaliya	Somalia	35
9	al-Mamlakah al-Urdunnīyah al-Hāshimīyah	Jordan	34
10	Repoblika Demokratika n'i Madagaskar	Madagascar	32

* *Some official names have been transliterated from languages that do not use the Roman alphabet; their length may vary according to the method used.*

TOP 10 ★
MOST COMMON PLACE NAMES IN THE US

	NAME	OCCURRENCES
1	Fairview	287
2	Midway	252
3	Riverside	180
4	Oak Grove	179
5	Five Points	155
6	Oakland	149
7	Greenwood	145
8 =	Bethel	141
=	Franklin	141
10	Pleasant Hill	140

Source: *US Geological Board*

TOP 10 MOST COMMON STREET NAMES IN THE US

1 2nd/Second Street **2** 3rd/Third Street **3** 1st/First Street **4** 4th/Fourth Street
5 Park Street **6** 5th/Fifth Street **7** Main Street **8** 6th/Sixth Street **9** Oak Street
10 7th/Seventh Street   Source: *US Bureau of the Census*

TOP 10 ★
TREES AFTER WHICH US STREETS ARE NAMED

	NAME	OCCURRENCES
1	Oak	6,946
2	Pine	6,170
3	Maple	6,103
4	Cedar	5,644
5	Elm	5,233
6	Walnut	4,799
7	Willow	4,017
8	Cherry	3,669
9	Hickory	3,297
10	Chestnut	2,994

Source: *US Bureau of the Census*

TOP 10 ★
PEOPLE AFTER WHOM US STREETS ARE NAMED

	NAME	OCCURRENCES
1	Washington	4,979
2	Lincoln	4,044
3	Jackson	3,725
4	Johnson	3,325
5	Jefferson	3,306
6	Smith	3,076
7	Franklin	2,882
8	Adams	2,856
9	Davis	2,769
10	Williams	2,682

Source: *US Bureau of the Census*

Did You Know? 1st/First Street is the third most common street name in the US only because many streets that would be so designated are instead called Main Street.

TOP 10 ★
LONGEST PLACE NAMES*

NAME	LETTERS

1 Krung thep mahanakhon bovorn ratanakosin mahintharayutthaya mahadilok pop noparatratchathani burirom udomratchanivetmahasathan amornpiman avatarnsathit sakkathattiyavisnukarmprasit   167

When the poetic name of Bangkok, capital of Thailand, is used, it is usually abbreviated to "Krung Thep" (city of angels).

2 Taumatawhakatangihangakoauauotamateaturipukakapikimaungahoronukupokaiw-henuakitanatahu   85

This is the longer version (the other has a mere 83 letters) of the Maori name of a hill in New Zealand. It translates as "The place where Tamatea, the man with the big knees, who slid, climbed and swallowed mountains, known as land-eater, played on the flute to his loved one."

3 Gorsafawddachaidraigddanheddogleddollônpenrhynareurdraethceredigion   67

A name contrived by the Fairbourne Steam Railway, Gwynedd, North Wales, for publicity purposes and in order to outdo its rival, No. 4. It means "The Mawddach station and its dragon teeth at the Northern Penrhyn Road on the golden beach of Cardigan Bay."

4 Llanfairpwllgwyngyllgogerychwyrndrobwllllantysiliogogogoch   58

This is the place in Gwynedd famed especially for the length of its train tickets. It means "St. Mary's Church in the hollow of the white hazel near to the rapid whirlpool of Llantysilio of the Red Cave." Questions have been raised about its authenticity, since its official name comprises only the first 20 letters, and the full name appears to have been invented as a hoax in the 19th century by a local poet, John Evans, known as Y Bardd Cocos. It also has Britain's longest Internet site name: http://www.llanfairpwllgwyngyllgogerychwyrndrobwllllllantysiliogogogoch.wales.com/llanfair

5 El Pueblo de Nuestra Señora la Reina de los Angeles de la Porciuncula   57

The site of a Franciscan mission and the full Spanish name of Los Angeles; it means "the town of Our Lady the Queen of the Angels of the Little Portion." Nowadays it is customarily known by its initial letters, "LA," making it also one of the shortest-named cities in the world.

6 Chargoggagoggmanchauggagoggchaubunagungamaugg   45

America's second longest place name, a lake near Webster, Massachusetts. Its Indian name, loosely translated, means "You fish on your side, I'll fish on mine, and no one fishes in the middle." It is said to be pronounced "Char-gogg-a-gogg (pause) man-chaugg-a-gogg (pause) chau-bun-a-gung-amaugg." It is, however, an invented extension of its real name (Chagungungamaug Pond, or "boundary fishing place"), devised in the 1920s by Larry Daly, the editor of the Webster Times.

7 = Lower North Branch Little Southwest Miramichi   40

Canada's longest place name – a short river in New Brunswick.

= Villa Real de la Santa Fe de San Francisco de Asis   40

The full Spanish name of Santa Fe, New Mexico, translates as, "Royal city of the holy faith of St. Francis of Assisi."

9 Te Whakatakanga-o-te-ngarehu-o-te-ahi-a-Tamatea   38

The Maori name of Hammer Springs, New Zealand; like the second name in this list, it refers to a legend of Tamatea, explaining how the springs were warmed by "the falling of the cinders of the fire of Tamatea." Its name is variously written either hyphenated or as a single word.

10 Meallan Liath Coire Mhic Dhubhghaill   32

The longest multiple name in Scotland, a place near Aultanrynie, Highland, this is alternatively spelled Meallan Liath Coire Mhic Dhughaill (30 letters).

* Including single-word, hyphenated, and multiple-word names

CITY OF ANGELS
The original 57-letter Spanish name of Los Angeles contrasts dramatically with its more common designation as "LA."

The Tallest Buildings

TOP 10 ★
TALLEST HABITABLE BUILDINGS

BUILDING/YEAR/ LOCATION	STOREYS	HEIGHT FT	M
1 Petronas Towers, 1996, Kuala Lumpur, Malaysia	96	1,482	452
2 Sears Tower, 1974, Chicago, US *with spires*	110	1,454 1,707	443 520
3 World Trade Center*, 1972, New York, US	110	1,368	417
4 World Finance Center, 2001, Hong Kong, China	88	1,312	400
5 Jin Mao Building, 1997, Shanghai, China *with spire*	93	1,255 1,378	382 420
6 Empire State Building, 1931, New York, US *with spire*	102	1,250 1,472	381 449
7 T & C Tower, 1997, Kao-hsiung, Taiwan	85	1,142	348
8 Amoco Building, 1973, Chicago, US	80	1,136	346
9 John Hancock Center, 1969, Chicago, US *with spires*	100	1,127 1,470	343 449
10 Shun Hing Square, 1996, Shenzen, China *with spires*	80	1,082 1,260	330 384

*Twin towers; the second tower, completed in 1973, has the same number of stories but is slightly smaller at 1,360 ft (415m), although its spire takes it up to 1,710 ft (521 m).

TOP 10 ★
TALLEST REINFORCED CONCRETE BUILDINGS

BUILDING/YEAR/ LOCATION	STOREYS	HEIGHT FT	M
1 Baiyoke II Tower, 1997, Bangkok, Thailand	89	1,046	319
2 Central Plaza, 1992, Hong Kong, China *with spire*	78	1,015 1,228	309 374
3 311 South Wacker Drive, 1990, Chicago, US	65	970	296
4 2 Prudential Plaza, 1990, Chicago, US *with spire*	64	901 978	275 298
5 NCNB, 1992, Charlotte, US	60	871	265
6 Water Tower Place, 1975, Chicago, US	74	859	262
7 Messeturm, 1990, Frankfurt, Germany	70	841	256
8 Citispire, 1989, New York, US	72	802	245
9 Rialto Tower, 1985, Melbourne, Australia	60	794	242
10 Tun Abdul Rasak Building, 1985, Penang, Malaysia	61	761	232

Reinforced concrete was patented in France on March 16, 1867 by Joseph Monier (1823–1906) and was later developed by another Frenchman, François Hennebique (1842–1921). The first American buildings constructed from it date from a century ago, and since then it has become one of the most important of all building materials. It is constructed from concrete slabs containing steel bars which expand and contract at the same rate as the concrete. This provides great tensile strength and fire resistance. These qualities make it the ideal construction material for bridge spans and skyscrapers.

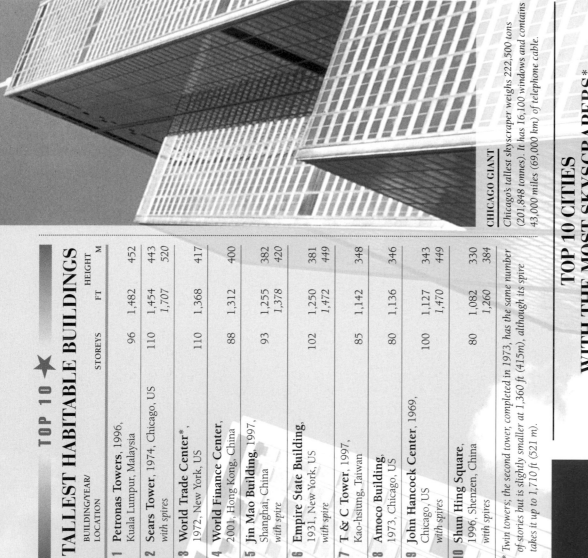

CHICAGO GIANT

Chicago's tallest skyscraper weighs 222,500 tons (201,848 tonnes). It has 16,100 windows and contains 43,000 miles (69,000 km) of telephone cable.

TOP 10 CITIES WITH THE MOST SKYSCRAPERS*
(City/country/skyscrapers)

1 New York City, US, 162   **2** Chicago, US, 72   **3** Hong Kong, China, 41
4 Shanghai, China, 38   **5** Tokyo, Japan, 29   **6** Houston, US, 27   **7** Singapore, 25
8 Los Angeles, US, 21   **9** Dallas, US, 19   **10** Sydney, Australia, 18

* Habitable buildings of more than 500 ft (152 m)

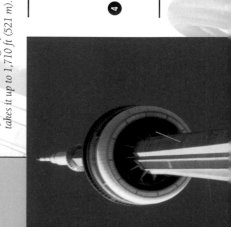

TOP 10 ★ TALLEST TELECOMMUNICATIONS TOWERS

	TOWER/YEAR/LOCATION	FT	M
1	CN Tower, 1975, Toronto, Canada	1,821	555
2	Ostankino Tower, 1967, Moscow, Russia	1,762	537
3	Oriental Pearl Broadcasting Tower, 1995, Shanghai, China	1,535	468
4	Menara Telecom Tower, 1996, Kuala Lumpur, Malaysia	1,381	421
5	Tianjin TV and Radio Tower, 1991, Tianjin, China	1,362	415
6	Central Radio and TV Tower, 1994, Beijing, China	1,328	405
7	TV Tower, 1983, Tashkent, Uzbekistan	1,230	375
8	Liberation Tower, 1998, Kuwait City, Kuwait	1,220	372
9	Alma-Ata Tower, 1983, Kazakhstan	1,214	370
10	TV Tower, 1969, Berlin, Germany	1,198	365

TOP 10 ★ TALLEST MASTS

	MAST/LOCATION	FT	M
1	KVLY Channel 11 TV Tower (formerly KTHI-TV), Blanchard/Fargo, North Dakota,	2,063	629
2	KSLA-TV Mast, Shreveport, Louisiana	1,898	579
3	= WBIR-TV Mast, Knoxvile, Tennessee	1,749	533
	= WTVM & WRBL TV Mast, Columbus, Georgia	1,749	533
5	KFVS TV Mast, Cape Girardeau, Missouri	1,676	511
6	WPSD-TV Mast, Paducah, Kentucky	1,638	499
7	WGAN TV Mast, Portland, Maine	1,619	493
8	KWTV TV Mast, Oklahoma City, Oklahoma	1,572	479
9	BREN Tower, Area 25, Nevada Test Site, Nevada	1,530	465
10	Omega Base Navigational Mast, Gippsland, Victoria, Australia	1,400	426

TOP 10 HIGHEST PUBLIC OBSERVATORIES

	BUILDING/LOCATION	OBSERVATORY	YEAR	FT	M
1	CN Tower, Toronto, Canada	Space deck	1975	447	1,465
2	World Trade Center, New York, NY	Rooftop Tower B	1973	415	1,360
3	Sears Tower, Chicago, IL	103rd floor	1974	412	1,353
4	Empire State Building, New York, NY	102nd floor Outdoor observatory	1931	381 320	1,250 1,050
5	Ostankino Tower, Moscow, Russia	5th floor turret	1967	360	1,181
6	Oriental Pearl Broadcasting Tower, Shanghai, China	VIP observation level Public observation level	1995	350 263	1,148 863
7	Jin Mao Building, Shanghai, China	88th floor	1997	340	1,115
8	John Hancock Center, Chicago, IL	94th floor	1968	314	1,030
9	Sky Central Plaza, Guanghshou, China	90th floor	1996	310	1,016
10	KL Tower, Kuala Lumpur, Malaysia	Revolving restaurant Public observation level	1995	282 276	925 907

TALLEST BY FAR
The world's tallest free-standing structure, the CN Tower in Toronto, Canada, attracts almost 2 million visitors a year to its space deck level at 1,465 ft (447 m).

Bridges & Other Structures

LONGEST ROAD TUNNELS

	TUNNEL/YEAR	LOCATION	LENGTH MILES	KM
1	**Laerdal**, 2000	Norway	15.22	24.50
2	**St. Gotthard**, 1980	Switzerland	10.14	16.32
3	**Arlberg**, 1978	Austria	8.69	13.98
4 =	**Fréjus**, 1980	France/Italy	8.02	12.90
=	**Pinglin Highway**, U/C	Taiwan	8.02	12.90
6	**Mont-Blanc**, 1965	France/Italy	7.21	11.60
7	**Gudvangen**, 1992	Norway	7.08	11.43
8	**Folgefonn**, 2001	Norway	6.90	11.10
9	**Kan-Etsu II**, 1991	Japan	6.87	11.06
10	**Kan-Etsu I**, 1986	Japan	6.79	10.93

U/C = under construction

TOP 10 ★

LONGEST STEEL ARCH BRIDGES

	BRIDGE/YEAR/LOCATION	LONGEST SPAN FT	M
1	**New River Gorge**, 1977, Fayetteville, West Virginia	1,700	518
2	**Kill Van Kull**, 1931, Bayonne, New Jersey/ Staten Island, New York	1,654	504
3	**Sydney Harbour**, 1932, Australia	1,650	503
4	**Fremont**, 1973, Portland, Oregon	1,257	383
5	**Port Mann**, 1964, Vancouver, Canada	1,200	366
6	**Thatcher Ferry**, 1962, Panama Canal	1,128	344
7	**Laviolette**, 1967, Quebec, Canada	1,100	335
8 =	**Runcorn–Widnes**, 1961, UK	1,082	330
=	**Zdákov**, 1967, Lake Orlik, Czech Republic	1,082	330
10 =	**Birchenough**, 1935, Fort Victoria, Zimbabwe	1,080	329
=	**Roosevelt Lake**, 1990, Arizona	1,080	329

SHANGHAI SURPRISE

One of the world's longest cable-stayed bridges, Shanghai's Yang Pu was built to ease traffic congestion on the city's busy inner ring road.

TOP 10 ★

LARGEST SPORTS STADIUMS

	STADIUM/LOCATION	CAPACITY
1	**Strahov Stadium**, Prague, Czech Republic	240,000
2	**Maracaña Municipal Stadium**, Rio de Janeiro, Brazil	220,000
3	**Rungnado Stadium**, Pyongyang, South Korea	150,000
4	**National Stadium of Iran**, Azadi, Iran	128,000
5	**Estádio Maghalaes Pinto**, Belo Horizonte, Brazil	125,000
6 =	**Estádio Morumbi**, São Paulo, Brazil	120,000
=	**Estádio da Luz**, Lisbon, Portugal	120,000
=	**Senayan Main Stadium**, Jakarta, Indonesia	120,000
=	**Yuba Bharati Krirangan**, Nr. Calcutta, India	120,000
10	**Estádio Castelâo**, Fortaleza, Brazil	119,000

These figures represent maximum capacities. In fact, new safety regulations introduced in many countries mean that actual audiences for most events are smaller. The Aztec Stadium, Mexico City, holds 107,000, with most of the seats under cover. The New Orleans Superdome is the largest indoor stadium, with a capacity of 97,365. The Michigan Football Stadium, Ann Arbor, MI, built in 1927, is the largest outdoor stadium in the US, with a seating capacity of 107,501. The largest stadium in the UK is Wembley Stadium, with a capacity of 80,000. This is being replaced with a new National Stadium, with a capacity of 90,000, scheduled for completion in 2003.

TOP 10 ★

LONGEST CABLE-STAYED BRIDGES

	BRIDGE/YEAR/LOCATION	LENGTH OF MAIN SPAN FT	M
1	**Tatara**, 1999, Onomichi–Imabari, Japan	2,920	890
2	**Pont de Normandie**, 1994, Le Havre, France	2,808	856
3	**Qinghzhou Minjiang**, 1996, Fozhou, China	1,985	605
4	**Yang Pu**, 1993, Shanghai, China	1,975	602
5 =	**Meiko–Chuo**, 1997, Nagoya, Japan	1,936	590
=	**Xu Pu**, 1997, Shanghai, China	1,936	590
7	**Skarnsundet**, 1991, Trondheim Fjord, Norway	1,739	530
8	**Tsurumi Tsubasa**, Yokohama, Japan	1,673	510
9 =	**Ikuchi**, 1994, Onomichi–Imabari, Japan	1,608	490
=	**Öresund**, 2000, Copenhagen–Malmö, Denmark/Sweden)	1,608	490

TOP 10 ★
LONGEST CANTILEVER BRIDGES

BRIDGE/YEAR/LOCATION	LONGEST SPAN	
	FT	M
1 Pont de Québec, 1917, Canada	1,800	549
2 Firth of Forth, 1890, Scotland	1,710	521
3 Minato, 1974, Osako, Japan	1,673	510
4 Commodore John Barry, 1974, New Jersey/Pennsylvania	1,622	494
5 =Greater New Orleans 1, 1958, Louisiana	1,575	480
=Greater New Orleans 2, 1988, Louisiana	1,575	480
7 Howrah, 1943, Calcutta, India	1,500	457
8 Gramercy, 1995, Louisiana	1,460	445
9 Transbay, 1936, San Francisco	1,400	427
10 Baton Rouge, 1969, Louisiana	1,235	376

TOP 10 ★
LONGEST UNDERWATER TUNNELS

TUNNEL/YEAR/LOCATION	LENGTH	
	MILES	KM
1 Seikan, 1988, Japan	33.49	53.90
2 Channel Tunnel, 1994, France/England	31.03	49.94
3 Dai–Shimizu, 1982, Japan	13.78	22.17
4 Shin–Kanmon, 1975, Japan	11.61	18.68
5 Great Belt Fixed Link (Eastern Tunnel), 1997, Denmark	4.97	8.00
6 Bømlafjord*, 2000, Norway	4.86	7.82
7 Oslofjord*, 2000, Norway	4.59	7.39
8 Severn, 1886, UK	4.36	7.01
9 Magerøysund*, 1999, Norway	4.27	6.87
10 Haneda, 1971, Japan	3.72	5.98

* Road; others rail

The need to connect the Japanese islands of Honshu, Kyushu, and Hokkaido has resulted in a wave of undersea tunnel building in recent years, with the Seikan the most ambitious project of all. Connecting Honshu and Hokkaido, 14.4 miles (23.3 km) of the tunnel is 328 ft (100 m) below the seabed. It took 24 years to complete.

TOP 10 ★
HIGHEST DAMS

DAM/RIVER/LOCATION	YEAR	HEIGHT	
		FT	M
1 Rogun, Vakhsh, Tajikistan	U/C	1,099	335
2 Nurek, Vakhsh, Tajikistan	1980	984	300
3 Grande Dixence, Dixence, Switzerland	1961	935	285
4 Inguri, Inguri, Georgia	1980	892	272
5 Vajont, Vajont, Italy	1960	860	262
6 =Manuel M. Torres (Chicoasén), Grijalva, Mexico	1980	856	261
=Tehri, Bhagirathi, India	U/C	856	261
8 Alvaro Obregon (El Gallinero), Tenasco, Mexico	1946	853	260
9 Mauvoisin, Drance de Bagnes, Switzerland	1957	820	250
10 Alberto Lleras C., Guavio, Colombia	1989	797	243

U/C = under construction

Source: *International Commission on Large Dams (ICOLD)*

TOP 10 ★
LONGEST SUSPENSION BRIDGES

BRIDGE/YEAR/LOCATION	LENGTH OF MAIN SPAN	
	FT	M
1 Akashi–Kaiko, 1998, Kobe–Naruto, Japan	6,529	1,990
2 Great Belt, 1997, Denmark	5,328	1,624
3 Humber Estuary, 1981, UK	4,626	1,410
4 Jiangyin, 1998, China	4,544	1,385
5 Tsing Ma, 1997, Hong Kong, China	4,518	1,377
6 Verrazano Narrows, 1964, New York	4,260	1,298
7 Golden Gate, 1937, San Francisco	4,200	1,280
8 Höga Kusten, 1997, Veda, Sweden	3,970	1,210
9 Mackinac Straits, 1957, Michigan	3,800	1,158
10 Minami Bisan-seto, 1988, Kojima–Sakaide, Japan	3,609	1,100

The Messina Strait Bridge between Sicily and Calabria, Italy, remains a speculative project but, if constructed according to plan, it will have by far the longest center span of any bridge at 10,892 ft (3,320 m). However, at 12,828 ft (3,910 m), Japan's Akashi–Kaiko bridge, completed in 1998 and with a main span of 6,528 ft (1,990 m), is the world's longest overall.

DAM RECORD BUSTER

An incongruous mural depicting Lenin celebrates this Soviet engineering accomplishment, the building of the world's second highest dam, the Nurek in Tajikistan.

Background image: **PONT DE QUÉBEC CANADA**

Where is the tallest mast outside the US?
see p.91 for the answer
A Germany
B Australia
C China

93

Word Power

LONGEST WORDS IN THE ENGLISH LANGUAGE*

WORD/MEANING   LETTERS

1 Ornicopytheobibliopsychocrystarroscioaerogenethliometeoroaustrohiero-anthropoichthyopyrosiderochpnomyoalectryoophiobotanopegohydrorhab-docrithoaleuroalphitohalomolybdocl erobeloaxinocoscinodactyliogeolitho-pessopsephocatoptrotephraoneirochiroonychodactyloarithstichooxogelo-scogastrogyrocerobletonooenoscapulinaniac   **310**

Medieval scribes used this word to refer to "A deluded human who practices divination or forecasting by means of phenomena, interpretation of acts, or other manifestations related to the following animate or inanimate objects and appearances: birds, oracles, Bible, ghosts, crystal gazing, shadows, air appearances, birth stars, meteors, winds, sacrificial appearances, entrails of humans and fishes, fire, red-hot irons, altar smoke, mice, grain picking by rooster, snakes, herbs, fountains, water, wands, dough, meal, barley, salt, lead, dice, arrows, hatchet balance, sieve, ring suspension, random dots, precious stones, pebbles, pebble heaps, mirrors, ash writing, dreams, palmistry, nail rays, finger rings, numbers, book passages, name letterings, laughing manners, ventriloquism, circle walking, wax, susceptibility to hidden springs, wine, and shoulder blades."

2 Lopadotemachoselachogaleokranioleipsanodrimhypotrimmatosilphioparao-melitokatakechymenokichlepikossyphophattoperisteralektryonopteke phall-iokigklopeleiolagoiosiraiobaphetraganopterygon   **182**

The English transliteration of a 170-letter Greek word that appears in The Ecclesiazusae (a comedy by the Greek playwright Aristophanes, c.448–380 BC). It is used as a description of a 17-ingredient dish.

3 Aequeosalinocalcalinosetaceoaluminosocupreovitriolic   **52**

Invented by a medical writer, Dr. Edward Strother (1675–1737), to describe the spa waters at Bath.

4 Osseocarnisanguineoviscericartilaginonervomedullary   **51**

Coined by writer and East India Company official Thomas Love Peacock (1785–1866), and used in his satire Headlong Hall (1816) as a description of the structure of the human body.

5 Pneumonoultramicroscopicsilicovolcanoconiosis   **45**

It first appeared in print (though ending in "-koniosis") in F. Scully's Bedside Manna [sic] (1936), then found its way into Webster's Dictionary and is now in the Oxford English Dictionary. It is said to mean a lung disease caused by breathing fine dust.

6 Hepaticocholecystostcholecystenterostomies   **42**

Surgical operations to create channels of communication between gall bladders and hepatic ducts or intestines.

7 Praetertranssubstantiationalistically   **37**

The adverb describing the act of surpassing the act of transubstantiation; the word is found in Mark McShane's novel Untimely Ripped (1963).

8 = Pseudoantidisestablishmentarianism   **34**

A word meaning "false opposition to the withdrawal of state support from a Church," derived from that perennial favorite long word, antidisestablishmentarianism (a mere 28 letters).

    = Supercalifragilisticexpialidocious   **34**

An invented word, but perhaps now eligible since it has appeared in the Oxford English Dictionary. It was popularized by the song of this title in the film Mary Poppins (1964), where it is used to mean "wonderful," but it was originally written in 1949 in an unpublished song by Parker and Young who spelled it "supercalafajalistickespialadojus" (32 letters).

10 = Encephalomyeloradiculoneuritis   **30**

A syndrome caused by a virus associated with encephalitis.

    = Hippopotomonstrosesquipedalian   **30**

Appropriately, the word that means "pertaining to an extremely long word."

    = Pseudopseudohypoparathyroidism   **30**

First used (hyphenated) in the US in 1952 and (unhyphenated) in Great Britain in The Lancet in 1962 to describe a medical case in which a patient appeared to have symptoms of pseudohypoparathyroidism, but with "no manifestations suggesting hypoparathyroidism."

* Excluding names of chemical compounds

MOST USED LETTERS IN WRITTEN ENGLISH

SURVEY*		#MORSE
e	1	e
t	2	t
a	3	a
o	4	i
i	5	n
n	6	o
s	7	s
r	8	h
h	9	r
l	10	d

* The order as indicated by a survey across approximately 1 million words appearing in a wide variety of printed texts, ranging from newspapers to novels.

The order estimated by Samuel Morse, the inventor in the 1830s of Morse code, based on his calculations of the respective quantities of type used by a printer. The number of letters in the printer's type trays ranged from 12,000 for "e" to 4,400 for "d," with only 200 for "z."

MOST COMMON WORDS IN ENGLISH

SPOKEN ENGLISH		WRITTEN ENGLISH
the	1	the
and	2	of
I	3	to
to	4	in
of	5	and
a	6	a
you	7	for
that	8	was
in	9	is
it	10	that

Various surveys have been conducted to establish the most common words in spoken English of various types, from telephone conversations to broadcast commentaries. Beyond the Top 10, words such as "yes" and "well" appear.

Did You Know? Honorificabilitudinitatibus (27 letters), which means "honorably," is the longest word used by Shakespeare; it appears in *Love's Labour's Lost* (Act V, Scene i).

TOP 10 ★ COUNTRIES WITH THE MOST ENGLISH-LANGUAGE SPEAKERS*

	COUNTRY	APPROXIMATE NO. OF SPEAKERS
1	US	232,910,000
2	UK	57,520,000
3	Canada	18,655,000
4	Australia	15,204,000
5	South Africa	3,900,000
6	Ireland	3,590,000
7	New Zealand	3,309,000
8	Jamaica	2,400,000
9	Trinidad and Tobago	1,199,000
10	Guyana	749,000

* Inhabitants for whom English is their mother tongue

The Top 10 represents the countries with the greatest numbers of inhabitants who speak English as their mother tongue. After the 10th entry, the figures dive to around or under 260,000, in the case of the Bahamas, Barbados, and Zimbabwe. In addition to these and others that make up a world total that is probably in excess of 500 million, there are perhaps as many as 1 billion who speak English as a second language: a large proportion of the population of the Philippines, for example, speaks English, and there are many countries, such as India, Nigeria, and other former British colonies in Africa, where English is either an official language or is widely understood.

THE ROSETTA STONE

Made in Egypt in around 200 BC and discovered in 1799 during the French occupation of Egypt, the Rosetta Stone was taken to England in 1801 and is now in the British Museum, London. It has the same inscription in three different alphabets – Egyptian hieroglyphics at the top, demotic Egyptian in the middle, and Greek below. After a painstaking study of the relationship between the different alphabets, French scholar Jean François Champollion (1790–1832) was able to decipher the hieroglyphics, all knowledge of which had previously been lost. The Rosetta Stone thus provided the key to our understanding of this ancient language.

SNAP SHOTS ★

TOP 10 ★ MOST WIDELY SPOKEN LANGUAGES

	LANGUAGE	APPROXIMATE NO. OF SPEAKERS
1	Chinese (Mandarin)	1,075,000,000
2	English	514,000,000
3	Hindustani	496,000,000
4	Spanish	425,000,000
5	Russian	275,000,000
6	Arabic	256,000,000
7	Bengali	215,000,000
8	Portuguese	194,000,000
9	Malay-Indonesian	176,000,000
10	French	129,000,000

According to mid-1999 estimates by Emeritus Professor Sidney S. Culbert of the University of Washington, in addition to those languages appearing in the Top 10, there are three further languages that are spoken by more than 100 million individuals: German (128 million), Japanese (126 million), and Urdu (105 million). A further 13 languages are spoken by 50–100 million people: Punjabi (94), Korean (78), Telugu (76), Tamil (74), Marathi (71), Cantonese (71), Wu (70), Vietnamese (67), Javanese (64), Italian (63), Turkish (61), Tagalog (58), and Thai (52).

TOP 10 MOST STUDIED FOREIGN LANGUAGES IN THE US*

① Spanish ② French ③ German ④ Japanese ⑤ Italian ⑥ Chinese (Mandarin) ⑦ Latin ⑧ Russian ⑨ Ancient Greek ⑩ Hebrew

* In US institutions of higher education
Source: *Modern Language Association of America*
These rankings are from the most recent survey conducted every five years, from colleges and universities in the fall of 1995

TOP 10 ★ LANGUAGES OFFICIALLY SPOKEN IN THE MOST COUNTRIES

	LANGUAGE	COUNTRIES
1	English	57
2	French	33
3	Arabic	23
4	Spanish	21
5	Portuguese	8
6 =	Dutch	4
=	German	4
8 =	Chinese (Mandarin)	3
=	Danish	3
=	Italian	3
=	Malay	3

There are many countries in the world with more than one official language – both English and French are recognized officially in Canada, for example. English is used in numerous countries as the lingua franca – the common language that enables people who speak mutually unintelligible languages to communicate with each other.

TOP 10 MOST CITED AUTHORS OF ALL TIME

(Author/country/dates)

1 **William Shakespeare**, UK, 1564–1616 **2** **Charles Dickens**, UK, 1812–70
3 **Sir Walter Scott**, UK, 1771–1832 **4** **Johann Goethe**, Germany, 1749–1832
5 **Aristotle**, Greece, 384–322 BC **6** **Alexandre Dumas (père)**, France, 1802–70
7 **Robert Louis Stevenson**, UK, 1850–94 **8** **Mark Twain**, US, 1835–1910
9 **Marcus Tullius Cicero**, Italy, 106–43 BC **10** **Honoré de Balzac**, France, 1799–1850

This Top 10 is based on a search of a major US library computer database, Citations, which includes books both by and about the author, with a total of more than 15,000 for Shakespeare.

TOP 10 ★
LARGEST LIBRARIES

	LIBRARY	LOCATION	FOUNDED	BOOKS
1	Library of Congress	Washington, DC	1800	23,994,965
2	National Library of China	Beijing, China	1909	20,000,000
3	National Library of Canada	Ottawa, Canada	1953	16,000,000
4	Deutsche Bibliothek*	Frankfurt, Germany	1990	15,997,000
5	British Library#	London, UK	1753	15,000,000
6	Harvard University Library	Cambridge, Massachusetts	1638	13,617,133
7	Vernadsky Central Scientific Library of the National Academy of Sciences	Kiev, Ukraine	1919	13,000,000
8	Russian State Library+	Moscow, Russia	1862	11,750,000
9	New York Public Library★	New York	1895	11,445,971
10	Bibliotheque Nationale de Paris	Paris, France	1400	11,000,000

* *Formed in 1990 through the unification of the Deutsche Bibliothek, Frankfurt (founded 1947) and the Deutsche Bucherei, Leipzig*

\# *Founded as part of the British Museum, 1753; became an independent body in 1973*

\+ *Founded 1862 as Rumyantsev Library, formerly State V. I. Lenin Library*

★ *Astor Library founded 1848, consolidated with Lenox Library and Tilden Trust to form New York Public Library in 1895*

The figures for books in such vast collections as held by the libraries listed above represent only a fraction of the total collections, which include manuscripts, microfilms, maps, prints, and records. The Library of Congress has perhaps more than 100 million cataloged items and the New York Public Library more than 26 million manuscripts, maps, audio-visual, and other cataloged items in addition to books.

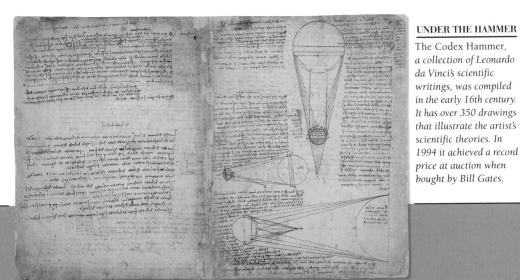

TOP 10 ★
MOST EXPENSIVE BOOKS AND MANUSCRIPTS EVER SOLD AT AUCTION

BOOK OR MANUSCRIPT/SALE	PRICE ($)*

1 *The Codex Hammer*, c.1508–10, Christie's, New York, Nov 11, 1994 — 30,800,000
This Leonardo da Vinci notebook was bought by Bill Gates, the billionaire founder of Microsoft.

2 *The Gospels of Henry the Lion*, c.1173–75, Sotheby's, London, Dec 6, 1983 — 10,841,000
At the time of its sale, this became the most expensive manuscript or book ever sold.

3 *The Birds of America*, **John James Audubon**, 1827–38, Christie's, New York, Mar 10, 2000 — 8,000,000
This holds the record for any natural history book.

4 *The Canterbury Tales*, **Geoffrey Chaucer**, c.1476–77, Christie's, London, July 8, 1998 — 7,696,720
Printed by William Caxton and bought by Paul Getty.

5 *The Gutenberg Bible*, 1455, Christie's, New York, Oct 22, 1987 — 5,390,000
This is one of the first books ever printed, by Johann Gutenberg and Johann Fust in 1455.

6 *The Northumberland Bestiary*, c.1250–60, Sotheby's, London, Nov 29, 1990 — 5,049,000
This holds the record for an English manuscript.

7 *The Burdett Psalter and Hours*, 1282–86, Sotheby's, London, June 23, 1998 — 4,517,640
This is the third most expensive illustrated manuscript ever sold.

8 **Autograph manuscript of nine symphonies by Wolfgang Amadeus Mozart**, c.1773–74, Sotheby's, London, May 22, 1987 — 3,854,000
This holds the record for any music manuscript.

9 *The Birds of America*, **John James Audubon**, 1827–38, Sotheby's, New York, June 6, 1989 — 3,600,000

10 *The Hours of Saint-Lô*, 1470, Sotheby's, New York, Apr 21, 1998 — 3,300,000

* *Excluding premiums*

UNDER THE HAMMER

The Codex Hammer, *a collection of Leonardo da Vinci's scientific writings, was compiled in the early 16th century. It has over 350 drawings that illustrate the artist's scientific theories. In 1994 it achieved a record price at auction when bought by Bill Gates.*

THE 10 ★
FIRST PUBLICATIONS PRINTED IN ENGLAND
AUTHOR/BOOK

1 *Propositio ad Carolum ducem Burgundiae**

2 Cato, *Disticha de Morbidus*

3 Geoffrey Chaucer, *The Canterbury Tales*

4 *Ordinale seu Pica ad usem Sarum ("Sarum Pie")*

5 John Lydgate, *The Temple of Glass*

6 John Lydgate, *Stans Puer Mensam*

7 John Lydgate, *The Horse, the Sheep and the Goose*

8 John Lydgate, *The Churl and the Bird*

9 *Infanta Salvatoris*

10 William Caxton, advertisement for "Sarum Pie"

* This work was printed before September 1476; all the others were printed in either 1476 or 1477.

THE 10 FIRST POCKET BOOKS*
(Author/title)

❶ James Hilton, *Lost Horizon*
❷ Dorothea Brande, *Wake Up and Live!*
❸ William Shakespeare, *Five Great Tragedies* ❹ Thorne Smith, *Topper*
❺ Agatha Christie, *The Murder of Roger Ackroyd* ❻ Dorothy Parker, *Enough Rope* ❼ Emily Brontë, *Wuthering Heights* ❽ Samuel Butler, *The Way of All Flesh* ❾ Thornton Wilder, *The Bridge of San Luis Rey* ❿ Felix Salten, *Bambi*

* All published in 1939

"BLURB"
American humorist Frank Gelett Burgess (1866–1951), best known as the author of the nonsense poem *I Never Saw a Purple Cow*, was also the inventor of the word "blurb" – the effusive text used on book jackets to describe the book within. In his book *Are You a Bromide?*, Burgess claimed that its author was Miss Belinda Blurb, whose work was said to be the sensation of the year.

WHY DO WE SAY ?

BEST RED AUTHOR
During the Cultural Revolution, Chinese leader Mao Tse-tung (Zedong) became the subject of a personality cult, with his bestselling Quotations ... (Little Red Book) *its most potent symbol.*

TOP 10 ★
LARGEST LIBRARIES IN THE US

LIBRARY/LOCATION	BOOKS
1 **Library of Congress**, Washington, DC	23,994,965
2 **Harvard University**, Cambridge, MA	13,617,133
3 **New York Public Library**, New York	11,445,971
4 **Yale University**, New Haven, CT	9,932,080
5 **Queens Borough Public Library**, New York	9,237,300
6 **University of Illinois**, Urbana, IL	9,024,928
7 **University of California**, Berkeley, CA	8,628,028
8 **Cincinnati and Hamilton County Public Library**, Cincinnati, OH	8,582,637
9 **Chicago Public Library**, Chicago, OH	8,100,000
10 **Free Library of Philadelphia**, PA	7,891,532

Source: *American Library Association*

TOP 10 ★
BESTSELLING BOOKS OF ALL TIME

BOOK/AUTHOR	FIRST PUBLISHED	APPROX. SALES
1 *The Bible*	c.1451–55	over 6,000,000,000
2 *Quotations from the Works of Mao Tse-tung* (dubbed *Little Red Book* by the Western press)	1966	900,000,000
3 *American Spelling Book* by Noah Webster	1783	up to 100,000,000
4 *The Guinness Book of Records*	1955	over 85,000,000*
5 *World Almanac*	1868	73,500,000*
6 *The McGuffey Readers* by William Holmes McGuffey	1836	60,000,000
7 *The Common Sense Book of Baby and Child Care* by Benjamin Spock	1946	over 50,000,000
8 *A Message to Garcia* by Elbert Hubbard	1899	up to 40,000,000
9 = *In His Steps: "What Would Jesus Do?"* by Rev. Charles Monroe Sheldon	1896	over 30,000,000
= *Valley of the Dolls* by Jacqueline Susann	1966	over 30,000,000

* Aggregate sales of annual publication

Which language is not among the world's Top 10?
see p.97 for the answer
A Japanese
B Spanish
C French

Toys & Games

TOP 10 TOYS OF 1999 IN THE US*

1. Furbys 2. Hot Wheels basic cars
3. Star Wars Episode 1 figure #1
4. Barbie Millennium 5. Pokémon booster packs 6. Furby Babies 7. Barbie Sun Jamer 4x4 8. Pokémon deck assistant
9. Sesame Street rock 'n' roll assistant
10. Pokémon Fossil booster packs

By value of sales
Source: *Toy Manufacturers of America, Inc.*

TOP 10 ★ BOARD GAMES IN THE US, 1999

	GAME	MANUFACTURER
1	Pokémon Monopoly	Parker Brothers
2	Monopoly	Parker Brothers
3	Trouble	Milton Bradley
4	Pokémon Master Trainer	Milton Bradley
5	Operation	Milton Bradley
6	Connect Four	Milton Bradley
7	Twister	Milton Bradley
8	Disney Wonderful World of Trivia	Mattel
9	Standard Scrabble	Milton Bradley
10	The Game of Life	Milton Bradley

Source: *NPD TRSTS Toys Tracking Service*

TOP 10 INTERACTIVE ENTERTAINMENT SOFTWARE TITLES IN THE US, 1999*

(Game/format)

1. Pokémon Blue, Gameboy#
2. Pokémon Red, Gameboy# 3. Pokémon Yellow, Gameboy# 4. Pokémon Pinball, Gameboy# 5. Pokémon Snap, Nintendo 64#
6. Donkey Kong 64, Nintendo 64#
7. Gran Turismo Racing, Sony Playstation+
8. Super Smash Brothers, Nintendo 64#
9. Driver, Sony Platstation+ 10. Spyro the Dragon, Sony Platstation+

*Ranked by units sold # Published by Nintendo
+ Published by Sony*
Source: *NPD TRSTS Toys Tracking Service*

THE 10 ★ TOYS INTRODUCED IN THE US IN 1999

	TOY	MANUFACTURER
1	Star Wars Episode 1 figure #1	Hasbro
2	Barbie Millennium	Mattel
3	Pokémon booster packs	Wizards of the Coast
4	Furby Babies	Tiger Electronics
5	Sesame Street rock 'n' roll assistant	Tyco Preschool
6	Pokémon Fossil booster packs	Wizards of the Coast
7	Disney Walk 'n' Wag Pluto	Mattel
8	Star Wars Episode 1 figure #2	Hasbro
9	Kawasaki new Ninja	Fisher-Price
10	Harley Davidson motorcycle	Fisher-Price

Source: *Toy Manufacturers of America, Inc.*

TOP 10 ★ MOST LANDED-ON SQUARES IN MONOPOLY®*

US GAME		UK GAME
Illinois Avenue	1	Trafalgar Square
Go	2	Go
B. & O. Railroad	3	Fenchurch Street Station
Free Parking	4	Free Parking
Tennessee Avenue	5	Marlborough Street
New York Avenue	6	Vine Street
Reading Railroad	7	King's Cross Station
St. James Place	8	Bow Street
Water Works	9	Water Works
Pennsylvania Railroad	5	Marylebone Station

Based on a computer analysis of the probability of landing on each square

Monopoly® is a registered trade mark of Parker Brothers division of Tonka Corporation, US.

TOP 10 ★ HIGHEST-SCORING SCRABBLE® WORDS

	WORD/PLAY	SCORE
1	QUARTZY	164/162

(i) *Play across a triple-word-score (red) square with the Z on a double-letter-score (light blue) square*
(ii) *Play across two double-word-score (pink) squares with Q and Y on pink squares*

| 2 | =BEZIQUE | 161/158 |

(i) *Play across a red square with either the Z or the Q on a light blue square*
(ii) *Play across two pink squares with the B and second E on two pink squares*

| | =CAZIQUE | 161/158 |

(i) *Play across a red square with either the Z or the Q on a light blue square*
(ii) *Play across two pink squares with the C and E on two pink squares*

| 4 | ZINKIFY | 158 |

Play across a red square with the Z on a light blue square

| 5 | =QUETZAL | 155 |

Play across a red square with either the Q or the Z on a light blue square

| | =JAZZILY | 155 |

(Using a blank as one of the Zs) Play across a red square with the non-blank Z on a light blue square

| | =QUIZZED | 155 |

(Using a blank as one of the Zs) Play across a red square with the non-blank Z or the Q on a light blue square

| 8 | =ZEPHYRS | 152 |

Play across a red square with the Z on a light blue square

| | =ZINCIFY | 152 |

Play across a red square with the Z on a light blue square

| | =ZYTHUMS | 152 |

Play across a red square with the Z on a light blue square

All the Top 10 words contain seven letters and therefore earn the premium of 50 for using all the letters in the rack. Being able to play them depends on there already being suitable words on the board to which they can be added. In an actual game, the face values of the perpendicular words to which they are joined would also be counted, but these are discounted here as the total score variations would be infinite. Scrabble was invented in the US during the Depression by an unemployed architect, Alfred Butts, and developed in the 1940s by James Brunot.

TOP 10 ★
MOST EXPENSIVE TOYS EVER SOLD AT AUCTION BY CHRISTIE'S EAST, NY

TOY/SALE	PRICE ($)*
1 "The Charles," a fire-hose-reel made by American manufacturer George Brown and Co., c.1875, Dec 1991	231,000
2 Märklin fire station, Dec 1991	79,200
3 Horse-drawn double-decker tram, Dec 1991	71,500
4 Mikado mechanical bank, Dec 1993	63,000
5 Märklin ferris wheel, June 1994	55,200
6 Girl skipping rope mechanical bank, June 1994	48,300
7 Märklin battleship, June 1994	33,350
8 Märklin battleship, June 1994	32,200
9= Bing keywind open phaeton tinplate automobile, Dec 1992	24,200
= Märklin fire pumper, Dec 1991	24,200

* Including 10 percent buyer's premium

Source: *Christie's East*

The fire-hose-reel at # 1 in this list is the record price paid at auction for a toy other than a doll. Models by the German tinplate maker Märklin, regarded by collectors as the Rolls-Royce of toys, similarly feature among the record prices of auction houses in the UK and other countries, where high prices have also been attained. On both sides of the Atlantic, pristine examples of high-quality mechanical toys (ideally in their original boxes, and unplayed with by the children for whom they were designed) command top dollar prices.

TOP 10 ★
MOST EXPENSIVE TEDDY BEARS SOLD AT AUCTION

BEAR/SALE	PRICE ($)*
1 "Teddy Girl," a 1904 Steiff bear, Christie's, London, Dec 5, 1994	169,928

This bear precisely doubled the previous world record for a teddy bear when it was acquired by Yoshiro Sekiguchi for a museum near Tokyo.

2 "Happy," a dual-plush Steiff teddy bear, 1926, Sotheby's, London, Sep 19, 1989	85,470

Although estimated at $1,000–$1,400, competitive bidding pushed the price up to the then world record, when it was acquired by collector Paul Volpp.

3 "Elliot," a blue Steiff bear, 1908, Christie's, London, Dec 6, 1993	74,275

Produced as a sample for Harrods.

4 "Teddy Edward," a golden mohair teddy bear, Christie's, London, Dec 9, 1996	60,176
5 Black Steiff teddy bear, c.1912, Sotheby's, London, May 18, 1990	45,327
6 Steiff, blank button, brown teddy bear, c.1905, Christie's, London, Dec 8, 1997	35,948
7 "Albert," a Steiff teddy bear, c.1910, Christie's, London, Dec 9, 1996	28,759
8 Steiff teddy bear, Christie's, London, Dec 9, 1996	26,962
9 "Theodore," a miniature Steiff teddy bear, 9 cm (3½ in) tall, c.1948, Christie's, London, Dec 11, 1995	22,705
10= "Black Jack," black Steiff teddy bear, Christie's, London, May 22, 1997	21,569
= Cinnamon Steiff teddy bear, c.1905, Christie's, London, May 23, 1997	21,569

* Prices include buyer's premium

"TEDDY BEAR"

While on a hunting trip, US President Theodore ("Teddy") Roosevelt refused to shoot a young bear. This became the subject of a famous cartoon by Clifford K. Berryman, published in the *Washington Post*. Immediately afterward, Morris Michtom, a New York shopkeeper, made stuffed bears and, with Roosevelt's permission, advertised them as "Teddy's Bears". Margarete Steiff, a German toymaker, soon began making her toy bears, exporting them to the US to meet demand.  **WHY DO WE SAY?**

TOP 10 ★
MOST EXPENSIVE DOLLS SOLD AT AUCTION

DOLL/SALE	PRICE ($)
1 Kämmer and Reinhardt doll, Sotheby's, London, Feb 8, 1994	282,750
2 Kämmer and Reinhardt bisque character doll, German, c.1909, Sotheby's, London, Oct 17, 1996 *(Previously sold at Sotheby's, London, February 16, 1989, for $140,171)*	169,117
3 Kämmer and Reinhardt bisque character doll, German, c.1909, Sotheby's, London, Oct 17, 1996	143,327
4 Albert Marque bisque character doll, Sotheby's, London, Oct 17, 1996	112,380
5 William and Mary wooden doll, English, c.1690, Sotheby's, London, Mar 24, 1987	110,396
6 Wooden doll, Charles II, 17th century, Christie's, London, May 18, 1989	103,850
7 Albert Marque bisque character doll, Sotheby's, London, Oct 17, 1996	91,748
8= Albert Marque bisque character doll, Christie's, London, May 23, 1997	89,581
= Pressed bisque swivel-head Madagascar doll, Sotheby's, London, Oct 17, 1996	88,310
10 Shellacked pressed bisque swivel-head doll, Sotheby's, London, Oct 17, 1996	71,117

TOP 10 TOY RETAIL OUTLETS IN THE US, 1999*
(Outlet type/percentage of market share)

❶ Discount stores, 41.5 ❷ National toy stores, 21.7 ❸ Other outlets (not toy stores), 12.8 ❹ Mail order, 5.3 ❺ Department stores, 4.1 ❻ Other toy stores, 3.7 ❼ Food/drug stores, 3.6 ❽ Card/gift/stationery stores, 3.1 ❾ Hobby/craft stores, 2.7 ❿ Variety stores, 1.5

* Ranked by dollar share perentage in 1998   Soure: *Toy Manufacturers of America Inc.*

Which comic book superhero first appeared in 1938?   **A** Batman
see p.119 for the answer   **B** Spider-Man
   C Superman

20th-Century Artists

TOP 10 ★
MOST EXPENSIVE PAINTINGS BY ANDY WARHOL

PAINTING*/SALE	PRICE ($)
1 Orange Marilyn, Sotheby's, New York, May 14, 1998	15,750,000
2 Shot Red Marilyn, Sotheby's, New York, May 3, 1989	3,700,000
3 Marilyn Monroe, Twenty Times, Sotheby's, New York, Nov 10, 1988	3,600,000
4 Marilyn X 100, Sotheby's, New York, Nov 17, 1992	3,400,000
5 Shot Red Marilyn, Sotheby's, New York, Nov 2, 1994	3,300,000
6 Big Torn Campbell's Soup Can, Christie's, New York, May 7, 1997	3,200,000
7 Orange Marilyn, Christie's, New York, Nov 19, 1998	2,500,000
8 Marion, Sotheby's, New York, May 18, 1999	2,400,000
9 Big Electric Chair, Christie's, London, June 30, 1999	2,370,000
10 Self Portrait, Christie's, New York, May 12, 1998	2,200,000

* Including silkscreen works

"FAMOUS FOR 15 MINUTES"

Andy Warhol's own fame has outlived his famous phrase. His works continuing to attain considerable prices at auction.

HIGH FIGURES

The distinctive elongated figures created by Swiss sculptor Alberto Giacometti (1901–66), shown at work in his studio in 1958, command high prices at auction.

TOP 10 ★
MOST EXPENSIVE SCULPTURES BY ALBERTO GIACOMETTI

SCULPTURE/SALE	PRICE ($)	SCULPTURE/SALE	PRICE ($)
1 La Forêt – Sept Figures et Une Tête, Sotheby's, New York, Nov 16, 1998	6,800,000	**6 Trois Hommes Qui Marchent**, Christie's, New York, May 11, 1988	3,500,000
2 L'Homme Qui Marche I, Christie's, London Nov 28, 1988	6,358,000	**7 Grande Femme Debout II**, Christie's, New York, May 12, 1987	3,300,000
3 Trois Hommes Qui Marchent I, Sotheby's, New York, Nov 11, 1999	5,200,000	**8 Trois Hommes Qui Marchent II**, Christie's, New York, May 14, 1997	3,200,000
4 Grande Femme Debout I, Christie's, New York, Nov 14, 1989	4,500,000	**9 Grande Femme Debout I**, Christie's, New York, May 12, 1987	2,800,000
5 Grande Femme Debout I, Christie's, New York, Nov 14, 1990	3,600,000	**10 L'Homme Qui Marche III – Walking Man III**, Christie's, New York, May 12, 1998	2,700,000

114

Did You Know? Between October 18 and December 4, 1961, Henri Matisse's painting *Le Bateau* hung upside down in the Museum of Modern Art, New York. An estimated 116,000 people passed through the gallery before anyone noticed.

TOP 10 ★
MOST EXPENSIVE SCULPTURES BY HENRY MOORE

SCULPTURE/SALE	PRICE ($)
1 = *Reclining Figure*, Christies, New York, May 13, 1999	3,700,000
= *Two-piece Reclining Figure, Points*, Christie's, New York, Nov 9, 1999	3,700,000
= *Working Model for UNESCO Reclining Figure*, Christie's, New York, May 15, 1990	3,700,000
4 *Reclining Figure, Angles*, Christie's, New York, Nov 13, 1996	2,400,000
5 *Draped Reclining Woman*, Sotheby's, New York, Nov 13, 1997	2,350,000
6 *Reclining Connected Forms*, Sotheby's, New York, May 17, 1990	2,200,000
7 = *Reclining Figure, Bone Skirt*, Sotheby's, New York, May 13, 1997	2,000,000
= *Working Model for Three Way Piece No. 3 Vertebrae*, Sotheby's, New York, May 17, 1990	2,000,000
9 = *Festival Reclining Figure*, Sotheby's, New York, May 11, 1994	1,850,000
= *Reclining Figure*, Sotheby's, New York, Nov 11, 1988	1,850,000

British sculptor Henry Spencer Moore (1898–1986) was a war artist before achieving international fame for his sculptures. Many of these were commissioned for public buildings, but those that have entered the marketplace have achieved consistently high prices.

TOP 10 ★
MOST EXPENSIVE PAINTINGS BY ROY LICHTENSTEIN

PAINTING/SALE	PRICE ($)
1 *Kiss II*, Christie's, New York, May 7, 1990	5,500,000
2 *Torpedo...Los*, Christie's, New York, Nov 7, 1989	5,000,000
3 *Tex!*, Christie's, New York, Nov 20, 1996	3,600,000
4 *Blang!*, Christie's, New York, May 7, 1997	2,600,000
5 *Kiss II*, Christie's, New York, May 3, 1995	2,300,000
6 *I...I'm Sorry!*, Sotheby's, New York, Nov 1, 1994	2,250,000
7 *The Ring*, Sotheby's, New York, Nov 19, 1997	2,000,000
8 = *I Can See the Whole Room... And There's Nobody in It*, Christie's, New York, Nov 9, 1988	1,900,000
= *Forest Scene*, Sotheby's, New York, Nov 19, 1996	1,900,000
10 *Girl With Piano*, Sotheby's, New York, Nov 17, 1992	1,650,000

SECOND KISS

Kiss II by pop artist Roy Lichtenstein (1923–97) gained a record $5.5 million at auction, followed closely at $5 million by Torpedo...Los. His work was partly inspired by images from comic strips.

TOP 10 ★
MOST EXPENSIVE PAINTINGS BY JACKSON POLLOCK

PAINTING*/SALE	PRICE ($)
1 *Number 8, 1950*, Sotheby's, New York, May 2, 1989	10,500,000
2 *Frieze*, Christie's, New York, Nov 9, 1988	5,200,000
3 *Search*, Sotheby's, New York, May 2, 1988	4,400,000
4 *Number 19, 1949*, Sotheby's, New York, May 2, 1989	3,600,000
5 *Number 31, 1949*, Christie's, New York, May 3, 1988	3,200,000
6 *Number 13*, Christie's, New York, Nov 7, 1990	2,800,000
7 *Number 26, 1950*, Sotheby's, New York, May 4, 1987	2,500,000
8 = *Number 20*, Sotheby's, New York, May 8, 1990	2,200,000
= *Number 19, 1948*, Christies, New York, May 4, 1993	2,200,000
= *Something of the Past*, Christie's, New York, May 7, 1996	2,200,000

* Includes mixed media compositions

Music

Hit Albums of the Decades

TOP 10 ALBUMS OF EACH YEAR IN THE 1960s IN THE US
(Year/album/artist or group)

1 1960 *The Sound of Music*, Original Cast **2** 1961 *Judy at Carnegie Hall*, Judy Garland, **3** 1962 *West Side Story*, Soundtrack **4** 1963 *John Fitzgerald Kennedy: A Memorial Album*, Documentary **5** 1964 *Meet The Beatles*, The Beatles **6** 1965 *Mary Poppins*, Soundtrack **7** 1966 *Whipped Cream & Other Delights*, Herb Alpert & The Tijuana Brass **8** 1967 *Sgt. Pepper's Lonely Hearts Club Band*, The Beatles **9** 1968 *The Beatles* ("White Album"), The Beatles **10** 1969 *Hair*, Broadway Cast

BRIDGING THE ATLANTIC

Simon and Garfunkel's single and album Bridge over Troubled Water *topped the UK and US charts simultaneously in March 1970.*

TOP 10 ★
ALBUMS OF THE 1960s IN THE US

ALBUM/ARTIST OR GROUP	YEAR RELEASED
1 *West Side Story* (Original Soundtrack), Various	1961
2 *Blue Hawaii* (Original Soundtrack), Elvis Presley	1961
3 *The Sound of Music* (Original Soundtrack), Various	1965
4 *Sgt. Pepper's Lonely Hearts Club Band*, The Beatles	1967
5 *More of the Monkees*, The Monkees	1967
6 *Days of Wine and Roses*, Andy Williams	1963
7 *G.I. Blues*, Elvis Presley	1960
8 *The Button-Down Mind Of Bob Newhart*, Bob Newhart	1960
9 *Whipped Cream & Other Delights*, Herb Alpert & The Tijuana Brass	1965
10 *A Hard Day's Night* (Original Soundtrack), The Beatles	1964

TOP 10 ★
ALBUMS OF THE 1970s IN THE US

ALBUM/ARTIST OR GROUP	YEAR RELEASED
1 *Rumours*, Fleetwood Mac	1977
2 *Their Greatest Hits, 1971–1975*, The Eagles	1976
3 *The Dark Side of the Moon*, Pink Floyd	1973
4 *Tapestry*, Carole King	1971
5 *Saturday Night Fever* (Original Soundtrack), Various	1977
6 *Led Zeppelin IV* (Untitled), Led Zeppelin	1971
7 *Boston*, Boston	1976
8 *Grease* (Original Soundtrack), Various	1978
9 *Frampton Comes Alive!*, Peter Frampton	1976
10 *Songs in the Key of Life*, Stevie Wonder	1976

TOP 10 ★
ALBUMS OF EACH YEAR IN THE 1970s IN THE US

YEAR	ALBUM/ARTIST OR GROUP
1970	*Bridge Over Troubled Water*, Simon and Garfunkel
1971	*Tapestry*, Carole King
1972	*American Pie*, Don McLean
1973	*Dark Side of the Moon*, Pink Floyd
1974	*John Denver's Greatest Hits*, John Denver
1975	*Captain Fantastic and the Brown Dirt Cowboy*, Elton John
1976	*Frampton Comes Alive*, Peter Frampton
1977	*Rumours*, Fleetwood Mac
1978	*Saturday Night Fever*, Soundtrack
1979	*Breakfast in America*, Supertramp

THRILLS GALORE

It has been estimated that Michael Jackson's Thriller *album has sold 25 million copies in the US and more than 45 million worldwide.*

TOP 10 ★
ALBUMS OF EACH YEAR IN THE 1990s IN THE US

YEAR	ALBUM/ARTIST OR GROUP
1990	*Please Hammer Don't Hurt 'Em*, MC Hammer
1991	*Ropin' the Wind*, Garth Brooks
1992	*Some Gave All*, Billy Ray Cyrus
1993	*The Bodyguard*, Whitney Houston/Soundtrack
1994	*The Sign*, Ace of Base
1995	*Cracked Rear View*, Hootie & the Blowfish
1996	*Jagged Little Pill*, Alanis Morissette
1997	*Spice*, Spice Girls
1998	*Titanic*, Soundtrack
1999	*Millennium*, Backstreet Boys

TOP 10 ★
ALBUMS OF THE 1980s IN THE US

ALBUM/ARTIST OR GROUP	YEAR RELEASED
1 *Thriller*, Michael Jackson	1982
2 *Born in the USA*, Bruce Springsteen	1984
3 *Dirty Dancing* (Original Soundtrack), Various	1987
4 *Purple Rain* (Original Soundtrack), Prince & The Revolution	1984
5 *Can't Slow Down*, Lionel Richie	1983
6 *Whitney Houston*, Whitney Houston	1985
7 *Hysteria*, Def Leppard	1987
8 *Slippery When Wet*, Bon Jovi	1986
9 *Appetite For Destruction*, Guns N' Roses	1988
10 *The Wall*, Pink Floyd	1979

TOP 10 ALBUMS OF EACH YEAR IN THE 1980s IN THE US
(Year/album/artist or group)

❶ 1980 *The Wall*, Pink Floyd ❷ 1981 *Hi Infidelity*, REO Speedwagon ❸ 1982 *Asia*, Asia ❹ 1983 *Thriller*, Michael Jackson ❺ 1984 *Purple Rain*, Prince & The Revolution ❻ 1985 *Like a Virgin*, Madonna ❼ 1986 *Whitney Houston*, Whitney Houston ❽ 1987 *Slippery When Wet*, Bon Jovi ❾ 1988 *Faith*, George Michael ❿ 1989 *Girl You Know It's True*, Milli Vanilli

MADONNA V HAMMER

While Madonna's The Immaculate Collection was the UK's top selling album of 1990, with nine weeks at No. 1, it was held off the top slot in the US by MC Hammer with Please Hammer Don't Hurt 'Em.

TOP 10 ALBUMS OF THE 1990s IN THE US
(Album/artist or group/year released)

❶ *The Bodyguard*, Soundtrack, 1992 ❷ *No Fences*, Garth Brooks, 1990 ❸ *Jagged Little Pill*, Alanis Morissette, 1995 ❹ *Cracked Rear View*, Hootie & the Blowfish, 1994 ❺ *Ropin' the Wind*, Garth Brooks, 1991 ❻ *Come on Over*, Shania Twain, 1997 ❼ *Breathless*, Kenny G, 1992 ❽ *II*, Boyz II Men, 1994 ❾ *The Woman in Me*, Shania Twain, 1995 ❿ *Pieces of You*, Jewel, 1997

Source: *RIAA*

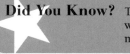

Did You Know? The album from the 1992 film *The Bodyguard* became a worldwide bestseller, its 16 million-plus sales in the US making it the country's bestselling soundtrack album ever.

Pop Stars of the 90s

TOP 10 ★ BOYZ II MEN SINGLES IN THE US

	TITLE	YEAR
1	I'll Make Love to You	1994
2	End of the Road	1992
3	On Bended Knee	1994
4	4 Seasons of Loneliness	1997
5	Motownphilly	1991
6	In the Still of the Nite	1992
7	A Song for Mama	1997
8	It's so Hard to Say Goodbye to Yesterday	1991
9	Water Runs Dry	1995
10	I Will Get There	1999

TOP 10 ★ MICHAEL BOLTON SINGLES IN THE US

	TITLE	YEAR
1	Said I Loved You ... But I Lied	1993
2	When a Man Loves a Woman	1991
3	Time, Love and Tenderness	1991
4	To Love Somebody	1992
5	Love is a Wonderful Thing	1991
6	How Can We Be Lovers	1990
7	When I'm Back on My Feet Again	1990
8	Missing You Now	1992
9	Go the Distance	1997
10	Can I Touch You ... There?	1995

TOP 10 ★ CELINE DION SINGLES IN THE US

	TITLE	YEAR
1	The Power of Love	1993
2	Because You Loved Me	1996
3	It's All Coming Back to Me Now	1996
4	My Heart Will Go On	1998
5	All By Myself	1997
6	Beauty and the Beast	1992
7	Where Does My Heart Beat Now	1990
8	That's the Way It Is	1999
9	If You Asked Me To	1992
10	When I Fall in Love	1993

TOP 10 ★ JANET JACKSON SINGLES IN THE US

	TITLE	YEAR
1	Again	1993
2	That's the Way Love Goes	1993
3	Together Again	1997
4	Love Will Never do Without You	1990
5	Escapade	1990
6	Black Cat	1990
7	Runaway	1995
8	If	1993
9	You Want This	1994
10	Any Time, Any Place	1994

TOP 10 ★ MARIAH CAREY SINGLES IN THE US

	TITLE	YEAR
1	Hero	1993
2	Always be My Baby	1996
3	Fantasy	1995
4	My All	1997
5	Honey	1997
6	Dreamlover	1993
7	I Still Believe	1999
8	Love Takes Time	1990
9	Vision of Love	1990
10	Heartbreaker	1999

TOP 10 MADONNA SINGLES IN THE US

(Single/year)

❶ Vogue, 1990 ❷ Justify My Love, 1990 ❸ Take a Bow, 1994 ❹ This Used to be My Playground, 1992 ❺ Erotica, 1992 ❻ Secret, 1994 ❼ I'll Remember, 1994 ❽ You'll See, 1995 ❾ Ray of Light, 1998 ❿ Frozen, 1998

Source: MRIB

TOP 10 ★ PRINCE SINGLES IN THE US

	TITLE	YEAR
1	Cream	1991
2	The Most Beautiful Girl in the World	1994
3	7	1992
4	Thieves in the Temple	1990
5	Gett Off	1991
6	Diamonds and Pearls	1991
7	1999	1992
8	I Hate U	1995
9	Money Don't Matter 2 Night	1992
10	Letitgo	1994

TOP 10 TLC SINGLES IN THE US

(Title/year)

❶ Waterfalls, 1995 ❷ Creep, 1995 ❸ Baby-Baby-Baby, 1992 ❹ Ain't 2 Proud 2 Beg, 1992 ❺ Unpretty, 1999 ❻ No Scrubs, 1999 ❼ Red Light Special, 1995 ❽ Diggin' on You, 1996 ❾ What About Your Friends, 1992 ❿ Hat 2 Da Back, 1993

TOP 10 ★
WHITNEY HOUSTON SINGLES
IN THE US

TITLE	YEAR
1 I Will Always Love You	1992
2 Exhale (Shoop Shoop)	1995
3 I Believe in You and Me	1996
4 Heartbreak Hotel*	1999
5 My Love Is Your Love	1999
6 I'm Your Baby Tonight	1990
7 All the Man That I Need	1990
8 I'm Every Woman	1993
9 It's Not Right but It's Okay	1999
10 I Have Nothing	1993

* With Faith Evans & Kelly Price

TOP 10 ★
JODECI SINGLES
IN THE US

TITLE	YEAR
1 Lately	1993
2 Cry for You	1994
3 Come and Talk to Me	1992
4 Freek 'N You	1995
5 Forever My Lady	1991
6 Get On Up	1996
7 Feenin'	1994
8 Love U 4 Life	1996
9 Stay	1992
10 Let's Go Through the Motions	1993

TOP 10 R. KELLY SINGLES IN THE US
(Single/year)

1 Bump and Grind, 1994 2 I Believe I Can Fly, 1997
3 I'm Your Angel*, 1998 4 Down Low (Nobody Has to Know)#, 1996 5 You Remind Me of Something, 1996
6 I Can't Sleep Baby (If I), 1996 7 You Body's Callin', 1994
8 Sex Me, Parts 1 & 2, 1993 9 Gotham City, 1997
10 If I Could Turn Back the Hands of Time, 1999

* With Celanie Dion   # Featuring Ronald Isley

GORGEOUS GEORGE
George Michael has achieved bestselling albums across two decades in both the UK and the US.

TOP 10 GEORGE
MICHAEL SINGLES
OF THE 1990s IN THE US
(Title/year)

1 I Want Your Sex, 1987 2 Faith, 1987
3 Don't Let the Sun Go Down on Me*, 1992
4 One More Try, 1988 5 Freedom, 1991
6 Fastlove, 1996 7 Jesus to a Child, 1996
8 Too Funky, 1992 9 Father Figure, 1988
10 Praying for Time, 1990

*With Elton John

Did You Know? Whitney Houston's mother, Cissy Houston, née Drinkard, began her musical career in a group called The Drinkard Sisters, with her nieces Dionne and Dee Dee Warwick.

Music Genres 2

IRISH ALBUMS IN THE UK

	TITLE/ARTIST	YEAR
1	*Talk on Corners*, Corrs	1997
2	*By Request*, Boyzone	1999
3	*The Joshua Tree*, U2	1987
4	*Where We Belong*, Boyzone	1998
5	*Watermark*, Enya	1988
6	*Shepherd Moons*, Enya	1991
7	*Rattle and Hum*, U2	1988
8	*Said and Done*, Boyzone	1995
9	*A Different Beat*, Boyzone	1996
10	*Achtung Baby!*, U2	1991

Source: *The Popular Music Database*

THE BOYS IN THE BAND

A string of UK No. 1 albums has secured Boyzone four of the Top 10 Irish albums of all time. The band was formed in Dublin in 1993 as Ireland's answer to Take That.

WORLD MUSIC ALBUMS IN THE US, 1999

	TITLE	ARTIST
1	*Sogno*	Andrea Bocelli
2	*Romanza*	Andrea Bocelli
3	*Buena Vista Social Club*	Buena Vista Social Club
4	*Tears of Stone*	Chieftains
5	*The Book of Secrets*	Loreena McKennitt
6	*Buena Vista Social Club*	Buena Vista Social Club Presents Ibrahim Ferrer
7	*The Irish Tenors*	John McDermott/ Anthony Kearns/Ronan Tynan
8	*Sueno* (with Spanish tracks)	Andrea Bocelli
9	*Romanza* (with Spanish tracks)	Andrea Bocelli
10	*Return To Pride Rock – Songs Inspired by Disney's The Lion King II*	Various Artists

Source: Billboard

JAZZ ALBUMS IN THE US

	ALBUM/ARTIST OR GROUP	YEAR
1	*Time Out Featuring Take Five*, Dave Brubeck Quartet	1960
2	*Hello Dolly*, Louis Armstrong	1964
3	*Getz & Gilberto*, Stan Getz and Joao Gilberto	1964
4	*Sun Goddess*, Ramsey Lewis	1975
5	*Jazz Samba*, Stan Getz and Charlie Byrd	1962
6	*Bitches Brew*, Miles Davies	1970
7	*The In Crowd*, Ramsey Lewis Trio	1965
8	*Time Further Out*, Dave Brubeck Quartet	1961
9	*Mack the Knife – Ella in Berlin*, Ella Fitzgerald	1960
10	*Exodus to Jazz*, Eddie Harris	1961

Did You Know? The first-ever rap album to reach a mass audience and achieve gold status was *Run-D.M.C.*, by the group of that name, on December 17, 1984.

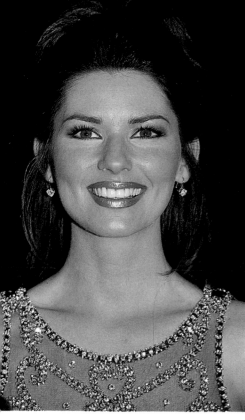

TWAIN MAKES HER MARK

Although it combines rock, pop, and country genres, Canadian-born Shania Twain's Come on Over ranks as the bestselling country album in the US.

TOP 10 ★
RAP SINGLES IN THE US

	TITLE/ARTIST	APPROX. SALES
1	*Whoomp! (There It Is)*, Tag Team	4,000,000
2	*I'll be Missing You*, Puff Daddy & Faith Evans (featuring 112)	3,000,000
3 =	*How Do U Want It*, 2Pac	2,000,000
=	*Tha Crossroads*, Bone Thugs-N-Harmony	2,000,000
=	*Gangsta's Paradise*, Coolio featuring L. V.	2,000,000
=	*Dazzey Duks*, Duice	2,000,000
=	*O.P.P.*, Naughty By Nature	2,000,000
=	*Baby Got Back*, Sir Mix-A-Lot	2,000,000
=	*Wild Thing*, Tone Loc	2,000,000
=	*Jump*, Kris Kross	2,000,000
=	*Rump Shaker*, Wreckx-N-Effect	2,000,000
=	*Can't Nobody Hold Me Down*, Puff Daddy	2,000,000

Source: *RIAA*

TOP 10 ★
COUNTRY ALBUMS IN THE US

	TITLE/ARTIST	APPROX. SALES
1	*Come on Over*, Shania Twain	17,000,000
2	*No Fences*, Garth Brooks	16,000,000
3	*Ropin' the Wind*, Garth Brooks	14,000,000
4	*Greatest Hits*, Kenny Rogers	12,000,000
5	*The Woman in Me*, Shania Twain	11,000,000
6	*The Hits*, Garth Brooks	10,000,000
7 =	*Some Gave All*, Billy Ray Cyrus	9,000,000
=	*Garth Brooks*, Garth Brooks	9,000,000
9 =	*Greatest Hits*, Patsy Cline	8,000,000
=	*In Pieces*, Garth Brooks	8,000,000
=	*The Chase*, Garth Brooks	8,000,000
=	*Wide Open Spaces*, Dixie Chicks	8,000,000

Source: *RIAA*

COOL GUY

Coolio (born Artis Ivey, 1963) sold over a million copies of his debut album, It Takes a Thief, achieving even greater success with his bestselling 1995 album, Gangsta's Paradise.

143

COUNTRY GOLD

In a recording career of over 30 years, Kenny Rogers has gained an impressive 28 gold and 44 platinum albums in the US.

MALE ARTISTS WITH THE MOST PLATINUM ALBUMS IN THE US

ARTIST	PLATINUM ALBUMS
1 Garth Brooks	97
2 Elvis Presley	75
3 Billy Joel	74
4 Elton John	58
5 =Michael Jackson	53
=Bruce Springsteen	53
7 George Strait	46
8 Kenny Rogers	44
9 Kenny G	41
10 Neil Diamond	35

Source: *RIAA*

Platinum singles and albums in the US are those that have achieved sales of 1 million units. The award has been made by the Recording Industry Association of America (RIAA) since 1976, when it was introduced in response to escalating music sales, as a result of which many discs were outselling the 500,000 required to achieve a gold award. In 1984 the RIAA introduced multiplatinum awards for certified sales of 2 million or more.

GROUPS WITH THE MOST PLATINUM ALBUMS IN THE US

GROUP	PLATINUM ALBUMS
1 The Beatles	90
2 Led Zeppelin	80
3 Pink Floyd	66
4 The Eagles	62
5 Aerosmith	51
6 Van Halen	50
7 Fleetwood Mac	46
8 Alabama	44
9 =AC/DC	42
=U2	42

Source: *The Popular Music Database*

GROUPS WITH THE MOST GOLD ALBUMS IN THE US

GROUP	GOLD ALBUMS
1 The Beatles	40
2 The Rolling Stones	37
3 Kiss	23
4 Rush	22
5 =Aerosmith	21
=Alabama	21
=Chicago	21
8 Jefferson Airplane/Starship	20
9 The Beach Boys	19
10 Santana	18

Source: *RIAA*

The RIAA's gold awards have been presented since 1958 to artists who have sold 500,000 of a single, album, or multidisc set. The first single to be so honored was Perry Como's *Catch a Falling Star*, and the first album was the soundtrack to *Oklahoma*. To date, more than 8,000 titles have been certified gold. Three further groups – AC/DC, Queen, and the Temptations – have each received 17 gold awards.

MALE ARTISTS WITH THE MOST GOLD ALBUMS IN THE US

ARTIST	GOLD ALBUMS
1 Elvis Presley	62
2 Neil Diamond	35
3 Elton John	32
4 Kenny Rogers	28
5 Frank Sinatra	26
6 Bob Dylan	24
7 =George Strait	23
=Willie Nelson	23
9 Hank Williams, Jr.	21
10 =Paul McCartney/Wings	20
=Rod Stewart	20

Source: *RIAA*

MALE ARTISTS WITH THE MOST GOLD ALBUMS IN THE UK

ARTIST	GOLD ALBUMS
1 =Elton John	20
=Cliff Richard	20
3 Rod Stewart	19
4 =Neil Diamond	17
=James Last	17
=Paul McCartney*	17
7 Mike Oldfield	16
8 =David Bowie	15
=Elvis Presley	15
10 Prince	13

* Including gold albums with Wings

Source: *BPI*

Did You Know? In the US, gold discs are those that have sold 500,000, while platinum are for sales of 1 million. The newer diamond award is for sales of 10 million.

ONE OF THE BEST

With eight gold and 17 platinum albums to her name, Tina Turner has secured a place in the top echelons of music.

TOP 10 ★
FEMALE ARTISTS WITH THE MOST PLATINUM ALBUMS IN THE UK

	ARTIST	PLATINUM ALBUMS
1	Madonna	35
2	Celine Dion	21
3	Whitney Houston	19
4	Tina Turner	17
5 =	Enya	12
=	Gloria Estefan	12
7 =	Kylie Minogue	10
=	Mariah Carey	10
=	Alanis Morissette	10
10	Kate Bush	9

Source: *BPI*

TOP 10 ★
FEMALE ARTISTS WITH THE MOST PLATINUM ALBUMS IN THE US

	ARTIST	PLATINUM ALBUMS
1	Barbra Streisand	49
2	Madonna	47
3 =	Whitney Houston	45
=	Mariah Carey	45
5	Celine Dion	34
6	Reba McEntire	24
7	Linda Ronstadt	23
8 =	Janet Jackson	19
=	Shania Twain	19
9 =	Sade	18
=	Gloria Estefan	18

Source: *RIAA*

TOP 10 ★
FEMALE ARTISTS WITH THE MOST GOLD ALBUMS IN THE UK

	ARTIST	GOLD ALBUMS
1	Diana Ross	17
2 =	Barbra Streisand	12
=	Madonna	12
4	Donna Summer	9
5 =	Mariah Carey	8
=	Tina Turner	8
7 =	Kate Bush	7
=	Cher	7
=	Celine Dion	7
10 =	Joan Armatrading	6
=	Janet Jackson	6

Source: *BPI*

TOP 10 ★
FEMALE ARTISTS WITH THE MOST GOLD ALBUMS IN THE US

	ARTIST	GOLD ALBUMS
1	Barbra Streisand	40
2	Reba McEntire	19
3	Linda Ronstadt	17
4	Olivia Newton-John	15
5 =	Aretha Franklin	13
=	Madonna	13
=	Dolly Parton	13
8 =	Gloria Estefan*	12
=	Anne Murray	12
=	Tanya Tucker	12

* *Includes hits with Miami Sound Machine*

Source: *RIAA*

GOLDEN SUMMER

Donna Summer has been making hit records for almost 30 years, during which time she has scored nine gold albums in the UK.

Oscar-winning Movie Music

THE 10 ★
"BEST SONG" OSCAR WINNERS OF THE 1940s

YEAR	TITLE/MOVIE
1940	*When You Wish Upon a Star*, Pinocchio
1941	*The Last Time I Saw Paris*, Lady Be Good
1942	*White Christmas*, Holiday Inn
1943	*You'll Never Know*, Hello, Frisco, Hello
1944	*Swinging on a Star*, Going My Way
1945	*It Might as Well Be Spring*, State Fair
1946	*On the Atchison, Topeka and Santa Fe*, The Harvey Girls
1947	*Zip-A-Dee-Doo-Dah*, Song of the South
1948	*Buttons and Bows*, The Pale Face
1949	*Baby, It's Cold Outside*, Neptune's Daughter

THE 10 ★
"BEST SONG" OSCAR WINNERS OF THE 1950s

YEAR	TITLE/MOVIE
1950	*Mona Lisa*, Captain Carey
1951	*In the Cool, Cool, Cool of the Evening*, Here Comes the Groom
1952	*High Noon (Do Not Forsake Me, Oh My Darling)*, High Noon
1953	*Secret Love*, Calamity Jane
1954	*Three Coins in the Fountain*, Three Coins in the Fountain
1955	*Love Is a Many-Splendored Thing*, Love Is a Many-Splendored Thing
1956	*Whatever Will Be, Will Be (Que Sera, Sera)*, The Man Who Knew Too Much
1957	*All the Way*, The Joker Is Wild
1958	*Gigi*, Gigi
1959	*High Hopes*, A Hole in the Head

Doris Day benefited strongly from these Oscars, scoring million-selling singles with *Secret Love* and *Whatever Will Be, Will Be*.

THE 10 ★
"BEST SONG" OSCAR WINNERS OF THE 1960s

YEAR	TITLE/MOVIE
1960	*Never on Sunday*, Never on Sunday
1961	*Moon River*, Breakfast at Tiffany's
1962	*Days of Wine and Roses*, Days of Wine and Roses
1963	*Call Me Irresponsible*, Papa's Delicate Condition
1964	*Chim Chim Cheree*, Mary Poppins
1965	*The Shadow of Your Smile*, The Sandpiper
1966	*Born Free*, Born Free
1967	*Talk to the Animals*, Dr. Dolittle
1968	*The Windmills of Your Mind*, The Thomas Crown Affair
1969	*Raindrops Keep Fallin' on My Head*, Butch Cassidy and the Sundance Kid

Both *The Windmills of Your Mind* and *Raindrops Keep Fallin' on My Head* hit the US Top 10. Sacha Distel's cover version of the 1969 Oscar winner charted five times in the UK in 1970.

TOP 10 ★
"BEST SONG" OSCAR-WINNING SINGLES IN THE US

	TITLE/ARTIST OR GROUP	YEAR
1	*You Light up My Life*, Debby Boone	1977
2	*Up Where We Belong*, Joe Cocker and Jennifer Warnes	1982
3	*Evergreen*, Barbra Streisand	1976
4	*My Heart Will Go On*, Celine Dion	1997
5	*I Just Called to Say I Love You*, Stevie Wonder	1984
6	*Arthur's Theme (Best That You Can Do)*, Christopher Cross	1981
7	*The Way We Were*, Barbra Streisand	1973
8	*A Whole New World*, Peabo Bryson and Regina Belle	1992
9	*Raindrops Keep Fallin' on My Head*, B. J. Thomas	1969
10	*(I've Had) The Time of My Life*, Bill Medley and Jennifer Warnes	1987

Source: *The Popular Music Database*

ALL IN A DAY'S WORK
Songs by Doris Day (real name Doris Kappelhoff), from films in which she also starred, produced a duo of Oscar winners in the 1950s.

OSCAR-WINNING PRINCE

A new phenomenon is that half the Oscar-winning songs of the past decade are from animated movies, such as the 1998 winner The Prince of Egypt.

THE 10 ⭐

"BEST SONG" OSCAR WINNERS OF THE 1970s

YEAR	TITLE/MOVIE
1970	*For All We Know*, Lovers and Other Strangers
1971	*Theme from "Shaft,"* Shaft
1972	*The Morning After*, The Poseidon Adventure
1973	*The Way We Were*, The Way We Were
1974	*We May Never Love Like This Again*, The Towering Inferno
1975	*I'm Easy*, Nashville
1976	*Evergreen*, A Star is Born
1977	*You Light up My Life*, You Light up My Life
1978	*Last Dance*, Thank God It's Friday
1979	*It Goes Like It Goes*, Norma Rae

THE 10 ⭐

"BEST SONG" OSCAR WINNERS OF THE 1980s

YEAR	TITLE/MOVIE
1980	*Fame*, Fame
1981	*Up Where We Belong*, An Officer and a Gentleman
1982	*Arthur's Theme (Best That You Can Do)*, Arthur
1983	*Flashdance... What a Feeling*, Flashdance
1984	*I Just Called to Say I Love You*, The Woman in Red
1985	*Say You, Say Me*, White Nights
1986	*Take My Breath Away*, Top Gun
1987	*(I've Had) The Time of My Life*, Dirty Dancing
1988	*Let the River Run*, Working Girl
1989	*Under the Sea*, The Little Mermaid

THE 10 ⭐

"BEST SONG" OSCAR WINNERS OF THE 1990s

YEAR	TITLE/MOVIE
1990	*Sooner or Later (I Always Get My Man)*, Dick Tracy
1991	*Beauty and the Beast*, Beauty and the Beast
1992	*Whole New World*, Aladdin
1993	*Streets of Philadelphia*, Philadelphia
1994	*Can You Feel the Love Tonight*, The Lion King
1995	*Colors of the Wind*, Pocahontas
1996	*You Must Love Me*, Evita
1997	*My Heart Will Go On*, Titanic
1998	*When You Believe*, The Prince of Egypt
1999	*You'll Be in My Heart*, Tarzan

 What is the most popular pop music movie?
see p.149 for the answer

A *Purple Rain*
B *La Bamba*
C *The Blues Brothers*

Soundtrack Smashes

TOP 10 ★
MUSICAL MOVIES*

	TITLE	YEAR
1	*Grease*	1978
2	*Saturday Night Fever*	1977
3	*The Sound of Music*	1965
4	*Footloose*	1984
5	*American Graffiti*	1973
6	*Mary Poppins*	1964
7	*Flashdance*	1983
8	*The Rocky Horror Picture Show*	1975
9	*Coal Miner's Daughter*	1980
10	*My Fair Lady*	1964

* *Traditional musicals (in which the cast actually sing) and movies in which a musical soundtrack is a major component of the movie are included*

MUSIC TO THE EARS

Despite being made over 35 years ago, The Sound of Music, starring British actress Julie Andrews, remains among the Top 10 highest-earning musicals of all time.

TOP 10 ★
JAMES BOND MOVIE THEMES IN THE US

	TITLE/ARTIST OR GROUP	YEAR
1	*A View to a Kill*, Duran Duran	1985
2	*Nobody Does It Better* (from *The Spy Who Loved Me*), Carly Simon	1977
3	*Live and Let Die*, Paul McCartney and Wings	1973
4	*For Your Eyes Only*, Sheena Easton	1981
5	*Goldfinger*, Shirley Bassey	1965
6	*Thunderball*, Tom Jones	1966
7	*All Time High* (from *Octopussy*), Rita Coolidge	1983
8	*You Only Live Twice*, Nancy Sinatra	1967
9	*Diamonds Are Forever*, Shirley Bassey	1972
10	*Goldfinger*, John Barry	1965

TOP 10 ORIGINAL SOUNDTRACK ALBUMS OF ALL TIME IN THE US
(Album/sales)

1 *The Bodyguard*, 17,000,000 **2** *Saturday Night Fever*, 15,000,000 **3** *Purple Rain*, 13,000,000 **4** *Dirty Dancing*, 11,000,000 **5** = *The Lion King*, 10,000,000; = *Titanic*, 10,000,000 **7** = *Grease*, 8,000,000; = *Footloose*, 8,000,000 **9** = *Top Gun*, 7,000,000; = *Waiting to Exhale*, 7,000,000

Source: *RIAA*

NOBODY DOES IT BETTER

Written by Marvin Hamlisch and Carole Bayer Sager, Carly Simon's song from The Spy Who Loved Me *was a US and UK hit.*

TOP 10 ★
ARTISTS WITH THE MOST "BEST SONG" OSCAR NOMINATIONS

ARTIST/WINS/YEARS	NOMINATIONS
1 Sammy Cahn, 4, 1942–75	26
2 Johnny Mercer, 4, 1938–71	18
3 =Paul Francis Webster, 3, 1944–76	16
=Alan and Marilyn Bergman, 2, 1968–95	16
5 James Van Heusen, 4, 1944–68	14
6 =Henry Warren, 3, 1935–57	11
=Henry Mancini, 2, 1961–86	11
=Ned Washington, 1, 1940–61	11
9 =Alan Menken, 4, 1986–97	10
=Sammy Fain, 2, 1937–77	10
=Leo Robin, 1, 1934–53	10
=Jule Styne, 1, 1940–68	10

It was not until 1934 that the category of "Best Song" was added to the many accolades bestowed on movies. The awards are often multiple, including the writers of the music and the lyrics.

THE 10 ★
FIRST DISNEY "BEST SONG" OSCAR WINNERS

YEAR	TITLE/MOVIE
1940	*When You Wish Upon a Star*, Pinocchio
1947	*Zip-a-Dee-Doo-Dah*, Song of the South
1964	*Chim Chim Cher-ee*, Mary Poppins
1989	*Under the Sea*, The Little Mermaid
1990	*Sooner or Later (I Always Get My Man)*, Dick Tracy
1991	*Beauty and the Beast*, Beauty and The Beast
1992	*Whole New World*, Aladdin
1994	*Can You Feel the Love Tonight*, The Lion King
1995	*Colors of the Wind*, Pocahontas
1996	*You Must Love Me*, Evita

TOP 10 ★
POP MUSIC MOVIES

	TITLE	YEAR
1	*The Blues Brothers*	1980
2	*Purple Rain*	1984
3	*La Bamba*	1987
4	*The Doors*	1991
5	*What's Love Got to Do With It?*	1993
6	*Xanadu*	1980
7	*The Jazz Singer*	1980
8	*Sgt. Pepper's Lonely Hearts Club Band*	1978
9	*Lady Sings the Blues*	1972
10	*Pink Floyd – The Wall*	1982

RAINING PRINCE

Produced in 1984, Prince's semi-autobiographical movie Purple Rain is one of the most successful pop music movies ever released.

MONEY FOR NOTHING

Much Ado About Nothing, starring Emma Thompson and Kenneth Branagh (who also directed it), achieved both critical and commercial success.

THE 10 ★ LATEST WINNERS OF TONY AWARDS FOR A PLAY

YEAR	PLAY
1999	Side Man
1998	Art
1997	The Last Night of Ballyhoo
1996	Master Class
1995	Love! Valour! Compassion!
1994	Angels in America Part II: Perestroika
1993	Angels in America Part I: Millennium Approaches
1992	Dancing at Lughnasa
1991	Lost in Yonkers
1990	The Grapes of Wrath

The Tony Awards, established by the American Theater Wing, honor outstanding Broadway plays and musicals, actors and actressses, music, costume and other contributions. They are named after the actress and director Antoinette Perry (1988–46), who headed the American Theater Wing during World War II.

THE 10 ★ LATEST WINNERS OF TONY AWARDS FOR A MUSICAL

YEAR	PLAY
1999	Fosse
1998	The Lion King
1997	Titanic
1996	Rent
1995	Sunset Boulevard
1994	Passion
1993	Kiss of the Spider Woman
1992	Crazy for You
1991	The Will Rogers Follies
1990	City of Angels

TOP 10 ★ FILMS OF SHAKESPEARE PLAYS

	FILM	YEAR
1	William Shakespeare's Romeo + Juliet	1996
2	Romeo and Juliet	1968
3	Much Ado About Nothing	1993
4	Hamlet	1990
5	Henry V	1989
6	Hamlet	1996
7	Richard III	1995
8	Othello	1995
9	The Taming of the Shrew	1967
10	Hamlet	1948

TOP 10 ★ MOST PRODUCED PLAYS BY SHAKESPEARE, 1961–99

	PLAY	PRODUCTIONS
1	A Midsummer Night's Dream	30
2	=Macbeth	26
	=Twelfth Night	26
4	Romeo and Juliet	25
5	The Taming of the Shrew	24
6	=As You Like It	23
	=Richard III	23
8	King Lear	22
9	=Hamlet	21
	=Much Ado About Nothing	21

TOP 10 MOST-FILMED PLAYS BY SHAKESPEARE

❶ Hamlet ❷ Romeo and Juliet ❸ Macbeth ❹ A Midsummer Night's Dream ❺ Julius Caesar ❻ Othello ❼ Richard III ❽ Henry V ❾ The Merchant of Venice ❿ Antony and Cleopatra

Counting modern versions, including those in foreign languages, but discounting made-for-TV films, parodies, and stories derived from the plays, it appears that *Hamlet* is the most-filmed of all Shakespeare's works, with some 70 releases to date, while *Romeo and Juliet* has been remade on at least 40 occasions.

 Which 1950s movie won the most "Best Picture" Oscars? *see p.166 for the answer* A *All About Eve* B *Ben-Hur* C *From Here to Eternity*

TOP 10 ★
LONGEST-RUNNING COMEDIES ON BROADWAY

	COMEDY/YEARS	PERFORMANCES
1	*Life With Father*, 1939–47	3,224
2	*Abie's Irish Rose*, 1922–27	2,327
3	*Gemini*, 1977–81	1,819
4	*Harvey*, 1944–49	1,775
5	*Born Yesterday*, 1946–49	1,642
6	*Mary, Mary*, 1961–64	1,572
7	*The Voice of the Turtle*, 1943–48	1,557
8	*Barefoot in the Park*, 1963–67	1,530
9	*Same Time Next Year*, 1975–78	1,454
10	*Brighton Beach Memoirs*, 1983–86	1,299

Source: *The League of American Theaters and Producers*

TOP 10 ★
LATEST PULITZER DRAMA AWARDS

YEAR*	AUTHOR/PLAY
2000	Jhumpa Lahiri, *Dinner With Friends*
1999	Margaret Edson, *Wit*
1998	Paula Vogel, *How I Learned to Drive*
1996	Jonathan Larson, *Rent*
1995	Horton Foote, *The Young Man from Atlanta*
1994	Edward Albee, *Three Tall Women*
1993	Tony Kushner, *Angels in America: Millennium Approaches*
1992	Robert Schenkkan, *The Kentucky Cycle*
1991	Neil Simon, *Lost in Yonkers*
1990	August Wilson, *The Piano Lesson*

* *No award was made in 1997*

The Pulitzer Drama Award is made for "an American play, preferably original and dealing with American life."

TOP 10 ★
LONGEST-RUNNING SHOWS ON BROADWAY

	SHOW/YEARS	PERFORMANCES
1	*Cats*, 1982–	7,200*
2	*A Chorus Line*, 1975–90	6,137
3	*Oh! Calcutta!*, 1976–89	5,962
4	*Les Misérables*, 1987–	5,378#
5	*The Phantom of the Opera*, 1988–	5,008#
6	*Miss Saigon*, 1991–	3,619#
7	*42nd Street*, 1980–89	3,486
8	*Grease*, 1972–80	3,388
9	*Fiddler on the Roof*, 1964–72	3,242
10	*Life With Father*, 1939–47	3,224

* *Total as at January 1, 2000; closed June 25, 2000 after record 7,397 performances*

Total as at January 1, 2000; still running

Source: *The League of American Theaters and Producers*

Cats became the longest-running Broadway show of all time on June 19, 1997, when it notched up its 6,138th performance. *Les Misérables* celebrated its 13th anniversary on March 12, 2000 with its 5,351st performance. By that date, it had been seen by 7.5 million people in New York and 42 million worldwide. *Life With Father*, the earliest show to be listed here, was a roaring success from the moment it opened. Its popularity had not been predicted, and after the lead parts were refused by major actors and actresses, the author, Howard Lindsay, and his wife, Dorothy Stickney, decided to play the roles themselves. They continued to do so, to rave reviews, for the following five years.

TOP 10 ★
LONGEST-RUNNING MUSICALS ON BROADWAY

	MUSICAL/YEARS	PERFORMANCES
1	*Cats*, 1982–2000	7,200*
2	*A Chorus Line*, 1975–90	6,137
3	*Les Misérables*, 1987–	5,278#
4	*The Phantom of the Opera*, 1988–	5,008#
5	*Miss Saigon*, 1901–	3,619#
6	*42nd Street*, 1980–89	3,486
7	*Grease*, 1972–80	3,388
8	*Fiddler on the Roof*, 1964–72	3,242
9	*Hello Dolly!*, 1964–71	2,844
10	*My Fair Lady*, 1956–62	2,717

* *Total as at January 1, 2000; closed June 25, 2000 after record 7,397 performances*

Total as at January 1, 2000; still running

Source: *The League of American Theaters and Producers*

OUT OF THEIR MISERY

Les Misérables has achieved the dual feat of being one of the longest-running musicals both in London and on Broadway.

TOP 10 HIGHEST-GROSSING MOVIES OF ALL TIME

	MOVIE	YEAR	GROSS INCOME ($) US	GROSS INCOME ($) WORLD
1	Titanic	1997	600,800,000	1,835,100,000
2	Star Wars: Episode I – The Phantom Menace	1999	431,100,000	922,600,000
3	Jurassic Park	1993	357,100,000	920,100,000
4	Independence Day	1996	306,200,000	811,200,000
5	Star Wars	1977/97	461,000,000	798,000,000
6	The Lion King	1994	312,900,000	767,900,000
7	E.T.: The Extra-Terrestrial	1982	399,800,000	704,800,000
8	Forrest Gump	1994	329,700,000	679,700,000
9	The Lost World: Jurassic Park	1997	229,100,000	614,400,000
10	Men in Black	1997	250,100,000	586,100,000

TOP 10 ★ MOVIE OPENINGS OF ALL TIME IN THE US

	MOVIE/RELEASE DATE	OPENING WEEKEND GROSS ($)
1	The Lost World: Jurassic Park, May 23, 1997	72,132,785
2	Star Wars: Episode I – The Phantom Menace, May 21, 1999	64,820,970
3	Toy Story 2, Nov 24, 1999	57,388,839
4	Austin Powers: The Spy Who Shagged Me, June 11, 1999	54,917,604
5	Batman Forever, June 16, 1995	52,784,433
6	Men in Black, July 2, 1997	51,068,455
7	Independence Day, July 3, 1996	50,228,264
8	Jurassic Park, June 11, 1993	47,059,560
9	Batman Returns, June 19, 1992	45,687,711
10	Mission: Impossible, May 22, 1996	45,436,830

MONSTER MOVIE
Jurassic Park *set new standards for animatronic action and reigned as the world's highest-earning movie for five years, before being toppled by* Titanic.

Did You Know? On May 19, 1999, *Star Wars: Episode I – The Phantom Menace* became the highest-earning movie in a single day, taking a total of $28,540,000 at 2,970 box offices across the US.

TOP 10 ★
HIGHEST-GROSSING MOVIES OF ALL TIME IN THE UK

	MOVIE	YEAR	UK GROSS (£)
1	Titanic	1998	68,532,000
2	The Full Monty	1997	51,992,000
4	Star Wars: Episode I – The Phantom Menace	1999	50,735,000
4	Jurassic Park	1993	47,140,000
5	Toy Story 2	2000	40,169,000
6	Independence Day	1996	36,800,000
7	Men In Black	1997	35,400,000
8	Notting Hill	1999	30,404,000
9	The World is Not Enough	1999	28,367,000
10	Four Weddings and a Funeral	1994	27,800,000

Inevitably, because of inflation, the top-grossing movies of all time are releases from the 1990s.

TOP 10 ★
HIGHEST-GROSSING MOVIES OF ALL TIME IN THE US

	MOVIE	YEAR	US GROSS ($)
1	Titanic	1997	600,800,000
2	Star Wars	1977/97	461,000,000
3	Star Wars: Episode I – The Phantom Menace	1999	431,100,000
4	E.T.: The Extra-Terrestrial	1982	399,800,000
5	Jurassic Park	1993	357,100,000
6	Forrest Gump	1994	329,700,000
7	The Lion King	1994	312,900,000
8	Return of the Jedi	1983/97	309,100,000
9	Independence Day	1996	306,200,000
10	The Empire Strikes Back	1980/97	290,200,000

Star Wars: Episode I – The Phantom Menace was the fastest-earning movie ever, taking over $100 million in its first five days. Box-office revenue reached $102.7 million

BEST OF BRITISH

The highest-earning British-made movie, The Full Monty, was successful both in the UK and worldwide, grossing in excess of $250 million.

BACK FROM THE FUTURE

In the second of the two Terminator movies, Arnold Schwarzenegger is a caring cyborg who protects a boy and his mother from a near-indestructible rival.

TOP 10 ★
MOVIE SEQUELS THAT EARNED THE GREATEST AMOUNT MORE THAN THE ORIGINAL*

	ORIGINAL	OUTEARNED BY
1	The Terminator	Terminator 2: Judgment Day
2	First Blood	Rambo: First Blood Part II / Rambo III
3	Lethal Weapon	Lethal Weapon 2 / Lethal Weapon 3 / Lethal Weapon 4
4	Austin Powers: International Man of Mystery	Austin Powers: The Spy Who Shagged Me
5	Die Hard	Die Hard 2 / Die Hard With a Vengeance
6	Rocky	Rocky III / Rocky IV
7	Raiders of the Lost Ark	Indiana Jones and the Last Crusade
8	Ace Ventura: Pet Detective	Ace Ventura: When Nature Calls
9	48 HRS	Another 48 HRS
10	Patriot Games	Clear and Present Danger

* Ranked by greatest differential between original and highest-earning sequel

Movies of the Decades

TOP 10 ★
MOVIES OF THE 1930s

1	Gone With the Wind*	1939
2	Snow White and the Seven Dwarfs	1937
3	The Wizard of Oz	1939
4	The Woman in Red	1935
5	King Kong	1933
6	San Francisco	1936
7 =	Hell's Angels	1930
=	Lost Horizon	1937
=	Mr. Smith Goes to Washington	1939
10	Maytime	1937

* Winner of "Best Picture" Academy Award

Gone With the Wind and Snow White and the Seven Dwarfs have generated more income than any other prewar movie. However, if the income of Gone With the Wind is adjusted to allow for inflation in the period since its release, it could be regarded as the most successful movie ever, earning some $885 million in the US alone.

TOP 10 ★
MOVIES OF THE 1940s

1	Bambi	1942
2	Pinocchio	1940
3	Fantasia	1940
4	Cinderella	1949
5	Song of the South	1946
6	The Best Years of Our Lives*	1946
7	The Bells of St. Mary's	1945
8	Duel in the Sun	1946
9	Mom and Dad	1948
10	Samson and Delilah	1949

* Winner of "Best Picture" Academy Award

With the top four movies of the decade classic Disney cartoons, the 1940s may be regarded as the "golden age" of the animated movie.

TALL STORY

In one of movie history's most famous scenes, King Kong fights off his attackers atop the newly opened Empire State Building. The movie was one of the 1930s' highest earners.

TOP 10 ★
MOVIES OF THE 1950s

1	Lady and the Tramp	1955
2	Peter Pan	1953
3	Ben-Hur*	1959
4	The Ten Commandments	1956
5	Sleeping Beauty	1959
6	Around the World in 80 Days*	1956
7 =	The Robe	1953
=	The Greatest Show on Earth*	1952
9	The Bridge on the River Kwai*	1957
10	Peyton Place	1957

* Winner of "Best Picture" Academy Award

While the popularity of animated movies continued, the 1950s was outstanding as the decade of the "big" picture (in cast and scale).

TOP 10 MOVIES OF THE 1960s

1 *One Hundred and One Dalmatians*, 1961 **2** *The Jungle Book*, 1967 **3** *The Sound of Music**, 1965 **4** *Thunderball*, 1965 **5** *Goldfinger*, 1964 **6** *Doctor Zhivago*, 1965 **7** *You Only Live Twice*, 1967 **8** *The Graduate*, 1968 **9** *Mary Poppins*, 1964 **10** *Butch Cassidy and the Sundance Kid*, 1969

* Winner of "Best Picture" Academy Award

TOP 10 ★
MOVIES OF THE 1990s

1	Titanic*	1997
2	Star Wars: Episode I – The Phantom Menace	1999
3	Jurassic Park	1993
4	Independence Day	1996
5	The Lion King	1994
6	Forrest Gump*	1994
7	The Lost World: Jurassic Park	1997
8	Men in Black	1997
9	The Sixth Sense	1999
10	Armageddon	1998

* Winner of "Best Picture" Academy Award

Each of the Top 10 movies of the 1990s has earned more than $550 million around the world.

BRINGING THE HOUSE DOWN

The White House sustains a direct hit from the invading spacecraft in a scene from Independence Day, *one of the top movies of the 1990s.*

TOP 10 ★
MOVIES OF THE 1970s

1	Star Wars	1977/97
2	Jaws	1975
3	Close Encounters of the Third Kind	1977/80
4	The Exorcist	1973/98
5	Moonraker	1979
6	The Spy Who Loved Me	1977
7	The Sting*	1973
8	Grease	1978
9	The Godfather*	1972
10	Saturday Night Fever	1977

* Winner of "Best Picture" Academy Award

In the 1970s, the arrival of Steven Spielberg and George Lucas set the scene for the high-adventure blockbusters whose domination has continued ever since. Lucas wrote and directed *Star Wars*, formerly the highest-earning movie of all time.

JAWS OF DEATH

Although it once held the record as the world's highest-earning movie, Jaws *was eventually beaten by* Star Wars, *directed by George Lucas.*

TOP 10 MOVIES OF THE 1980s

① *E.T.: The Extra-Terrestrial*, 1982 **②** *Indiana Jones and the Last Crusade*, 1989 **③** *Batman*, 1989 **④** *Rain Man*, 1988 **⑤** *Return of the Jedi*, 1983 **⑥** *Raiders of the Lost Ark*, 1981 **⑦** *The Empire Strikes Back*, 1980 **⑧** *Who Framed Roger Rabbit*, 1988 **⑨** *Back to the Future*, 1985 **⑩** *Top Gun*, 1986

Which actress provided the voice of Tzipporah in *The Prince of Egypt*?
see p.176 for the answer

A Julia Roberts
B Demi Moore
C Michelle Pfeiffer

ACTING HIS AGE

Septuagenarian actor John Gielgud secured a "Best Supporting Actor" Oscar for his role as Hobson, the acerbic valet to the lead character star of Arthur.

"OSCAR"

Founded on May 4, 1927, the Hollywood-based Academy of Motion Picture Arts and Sciences proposed improving the image of the movie industry by issuing "awards for merit or distinction" in various categories. The award itself, a statuette designed by Cedric Gibbons, was modeled by a young artist, George Stanley. The gold-plated naked male figure holds a sword and stands on a reel of film. It was simply called "the statuette" until 1931, when Academy librarian Margaret Herrick commented, "It looks like my Uncle Oscar!" – and the name stuck.  **WHY DO WE SAY?**

THE 10 "BEST ACTRESS" OSCAR WINNERS OF THE 1950s

(Year/actress/movie)

1. **1950** Judy Holiday, *Born Yesterday*
2. **1951** Vivien Leigh, *A Streetcar Named Desire*
3. **1952** Shirley Booth, *Come Back, Little Sheba*
4. **1953** Audrey Hepburn, *Roman Holiday*
5. **1954** Grace Kelly, *The Country Girl*
6. **1955** Anna Magnani, *The Rose Tattoo*
7. **1956** Ingrid Bergman, *Anastasia*
8. **1957** Joanne Woodward, *The Three Faces of Eve*
9. **1958** Susan Hayward, *I Want to Live*
10. **1959** Simone Signoret, *Room at the Top*

THE 10 ★ "BEST ACTOR" OSCAR WINNERS OF THE 1950s

YEAR	ACTOR/MOVIE
1950	Jose Ferrer, *Cyrano de Bergerac*
1951	Humphrey Bogart, *The African Queen*
1952	Gary Cooper, *High Noon*
1953	William Holden, *Stalag 17*
1954	Marlon Brando, *On the Waterfront**
1955	Ernest Borgnine, *Marty**
1956	Yul Brynner, *The King and I*
1957	Alec Guinness, *The Bridge on the River Kwai**
1958	David Niven, *Separate Tables*
1959	Charlton Heston, *Ben-Hur**

* Winner of "Best Picture" Oscar

THE 10 ★ "BEST ACTRESS" OSCAR WINNERS OF THE 1960s

YEAR	ACTRESS/MOVIE
1960	Elizabeth Taylor, *Butterfield 8*
1961	Sophia Loren, *Two Women*
1962	Anne Bancroft, *The Miracle Worker*
1963	Patricia Neal, *Hud*
1964	Julie Andrews, *Mary Poppins*
1965	Julie Christie, *Darling*
1966	Elizabeth Taylor, *Who's Afraid of Virginia Woolf?*
1967	Katharine Hepburn, *Guess Who's Coming to Dinner*
1968 =	Katharine Hepburn*, *The Lion in Winter*
=	Barbra Streisand*, *Funny Girl*
1969	Maggie Smith, *The Prime of Miss Jean Brodie*

* The only tie for "Best Actress"

TOP 10 ★
OLDEST OSCAR-WINNING ACTORS AND ACTRESSES

	ACTOR OR ACTRESS	AWARD/MOVIE	YEAR	AGE*
1	Jessica Tandy	"Best Actress" (*Driving Miss Daisy*)	1989	80
2	George Burns	"Best Supporting Actor" (*The Sunshine Boys*)	1975	80
3	Melvyn Douglas	"Best Supporting Actor" (*Being There*)	1979	79
4	John Gielgud	"Best Supporting Actor" (*Arthur*)	1981	77
5	Don Ameche	"Best Supporting Actor" (*Cocoon*)	1985	77
6	Peggy Ashcroft	"Best Supporting Actress" (*A Passage to India*)	1984	77
7	Henry Fonda	"Best Actor" (*On Golden Pond*)	1981	76
8	Katharine Hepburn	"Best Actress" (*On Golden Pond*)	1981	74
9	Edmund Gwenn	"Best Supporting Actor" (*Miracle on 34th Street*)	1947	72
10	Ruth Gordon	"Best Supporting Actress" (*Rosemary's Baby*)	1968	72

* At the time of the Award ceremony; those of apparently identical age have been ranked according to their precise age in days at the time of the ceremony

THE 10 ★
LATEST RECIPIENTS OF THE MTV "BEST RAP VIDEO" AWARD

YEAR	ARTIST/TITLE
1999	Jay-Z featuring Ja Rule/Amil-lion, *Can I Get a…*
1998	Will Smith, *Gettin' Jiggy Wit it*
1997	The Notorious B.I.G., *Hypnotize*
1996	Coolio featuring LV, *Gangsta's Paradise*
1995	Dr. Dre, *Keep Their Heads Ringin'*
1994	Snoop Doggy Dogg, *Doggy Dogg World*
1993	Arrested Development, *People Everyday*
1992	Arrested Development, *Tennessee*
1991	L. L. Cool J, *Mama Said Knock You Out*
1990	MC Hammer, *U Can't Touch This*

Launched in 1981, MTV introduced its video awards three years later. The "Best Rap Video" category was added in 1989, when the winner was DJ Jazzy Jeff and the Fresh Prince for *Parents Just Don't Understand*.

THE 10 FIRST ARTISTS TO APPEAR IN PEPSI-COLA COMMERCIALS

1 Michael Jackson 2 Lionel Richie 3 Glenn Frey
4 Robert Palmer 5 Linda Ronstadt 6 Tina Turner
7 David Bowie 8 Gloria Estefan 9 MC Hammer
10 Ray Charles

THE 10 ★
FIRST ARTISTS TO FEATURE IN A COCA-COLA TELEVISION COMMERCIAL

	ACT/JINGLE	YEAR
1	**McGuire Sisters**, *Pause for a Coke*	1958
2 =	**Brothers Four***, *Refreshing New Feeling*	1960
=	**Anita Bryant**, *Refreshing New Feeling*	1960
=	**Connie Francis**, *Refreshing New Feeling*	1960
5 =	**Fortunes**, *Things Go Better With Coke*	1963
=	**Limeliters***, *Things Go Better With Coke*	1963
7	**Ray Charles**, *Things Go Better With Coke*	1969
8 =	**Bobby Goldsboro**, *It's the Real Thing*	1971
=	**New Seekers***, *It's the Real Thing*	1971
10	**Dottie West***, *It's the Real Thing (Country Sunshine)*	1972

* Artist(s) provided only the audio soundtrack for the commercial

ALL IN THE FAMILY
David Cassidy and real-life stepmother Shirley Jones starred in the popular TV series The Partridge Family, *screened from 1970 to 1974.*

TOP 10 ★
HIGHEST-RATED NETWORKED MUSIC TELEVISION SERIES IN THE US, 1950–99

	PROGRAMME	YEAR	PERCENT OF TV AUDIENCE*
1	*Stop the Music*	1951	34.0
2	*Your Hit Parade*	1958	33.6
3	*The Perry Como Show*	1956	32.6
4	*Name That Tune*	1958	26.7
5	*The Dean Martin Show*	1966	24.8
6	*The Sonny & Cher Hour*	1973	23.3
7	*The Partridge Family*	1972	22.6
8	*The Glen Campbell Goodtime Hour*	1968	22.5
9	*The Johnny Cash Show*	1969	21.8
10	*Cher*	1975	21.3

* *Percentage of American households with TV sets watching the broadcast: the total number of households rose from 3.8 million in 1950 to 99.4 million in 1999.*

© 2000, Nielsen Media Research

What was unique about *The Milky Way* cartoon?
see p.186 for the answer

A It was the first non-Disney animation to win an Oscar
B It was the first animated movie made in color
C It was the longest movie ever made

POWER TO THE PEOPLE

In the 20th century, the creation of national grids for the transmission of electricity brought power to even the remotest communities.

TOP 10 ★
ELECTRICITY-CONSUMING COUNTRIES

COUNTRY	CONSUMPTION KW/HR
1 US	3,278,500,000,000
2 China	955,980,000,000
3 Japan	904,600,000,000
4 Russia	712,400,000,000
5 Germany	477,270,000,000
6 Canada	475,120,000,000
7 India	397,280,000,000
8 France	375,550,000,000
9 Brazil	322,650,000,000
10 UK	309,590,000,000

Source: *Energy Information Administration*

TOP 10 ★
ITEMS OF DOMESTIC GARBAGE IN THE US

ITEM	TONS PER ANNUM
1 Yard trimmings	29,750,000
2 Corrugated boxes	28,800,000
3 Food waste	14,000,000
4 Newspapers	13,100,000
5 Miscellaneous durables	12,000,000
6 Wood packaging	10,600,000
7 Furniture and furnishings	7,200,000
8 Other commercial printing	7,100,000
9 Office-type papers	6,800,000
10 Paper folding cartons	5,300,000

Source: *Environmental Protection Agency*

THE 10 ★
COUNTRIES EMITTING THE MOST SULFUR DIOXIDE

COUNTRY	ANNUAL SO₂ EMISSIONS PER HEAD		
	LB	OZ	KG
1 Czech Republic	329	6	149.4
2 Former Yugoslavia	304	11	138.2
3 Bulgaria	257	8	116.8
4 Canada	229	4	104.0
5 Hungary	179	7	81.4
6 =Romania	174	10	79.2
=US	174	10	79.2
8 Poland	156	12	71.1
9 Slovakia	154	5	70.0
10 Belarus	126	12	57.5

Source: *World Resources Institute*

Sulfur dioxide, the principal cause of acid rain, is produced by fuel combustion in factories and especially by power stations.

THE 10 ★
COUNTRIES EMITTING THE MOST CARBON DIOXIDE

COUNTRY	ANNUAL CO₂ EMISSIONS PER HEAD (TONS)
1 Qatar	57.50
2 United Arab Emirates	39.89
3 Kuwait	27.81
4 Luxembourg	22.17
5 US	21.68
6 Singapore	21.43
7 Bahrain	20.42
8 Trinidad and Tobago	19.17
9 Australia	18.68
10 Brunei	18.60

Source: *Carbon Dioxide Information Analysis Center*

CO₂ emissions derive from three principal sources – fossil fuel burning, cement manufacturing, and gas flaring.

TOP 10 ★
COAL-CONSUMING COUNTRIES

COUNTRY	1998 CONSUMPTION IN TONS OF OIL EQUIVALENT
1 China	678,170,800
2 US	588,137,400
3 India	169,267,200
4 Russia	113,285,600
5 Japan	97,416,800
6 South Africa	96,865,800
7 Germany	93,339,400
8 Poland	67,111,800
9 Australia	50,771,600
10 UK	44,851,400

Source: *BP Statistical Review of World Energy 1999*

POWER PLANT

Opened in 1985–86, Pacific Gas and Electric's Diablo Canyon Nuclear Power Station, California, is one of the US's 104 reactors.

TOP 10 COUNTRIES WITH THE MOST NUCLEAR REACTORS

(Country/reactors)

① US, 104 **②** France, 58 **③** Japan, 53 **④** UK, 35 **⑤** Russia, 29 **⑥** Germany, 20 **⑦** Ukraine, 16 **⑧** South Korea, 15 **⑨** Canada, 14 **⑩** Sweden, 12

Source: *International Atomic Energy Agency*
There are some 434 nuclear power stations in operation in a total of 32 countries around the world, with a further 36 under construction. Lithuania has the greatest reliance on nuclear power, obtaining 77.2 percent of its electricity from nuclear sources.

TOP 10 ★
ENERGY-CONSUMING COUNTRIES

COUNTRY	1998 ENERGY CONSUMPTION*					
	OIL	GAS	COAL	NUCLEAR	HEP#	TOTAL
1 US	939.6	607.4	588.1	201.6	29.4	2,365.8
2 China	209.7	19.1	678.1	4.2	18.8	930.0
3 Russia	134.7	361.7	113.2	29.6	14.9	654.3
4 Japan	281.0	68.8	97.4	92.5	10.4	550.1
5 Germany	150.5	78.9	93.3	45.9	1.9	370.6
6 India	94.8	23.0	169.2	3.0	7.9	298.2
7 France	104.1	37.1	16.6	110.2	6.2	274.5
8 UK	88.7	88.0	44.8	28.4	0.7	250.7
9 Canada	91.7	69.7	28.5	20.3	31.5	241.6
10 South Korea	102.8	15.5	39.7	25.4	0.5	184.1
World	3,734.0	2,222.0	2,445.7	690.5	249.0	9,342.0

* *Millions of tons of oil equivalent*   # *Hydroelectric power*
Source: BP Statistical Review of World Energy 1999

THE 10 MOST DEFORESTING COUNTRIES

(Country/average annual forest loss 1990–95 in sq miles/sq km)

① Brazil, 9,862/25,544 **②** Indonesia, 4,186/10,844 **③** Dem. Rep. of Congo, 2,857/7,400 **④** Bolivia, 2,244/5,814 **⑤** Mexico, 1,961/5,080 **⑥** Venezuela, 1,943/5,034 **⑦** Malaysia, 1,545/ 4,002 **⑧** Myanmar, 1,495/3,874 **⑨** Sudan, 1,361/3,526 **⑩** Thailand, 1,271/3,294

Source: *Food and Agriculture Organization of the United Nations*

TOP 10 ★
NATURAL GAS-CONSUMING COUNTRIES

COUNTRY	1998 CONSUMPTION	
	BILLION CU FT	BILLION CU M
1 US	24,005.4	612.4
2 Russia	14,297.9	364.7
3 UK	3,479.7	88.8
4 Germany	3,118.3	79.6
5 Canada	2,756.8	70.3
6 Japan	2,722.0	69.4
7 Ukraine	2,695.8	68.8
8 Italy	2,242.9	57.2
9 Iran	2,025.1	51.7
10 Saudi Arabia	1,803.0	46.0
World total	87,816.6	2,240.2

Source: BP Statistical Review of World Energy 1999

TOP 10 ★
OIL-CONSUMING COUNTRIES

COUNTRY	1998 CONSUMPTION TONS
1 US	939,611,000
2 Japan	281,010,000
3 China	209,710,600
4 Germany	150,533,200
5 Russia	134,774,600
6 Italy	104,359,400
7 France	104,168,500
8 South Korea	102,816,600
9 =Brazil	88,711,000
=Canada	91,712,300

Source: BP Statistical Review of World Energy 1999

In which year was Coca-Cola introduced?
see p.220 for the answer

A 1886
B 1902
C 1927

Sweet Treats

A MARS A DAY ...
Mars's first product, the Milky Way bar, was renamed Mars bar when launched in the UK in 1932. The name did not appear in the US until 1940, when a new bar was introduced.

THE 10 ★
FIRST MARS PRODUCTS

	PRODUCT	YEAR INTRODUCED
1=	Milky Way bar	1923
=	Snickers bar (non-chocolate)	1923
3	Snickers bar (chocolate)	1930
4	3 Musketeers bar	1932
5	Maltesers	1937
6	Kitekat (catfood; now Whiskas)	1939
7	Mars almond bar	1940
8	M&M's plain chocolate candies	1941
9	Uncle Ben's converted brand rice	1942
10=	M&M's peanut chocolate candies	1954
=	Pal (dogfood)	1954

American candy manufacturer Franklin C. Mars set up his first business in Tacoma, Washington, in 1911, and formed the Mar-O-Bar company in Minneapolis in 1922, with the first of its products, the Milky Way bar. The founder's son, Forrest E. Mars, set up in the UK in 1932, merging the firm with its American counterpart in 1964. Strangely, outside the US the Milky Way bar is known as a Mars bar, while in the UK a Milky Way is a rather different product, introduced in 1935. In the UK, the Snickers bar began life as a Marathon, but was renamed to bring it in line with the US.

TOP 10 ★
SUGAR-CONSUMING COUNTRIES

	COUNTRY	LB	OZ	KG
		ANNUAL CONSUMPTION PER CAPITA		
1	Israel	220	14	100.2
2	Belize	156	1	70.8
3	Trinidad and Tobago	134	11	61.1
4	Cuba	129	7	58.7
5	Barbados	127	14	58.0
6	Brazil	124	9	56.5
7	Swaziland	119	8	54.2
8=	Costa Rica	118	3	53.6
=	Malta	118	3	53.6
10	Iceland	117	8	53.3
	World average	44	8	20.2
	US	71	10	32.5

Source: *Food and Agriculture Organization of the United Nations*

TOP 10 ★
CHOCOLATE BRANDS IN THE US

	BRAND/MANUFACTURER	MARKET SHARE % (1998)
1	**Snickers**, Mars	10.6
2	**Reese's Peanut Butter Cup**, Hershey Chocolate	8.7
3	**M&Ms**, Mars	5.1
4	**Kit Kat**, Hershey Chocolate	4.5
5	**Russell Stover**, Russell Stover Candies	4.0
6	**Milky Way**, Mars	3.7
7=	**Twix**, Mars	2.9
=	**York**, Hershey Chocolate	2.9
9	**Hershey's Milk Chocolate**, Hershey Chocolate	2.8
10=	**Three Musketeers**, Mars	2.6
=	**Hershey's Bar with Almonds**, Hershey Chocolate	2.6

Source: *Euromonitor*

TOP 10 ★
CANDY MANUFACTURERS IN THE US*

	MANUFACTURER	MARKET SHARE %*
1	Hershey Chocolate	26.2
2	Mars	19.9
3	Nestlé	5.7
4	William Wrigley Jr. Co.	4.8
5	Warner-Lambert	3.8
6	RJR Nabisco	3.7
7	Russell Stover Candies	3.5
8	Favorite Brands	2.8
9	Brach & Brock Confections	1.9
10	Tootsie Roll Industries	1.6

* Based on $ sales volume

Source: *Euromonitor*

Background image: **CHOCOLATE SELECTION**

TOP 10 ★
CHOCOLATE-CONSUMING NATIONS

	COUNTRY	TOTAL COCOA CONSUMPTION TONS
1	US	721,000
2	Germany	318,700
3	UK	211,600
4	France	195,400
5	Japan	137,000
6	Brazil	132,700
7	Russia	131,500
8	Italy	100,500
9	Canada	86,000
10	Spain	76,800
	World	2,999,600

Europe has the highest intake of the continents, with a cocoa consumption of 1,490,000 tons; the Americas are next with 1,158,000; then Asia and Oceania with 326,000; and lastly Africa, where only 65,000 tons are consumed across the entire continent.

TOP 10 ★
ICE CREAM-CONSUMING COUNTRIES

	COUNTRY	PRODUCTION PER CAPITA PINTS	LITERS
1	New Zealand	55.98	26.48
2	US	46.59	22.04
3	Canada	39.70	18.78
4	Australia	37.83	17.90
5	Belgium	31.09	14.71
6	Sweden	29.66	14.03
7	Finland	29.42	13.92
8	Norway	28.20	13.34
9	Denmark	21.64	10.24
10	Israel	15.93	7.23

Source: *International Dairy Foods Association*

Global statistics for ice cream consumption are hard to come by, but this list presents recent and reliable estimates for per capita production of ice cream and related products.

TOP 10 ★
SUGAR PRODUCERS, 1999

	COUNTRY	TONNES*
1	Brazil	20,995,000
2	India	16,826,000
3	China	8,958,000
4	US	7,556,000
5	Australia	5,778,000
6	Mexico	4,985,000
7	France	4,891,000
8	Thailand	4,314,000
9	Germany	4,054,000
10	Pakistan	3,817,000
	World	133,089,042

* *Raw centrifugal sugar*

Source: *Food and Agriculture Organization of the United Nations*

TOP 10 CONSUMERS OF KELLOGG'S CORNFLAKES*

1 Ireland 2 UK 3 Australia
4 Denmark 5 Sweden 6 Norway
7 Canada 8 US 9 Mexico
10 Venezuela

* *Based on per capita consumption*

In 1894, the brothers Will Keith Kellogg and Dr. John Harvey Kellogg discovered, by accident, that boiled and rolled wheat dough turned into flakes if left overnight; once baked, they became a tasty cereal. In 1898, they replaced wheat with corn, thereby creating the Cornflakes we know today. Will Keith Kellogg went into business manufacturing Cornflakes, with his distinctive signature on the packet. Today, Cornflakes remain Kellogg's bestselling product.

CEREAL SUCCESS

One of the world's most popular breakfast foods, Kellogg's Cornflakes have a history spanning more than a century.

Alcoholic & Soft Drinks

TOP 10 ★
SOFT DRINK BRANDS IN THE US

BRAND	ANNUAL SALES (GALLONS)*
1 Coca-Cola Classic	3,122,100,000
2 Pepsi	2,199,200,000
3 Diet Coke	1,303,400,000
4 Mountain Dew	1,017,600,000
5 Sprite	992,800,000
6 Dr. Pepper	899,100,000
7 Diet Pepsi	759,600,000
8 7-Up	316,400,000
9 Caffeine-Free Diet Coke	272,800,000
10 Minute Maid Regular and Diet	189,400,000

Wholesale sales

Source: *Beverage Marketing Corporation*

TOP 10 ★
SOFT DRINK-CONSUMING COUNTRIES*

COUNTRY	ANNUAL CONSUMPTION PER CAPITA	
	PINTS	LITERS
1 US	447.6	212
2 =Iceland	290.4	138
=Mexico	290.4	138
4 Malta	267.6	127
5 Norway	254.4	121
6 Canada	246.0	117
7 Australia	242.4	115
8 Israel	232.8	110
9 Chile	223.2	106
10 Ireland	222.0	103

Carbonated only

Source: *Zenith International*

As one might expect, affluent Western countries feature prominently in this list and, despite the spread of the so-called "Coca-Cola culture," former Eastern Bloc and Third World countries rank very low — some African nations recording extremely low consumption figures of less than 2 pints (1 liter) per annum.

THE 10 FIRST COCA-COLA PRODUCTS
(Product/date introduced)

1 **Coca-Cola**, May 1886   **2** **Fanta**, June 1960   **3** **Sprite**, Feb 1961   **4** **TAB**, May 1963   **5** **Fresca**, Feb 1966   **6** **Mr. PiBB***, June 1972   **7** **Hi-C Soft Drinks**, Aug 1977   **8** **Mello Yello**, Mar 1979   **9** **Ramblin' Root Beer**, June 1979   **10** **Diet Coke**, July 1982

* Mr. PiBB without Sugar launched Sep 1974; changed name to Sugar-free Mr. PiBB, 1975

TOP 10 ★
ALCOHOL-CONSUMING COUNTRIES

COUNTRY	ANNUAL CONSUMPTION PER CAPITA (100 PERCENT ALCOHOL)	
	PINTS	LITERS
1 Luxembourg	28.1	13.3
2 Portugal	23.6	11.2
3 =France	22.8	10.8
= Ireland	22.8	10.8
5 Germany	22.3	10.6
6 Czech Republic	21.5	10.2
7 Spain	21.2	10.1
8 =Denmark	20.0	9.5
=Romania	20.0	9.5
10 Hungary	19.8	9.4
US	13.7	6.5

Source: *Productschap voor Gedistilleerde Dranken*

TOP 10 BRANDS OF IMPORTED BEER IN THE US
(Brand/country/1998 imports in gallons)

1 **Corona Extra**, Mexico, 53,800,000   **2** **Heineken**, Germany, 42,300,000   **3** **LaBatt's**, Canada, 12,300,000   **4** **Becks**, Germany, 10,300,000   **5** **Molson Ice**, Canada, 9,900,000   **6** **Guinness/Stout**, Ireland, 8,400,000   **7** **Tecate**, Mexico, 8,300,000   **8** **= Molsen**, Canada, 8,200,000; **= Foster's**, Australia, 8,200,000   **10** **Bass**, England, 6,300,000

Source: *Beverage Marketing Corporation*

GRAPE HARVEST

Although Italy's wine production has led the world, it has recently been overtaken by that of France, which produced almost 6 million tons in 1999.

TOP 10 ★
WINE-DRINKING COUNTRIES

COUNTRY	ANNUAL CONSUMPTION PER CAPITA	
	PINTS	LITERS
1 Luxembourg	147.4	70.0
2 France	122.6	58.1
3 Portugal	112.3	53.2
4 Italy	109.8	52.0
5 Switzerland	91.2	43.2
6 Argentina	81.8	38.8
7 Greece	75.7	35.9
8 Spain	75.1	35.6
9 Austria	63.5	30.1
10 Denmark	61.2	29.0
US	15.6	7.4

Source: *Productschap voor Gedistilleerde Dranken*

The US still does not make it into the Top 10 or even Top 30 wine-drinking countries in the world.

TOP 10 ⭐
BEER-DRINKING COUNTRIES

	COUNTRY	ANNUAL CONSUMPTION PER CAPITA	
		PINTS	LITERS
1	Czech Republic	341.6	161.8
2	Ireland	317.7	150.5
3	Germany	268.9	127.4
4	Luxembourg	234.1	110.9
5	Austria	229.3	108.6
6	Denmark	221.6	105.0
7	UK	209.9	99.4
8	Belgium	206.9	98.0
9	Australia	199.4	94.5
10	Slovak Republic	193.8	91.8
	US	173.0	82.0

Source: *Productschap voor Gedistilleerde Dranken*

Despite its position as the world's leading producer of beer, the US misses being placed in the Top 10 – it is ranked in 13th position.

HERE FOR THE BEER

During the 1990s, beer consumption in Ireland rose by 20 percent, elevating the country from eighth to second place among the world's beer consumers.

TOP 10 ⭐
CHAMPAGNE-IMPORTING COUNTRIES

	COUNTRY	BOTTLES IMPORTED (1999)
1	UK	32,261,232
2	US	23,700,839
3	Germany	17,496,865
4	Belgium	10,753,197
5	Italy	9,431,994
6	Switzerland	8,658,165
7	Japan	3,946,155
8	Canada	2,462,938
9	Spain	1,731,055
10	Australia	1,686,231

In 1998 France consumed 179,004,405 bottles of champagne and exported 113,453,686. In that year Canada increased its imports by a record 45 percent, entering the Top 10 for the first time.

TOP 10 ⭐
MILK-DRINKING COUNTRIES*

	COUNTRY	ANNUAL CONSUMPTION PER CAPITA	
		PINTS	LITERS
1	Iceland	314.8	149.1
2	=Finland	294.1	139.3
	=Ireland	294.1	139.3
4	Norway	244.5	115.8
5	UK	241.7	114.4
6	Sweden	138.6	113.0
7	New Zealand	209.9	99.4
8	US	202.7	96.0
9	Spain	193.3	91.5
10	Switzerland	192.6	91.2

* Those reporting to the International Dairy Federation
Source: *National Dairy Council*

TOP 10 ⭐
COFFEE-DRINKING COUNTRIES

	COUNTRY	ANNUAL CONSUMPTION PER CAPITA			
		LB	OZ	KG	CUPS*
1	Finland	25	13	11.71	1,756
2	Denmark	21	14	9.57	1,435
3	Norway	20	15	9.52	1,428
4	Sweden	18	10	8.47	1,270
5	Austria	17	11	8.04	1,206
6	Netherlands	17	3	7.82	1,173
7	Germany	15	9	7.07	1,060
8	Switzerland	15	1	6.85	1,027
9	France	11	14	5.39	808
10	Italy	11	5	5.13	772

* Based on 150 cups per 2 lb 3 oz (1 kg)
Source: *International Coffee Organization*

 **Did You Know?** Until the invention of pasteurization, milk-drinkers risked contracting the disease scrofula. It was known as "King's Evil," because it was believed the only cure was to be touched by a king.

Rail Transportation

TOP 10 ★
LONGEST RAIL NETWORKS

	LOCATION	TOTAL RAIL LENGTH MILES	KM
1	US	149,129	240,000
2	Russia	93,205	150,000
3	Canada	42,112	67,773
4	China	40,327	64,900
5	India	39,093	62,915
6	Germany	28,769	46,300
7	Australia	23,962	38,563
8	Argentina	23,506	37,830
9	France	19,901	32,027
10	Mexico	19,292	31,048

RAILROAD

Although the US still has the longest rail network in the world, US rail mileage has declined considerably since its 1916 peak of 254,000 miles (408,773 km).

THE 10 ★
WORST RAIL DISASTERS IN THE US

LOCATION/DATE/INCIDENT	NO. KILLED

1 =Chatsworth, Illinois, Aug 10, 1887 — 101
A trestle bridge caught fire and collapsed as the Toledo, Peoria & Western train was passing over. In the crash, 81 people were killed immediately and a further 20 died later, while as many as 372 were injured.

=Nashville, Tennessee, July 9, 1918 — 101
On the Nashville, Chattanooga, and St. Louis Railway, a head-on collision resulted in a deathtoll that remains equal to the worst in US history, with an additional 171 people injured.

3 Brooklyn, New York, Nov 1, 1918 — 97
A subway train was derailed in the Malbone Street tunnel.

4 =Eden, Colorado, Aug 7, 1904 — 96
A bridge washed away during a flood smashed Steele's Hollow Bridge as the World's Fair Express was crossing.

=Wellington, Washington, Mar 1, 1910 — 96
On February 25, two electric trains were held up by a snowdrift that blocked Cascade Tunnel, forcing the passengers to camp in the cars. At dawn on March 1st, an avalanche swept them into a canyon.

6 =Bolivar, Texas, Sep 8, 1900 — 85
A train traveling from Beaumont encountered the hurricane that destroyed Galveston, killing 6,000. Attempts to load the train onto a ferry were abandoned, and it off set back to Beaumont, but was destroyed by the storm.

=Woodbridge, New Jersey, Feb 6, 1951 — 85
A Pennsylvania Railroad's Broker Special, traveling at excessive speed, passed over a temporary trestle, causing it to collapse. The rear cars of the train fell off the trestle, injuring a further 330.

8 =Ashtabula, Ohio, Dec 29, 1876 — 84
A bridge collapsed in a snow storm and the Lake Shore train fell into the Ashtabula River. The death toll may have been as high as 92.

9 =Frankford Junction, Pennsylvania, Sep 6, 1943 — 79
Pennsylvania's worst railroad accident occurred when a wheel locked and the train was derailed, with 100 injured.

=Richmond Hill, New York, Nov 22, 1950 — 79
A Long Island Railroad commuter train rammed into the rear of another, leaving 79 dead and 352 injured.

Did You Know? The world's first passenger rail fatality occurred on the Stockton and Darlington Railway on March 19, 1828, when a boiler explosion killed the driver, John Gillespie.

top10

TOP 10 ★
FASTEST RAIL JOURNEYS*

	JOURNEY/COUNTRY/TRAIN	DISTANCE MILES	KM	SPEED MPH	KM/H
1	Hiroshima–Kokura, Japan, Nozomi 500	119.3	192.0	162.7	261.8
2	Massy–St. Pierre des Corps, France, 7 TGV	128.5	206.9	157.4	253.3
3	Brussels–Paris, Belgium/France, Thalys 9342	194.7	313.4	140.7	226.5
4	Madrid–Seville, Spain, 5 AVE	292.4	470.5	129.9	209.1
5	Karlsruhe–Mannheim, Germany, 2 trains	44.1	71.0	120.4	193.8
6	London–York, UK, 1 IC225	188.5	303.4	112.0	180.2
7	Skövde–Södertälje, Sweden, 3 X2000	172.1	277.0	106.4	171.3
8	Piacenza–Parma, Italy, ES 9325	35.4	57.0	106.2	171.0
9	North Philadelphia–Newark Penn, US, 1 NE Direct	76.0	122.4	95.0	153.0
10	Salo–Karjaa, Finland, S220 132	33.0	53.1	94.3	151.7

* Fastest journey for each country; all those in the Top 10 have other similarly or equally fast services   Source: Railway Gazette International

THE 10 FIRST CITIES IN NORTH AMERICA TO HAVE SUBWAY SYSTEMS
(City/year opened)

1 New York, 1867   **2** Chicago, 1892
3 Boston, 1901   **4** Philadelphia, 1908   **5** Toronto, 1954
6 Cleveland, 1955   **7** Montreal, 1966   **8** San Francisco, 1972
9 Washington, D.C., 1976
10 Atlanta, 1979

TOP 10 ★
BUSIEST UNDERGROUND RAILROAD NETWORKS

	CITY	YEAR OPENED	TRACK LENGTH MILES	KM	STATIONS	PASSENGERS PER ANNUM
1	Moscow	1935	153	243.6	150	3,183,900,000
2	Tokyo	1927	106	169.1	154	2,112,700,000
3	Mexico City	1969	112	177.7	154	1,422,600,000
4	Seoul	1974	84	133.0	112	1,354,000,000
5	Paris	1900	127	201.4	372	1,170,000,000
6	New York	1867	249	398.0	469	1,100,000,000
7	Osaka	1933	66	105.8	99	988,600,000
8	St. Petersburg	1955	58	91.7	50	850,000,000
9	Hong Kong	1979	27	43.2	38	804,000,000
10	London	1863	247	392.0	245	784,000,000

THE 10 ★
WORST RAIL DISASTERS

LOCATION/DATE/INCIDENT   NO. KILLED

1 Bagmati River, India, June 6, 1981   c.800
The carriages of a train traveling from Samastipur to Banmukhi in Bihar plunged off a bridge over the Bagmati River, near Mansi, when the driver braked, apparently to avoid hitting a sacred cow. Although the official death toll was said to have been 268, many authorities have claimed that the train was so massively overcrowded that the actual figure was in excess of 800, making it probably the worst rail disaster of all time.

2 Chelyabinsk, Russia, June 3, 1989   up to 800
Two passenger trains, laden with vacationers heading to and from Black Sea resorts, were destroyed when liquid gas from a nearby pipeline exploded.

3 Guadalajara, Mexico, Jan 18, 1915   over 600
A train derailed on a steep incline, but political strife in the country meant that full details of the disaster were suppressed.

4 Modane, France, Dec 12, 1917   573
A troop-carrying train ran out of control and was derailed. It has been claimed that the train was overloaded and that as many as 1,000 may have died.

5 Balvano, Italy, Mar 2, 1944   521
A heavily laden train stalled in the Armi Tunnel, and many passengers were asphyxiated. Like the disaster at Torre (No. 6), wartime secrecy prevented full details from being published.

6 Torre, Spain, Jan 3, 1944   over 500
A double collision and fire in a tunnel resulted in many deaths – some have put the total as high as 800.

7 Awash, Ethiopia, Jan 13, 1985   428
A derailment hurled a train laden with some 1,000 passengers into a ravine.

8 Cireau, Romania, Jan 7, 1917   374
An overcrowded passenger train crashed into a military train and was derailed.

9 Quipungo, Angola, May 31, 1993   355
A trail was derailed by UNITA guerrilla action.

10 Sangi, Pakistan, Jan 4, 1990   306
A train was diverted on to the wrong line, resulting in a fatal collision.

PARIS METRO
Now 100 years old, the Paris Metro – with its distinctive Art Deco entrances – is among the world's longest and most used underground railroad systems.

Air Transportation

WORST AIRSHIP DISASTERS

LOCATION/DATE/INCIDENT	NO. KILLED
1 Off the Atlantic coast, US, Apr 4, 1933	73
US Navy airship Akron crashed into the sea in a storm, leaving only three survivors in the world's worst airship tragedy.	
2 Over the Mediterranean, Dec 21, 1923	52
French airship Dixmude is assumed to have been struck by lightning and to have broken up and crashed into the sea. Wreckage, believed to be from the airship, was found off Sicily 10 years later.	
3 Near Beauvais, France, Oct 5, 1930	50
British airship R101 crashed into a hillside leaving 48 dead, with two dying later, and six survivors.	
4 Off the coast near Hull, UK, Aug 24, 1921	44
Airship R38, sold by the British government to the US and renamed USN ZR-2, broke in two on a training and test flight.	
5 Lakehurst, New Jersey, May 6, 1937	36
German Zeppelin Hindenburg caught fire when mooring.	
6 Hampton Roads, Virginia, Feb 21, 1922	34
Roma, an Italian airship bought by the US Army, crashed, killing all but 11 men on board.	
7 Berlin, Germany, Oct 17, 1913	28
German airship LZ18 crashed after engine failure during a test flight at Berlin-Johannisthal.	
8 Baltic Sea, Mar 30, 1917	23
German airship SL9 was struck by lightning on a flight from Seerappen to Seddin and crashed into the sea.	
9 Mouth of the Elbe River, Germany, Sep 3, 1915	19
German airship L10 was struck by lightning and plunged into the sea.	
10= Off Heligoland, Sep 9, 1913	14
German Navy airship L1 crashed into the sea, leaving six survivors.	
= Caldwell, Ohio, Sep 3, 1925	14
US dirigible Shenandoah, the first airship built in the US and the first to use safe helium instead of inflammable hydrogen, broke up in a storm, scattering sections over a large area of the Ohio countryside.	

WORST AIR DISASTERS CAUSED BY HIJACKINGS AND BOMBS

LOCATION/DATE/INCIDENT	NO. KILLED
1 Off the Irish coast, June 23, 1985	329
An Air India Boeing 747, on a flight from Vancouver to Delhi, exploded in midair, perhaps as a result of a terrorist bomb, resulting in the worst-ever air disaster over water.	
2 Lockerbie, Scotland, Dec 21, 1988	270
(See Worst Air Disasters, No. 10)	
3 Tenere Desert, Niger, Sep 19, 1989	170
A Union de Transports Ariens DC-10, flying out of Ndjamena, Chad, exploded over Niger. French investigators implicated Libyan and Syrian terrorists.	
4 Baiyun Airport, China, Oct 2, 1990	132
A Xiamen Airlines Boeing 737 was hijacked in flight and, during an enforced landing, crashed into a taxiing 757.	
5 Comoro Islands, Indian Ocean, Nov 23, 1996	127
An Ethiopian Airlines Boeing 767 was hijacked and ditched in the sea when it ran out of fuel.	
6 Andaman Sea, off Myanmar (Burma), Nov 29, 1987	115
A Korean Air Boeing 707 exploded in midair. Two North Korean terrorists were captured, one of whom committed suicide, while the other was sentenced to death but later pardoned.	
7 Near Abu Dhabi, United Arab Emirates, Sep 23, 1983	111
A Gulf Air Boeing 737 exploded as it prepared to land. Evidence indicated that the explosion had been caused by a bomb in the cargo hold.	
8 Near El Dorado Airport, Bogota, Colombia, Nov 27, 1989	110
An AVIANCA Boeing 727 exploded soon after takeoff in a drug cartel-related bombing.	
9 Near Johor Baharu, Malaysia, Dec 4, 1977	100
A Malaysian Airline System Boeing 737 plunged to earth and exploded. Investigators concluded that the pilots had been shot.	
10 Near Kefallinia, Greece, Sep 8, 1974	88
A Trans World Airlines Boeing 707 plunged into the Ionian Sea after an explosion resulted in loss of control.	

"BLACK BOX"

During World War II, the British Royal Air Force slang term for the radar apparatus that aided navigators and bomb-aimers was "black box," the mystery and secrecy surrounding this invention emphasized by its color. The name was later applied to the flight data recorder on a modern airliner, the device that records all the aircraft's principal actions. In fact, to make them easier to find after a crash, black boxes are now customarily painted a luminous orange.

WHY DO WE SAY?

FIERY FINALE

Astonishingly, 61 of the 97 people on board the Hindenburg survived its explosion, but the awesome and terrible images of the catastrophe ended the airship era.

Background image: **CHARLES DE GAULLE AIRPORT, PARIS, FRANCE**

TOP 10 ★
BUSIEST INTERNATIONAL AIRPORTS

AIRPORT/LOCATION	PASSENGERS PER ANNUM
1 London Heathrow, London, UK	50,612,000
2 Frankfurt, Frankfurt, Germany	32,333,000
3 Charles de Gaulle, Paris, France	31,549,000
4 Schiphol, Amsterdam, Netherlands	30,832,000
5 Hong Kong, Hong Kong, China	28,316,000
6 London Gatwick, Gatwick, UK	24,835,000
7 Singapore International, Singapore	23,799,000
8 New Tokyo International (Narita), Tokyo, Japan	22,941,000
9 J. F. Kennedy International, New York, US	17,378,000
10 Zurich, Zurich, Switzerland	16,747,000

Source: *International Civil Aviation Organization*

In addition to New York's JFK, only six airports in the US handle more than 5 million international passengers a year: notably Miami, Los Angeles, Chicago O'Hare, San Francisco, Honolulu, and New York Newark.

THE 10 ★
WORST AIR DISASTERS

LOCATION/DATE/INCIDENT	NO. KILLED

1 Tenerife, Canary Islands, Mar 27, 1977 — 583
Two Boeing 747s (Pan Am and KLM, carrying 364 passengers and 16 crew and 230 passengers and 11 crew, respectively) collided and caught fire on the runway of Los Rodeos airport after the pilots received incorrect control-tower instructions.

2 Mt. Ogura, Japan, Aug 12, 1985 — 520
A JAL Boeing 747 on an internal flight from Tokyo to Osaka crashed, killing all but four on board in the worst-ever disaster involving a single aircraft.

3 Charkhi Dadri, India, Nov 12, 1996 — 349
Soon after taking off from New Delhi's Indira Gandhi International Airport, a Saudi Airways Boeing 747 collided with a Kazakh Airlines Ilyushin IL76 cargo aircraft on its descent and exploded, killing all 312 on the Boeing and 37 on the Ilyushin in the world's worst midair crash.

4 Paris, France, Mar 3, 1974 — 346
A Turkish Airlines DC-10 crashed at Ermenonville, north of Paris, immediately after takeoff for London, with many English rugby supporters among the dead.

5 Off the Irish coast, June 23, 1985 — 329
An Air India Boeing 747 on a flight from Vancouver to Delhi exploded in midair, perhaps as a result of a terrorist bomb.

6 Riyadh, Saudi Arabia, Aug 19, 1980 — 301
A Saudia (Saudi Arabian) Airlines Lockheed Tristar caught fire during an emergency landing.

7 Kinshasa, Zaïre, Jan 8, 1996 — 298
A Zaïrean Antonov-32 cargo plane crashed shortly after takeoff, killing shoppers in a market.

8 Off the Iranian coast, July 3, 1988 — 290
An Iran Air A300 airbus was shot down in error by a missile fired by the USS Vincennes.

9 Chicago, US, May 25, 1979 — 273
An engine fell off an American Airlines DC-10 as it took off from Chicago O'Hare airport; the plane plunged out of control, killing all 271 on board and two on the ground, in the US's worst-ever air disaster.

10 Lockerbie, Scotland, Dec 21, 1988 — 270
Pan Am Flight 103 from London Heathrow to New York exploded in midair as a result of a terrorist bomb, killing 243 passengers, 16 crew, and 11 on the ground in the UK's worst-ever air disaster.

TOP 10 COUNTRIES WITH THE MOST AIRPORTS
(Country/airports)

❶ **US**, 14,459 ❷ **Brazil**, 3,265
❸ **Russia**, 2,517 ❹ **Mexico**, 1,805
❺ **Argentina**, 1,374 ❻ **Canada**, 1,395
❼ **Bolivia**, 1,130 ❽ **Colombia**, 1,120
❾ **Paraguay**, 941 ❿ **South Africa**, 749

Source: *Central Intelligence Agency*
Airports, as defined by the CIA, range in size from those with paved runways over 10,000 ft (3,048 m) in length to those with only short landing strips. Among European countries those with the most airports are Germany (618), France (474), and the UK (387).

TOP 10 AIRLINE-USING COUNTRIES
(Country/passenger miles per annum*/passenger km per annum*)

❶ **US**, 599.332 billion/964.533 billion ❷ **UK**, 98.111 billion/157.895 billion
❸ **Japan**, 93.856 billion/151.048 billion ❹ **Germany**, 53.555 billion/86.189 billion
❺ **France**, 52.614 billion/84.675 billion ❻ **Australia**, 47.145 billion/75.873 billion
❼ **China**, 45.337 billion/72.964 billion ❽ **Netherlands**, 41.424 billion/66.666 billion
❾ **Canada**, 38.439 billion/61.862 billion ❿ **Rep. of Korea**, 36.892 billion/59.372 billion

* *Total distance traveled by scheduled aircraft of national airlines multiplied by number of passengers carried*
Source: *International Civil Aviation Organization*

Which country has the world's fastest scheduled rail service?
see p.232 for the answer
A France
B USA
C Japan

Sports

SYDNEY 2000

Indigenous Australian creatures welcome the world to the 27th Olympiad, held in Sydney from September 15 to October 1, 2000.

TM © SOCOG 1996

TOP 10 ★
LONGEST-STANDING CURRENT OLYMPIC TRACK AND FIELD RECORDS

EVENT	WINNING DISTANCE, TIME, OR SCORE	COMPETITOR/ COUNTRY	DATE SET
1 Men's long jump	8.90 m	Bob Beamon, US	Oct 18, 1968
2 Women's shot put	22.41 m	Ilona Slupianek, East Germany	July 24, 1980
3 Women's 800 meters	1 min 53.43 sec	Nadezhda Olizarenko, USSR	July 27, 1980
4 = Women's 4 x 100 meters	41.60 sec	East Germany	Aug 1, 1980
= Men's 1500 meters	3 min 32.53 sec	Sebastian Coe, GB	Aug 1, 1980
6 Women's marathon	2 hr 24 min 52 sec	Joan Benoit, US	Aug 5, 1984
7 Decathlon	8,847 points	Daley Thompson, GB	Aug 9, 1984
8 Men's 5,000 meters	13 min 05.59 sec	Said Aouita, Morocco	Aug 11, 1984
9 Men's marathon	2 hr 9 min 21 sec	Carlos Lopes, Portugal	Aug 12, 1984
10 = Men's shot put	22.47 m	Ulf Timmermann, East Germany	Sep 23, 1988
= Men's 20-km walk	1 hr 19 min 57 sec	Jozef Pribilinec, Czechoslovakia	Sep 23, 1988

Bob Beamon's record-breaking jump in 1968 is regarded as one of the greatest achievements in athletics. He was aided by Mexico City's rarefied atmosphere, but to add a staggering 21¾ in (55.25 cm) to the old record, and win the competition by 28½ in (72.39 cm), was no mean feat. Beamon's jump of 29 ft 2½ in (8.90 m) was the first beyond both 28 and 29 ft (8.53 and 8.84 m). The next 28-ft (8.53-m) jump in the Olympics was not until 1980, 12 years after Beamon's leap.

THE 10 OLYMPIC DECATHLON EVENTS

1 100 meters **2** Long jump **3** Shot put **4** High jump **5** 400 meters
6 110 meter hurdles **7** Discus
8 Pole vault **9** Javelin **10** 1500 meters

TOP 10 ★
OLYMPIC SPORTS IN WHICH GREAT BRITAIN HAS WON THE MOST MEDALS

SPORT	GOLD	SILVER	BRONZE	TOTAL
1 Track and field	47	79	57	183
2 Swimming	18	23	30	71
3 = Cycling	9	21	16	46
= Tennis	16	14	16	46
5 Shooting	13	14	18	45
6 Boxing	12	10	21	43
7 Rowing	19	15	7	41
8 Yachting	14	12	9	35
9 Equestrian	5	7	9	21
10 Wrestling	3	4	10	17

TOP 10 ★
OLYMPIC SPORTS IN WHICH THE US HAS WON THE MOST MEDALS

SPORT	GOLD	SILVER	BRONZE	TOTAL
1 Track and field	299	216	177	692
2 Swimming	230	176	137	543
3 Diving	46	40	41	127
4 Wrestling	46	38	25	109
5 Boxing	47	21	34	102
6 Shooting	45	26	21	92
7 Gymnastics	26	23	28	77
8 Rowing	29	28	19	76
9 Yachting	16	19	16	51
10 Speed skating	22	16	10	48

Background image: **THE OLYMPIC STADIUM IN SYDNEY**

TOP 10 ★
COUNTRIES WITH THE MOST SUMMER OLYMPICS MEDALS, 1896–1996

COUNTRY	GOLD	MEDALS SILVER	BRONZE	TOTAL
1 US	833	634	548	2,015
2 Soviet Union*	485	395	354	1,234
3 Great Britain	177	233	225	635
4 France	176	181	203	562
5 Germany #	151	181	184	516
6 Sweden	134	152	173	459
7 Italy	166	136	142	444
8 Hungary	142	128	155	425
9 East Germany	153	130	127	410
10 Australia	87	85	122	294

* Includes Unified Team of 1992; does not include Russia since this date

 # Not including West/East Germany 1968–88

The medals table was led by the host nations at the first three Games: Greece in 1896, France in 1900, and the US in 1904. Germany led at the 1936 Games, after which the US and the Soviet Union vied for preeminence.

TOP 10 SUMMER OLYMPICS ATTENDED BY THE MOST COMPETITORS, 1896–1996
(City/year/competitors)

1 Atlanta, 1996, 10,310   **2** Barcelona, 1992, 9,364   **3** Seoul, 1988, 9,101
4 Munich, 1972, 7,156   **5** Los Angeles, 1984, 7,058   **6** Montreal, 1976, 6,085
7 Mexico City, 1968, 5,530   **8** Rome, 1960, 5,346   **9** Moscow, 1980, 5,326
10 Tokyo, 1964, 5,140

The first Games in 1896 were attended by just 311 competitors, all men, representing 13 countries. Women took part for the first time four years later at the Paris Games.

TOP 10 ★
MEDAL WINNERS IN A SUMMER OLYMPICS CAREER

MEDALLIST	COUNTRY	SPORT	YEARS	GOLD	MEDALS SILVER	BRONZE	TOTAL
1 Larissa Latynina	USSR	Gymnastics	1956–64	9	5	4	18
2 Nikolay Andrianov	USSR	Gymnastics	1972–80	7	5	3	15
3 =Edoardo Mangiarotti	Italy	Fencing	1936–60	6	5	2	13
=Takashi Ono	Japan	Gymnastics	1952–64	5	4	4	13
=Boris Shakhlin	USSR	Gymnastics	1956–64	7	4	2	13
6 =Sawao Kato	Japan	Gymnastics	1968–76	8	3	1	12
=Paavo Nurmi	Finland	Athletics	1920–28	9	3	0	12
8 =Viktor Chukarin	USSR	Gymnastics	1952–56	7	3	1	11
=Vera Cáslavská	Czechoslovakia	Gymnastics	1964–68	7	4	0	11
=Carl Osborn	US	Shooting	1912–24	5	4	2	11
=Mark Spitz	US	Swimming	1968–72	9	1	1	11
=Matt Biondi	US	Swimming	1984–92	8	2	1	11

"OLYMPICS"

What we call the Olympics is a modern revival of games that took place at Olympia in Greece from as early as 1370 BC, as part of a religious festival held every four years. Originally foot races were the only events, and the earliest record is that of Coroibis of Olis, winner of a 186-yd (170-m) race in 776 BC. New sports were progressively added, but the Games were banned in AD 393 by Emperor Theodosius I. The Olympics were reborn with the first modern games held in Athens in 1896.

WHY DO WE SAY ?

MEDAL WINNER
Russian gymnast Nikolay Andrianov's tally of 15 individual and team medals won in three Olympics makes him the most decorated male athlete of all time.

Did You Know? Several unusual Olympic events have been discontinued, including underwater swimming, long jump and high jump on horseback, club-swinging, and stone-throwing.

Sporting Heroes

MOST POINTS SCORED BY MICHAEL JORDAN IN A GAME

	TEAM	DATE	POINTS
1	Cleveland Cavaliers	Mar 28, 1990	69
2	Orlando Magic	Jan 16, 1993	64
3	Boston Celtics	Apr 20, 1986	63
4=	Detroit Pistons	Mar 4, 1987	61
=	Atlanta Hawks	Apr 16, 1987	61
6	Detroit Pistons	Mar 3, 1988	59
7	New Jersey Nets	Feb 6, 1987	58
8	Washington Bullets	Dec 23, 1992	57
9=	Philadelphia 76ers	Mar 24, 1987	56
=	Miami Heat	Apr 29, 1992	56

Source: *NBA*

SEASONS BY WAYNE GRETZKY

	SEASON	GOALS	ASSISTS	POINTS
1	1985–86	52	163	215
2	1981–82	92	120	212
3	1984–85	73	135	208
4	1983–84	87	118	205
5	1982–83	71	125	196
6	1986–87	62	121	183
7	1988–89	54	114	168
8	1980–81	55	109	164
9	1990–91	41	122	163
10	1987–88	40	109	149

Wayne Gretzky, who retired in 1999 after 20 seasons in the NHL, is considered to be the greatest ice-hockey player of all time. He gained more records than any player in history, including the most goals, assists, and points in a career.

ICE MAN

Wayne Gretzky (pictured here during his 1984–85 season with the Edmonton Oilers) holds more career records than any player in ice-hockey history.

THE 10 LATEST WINNERS OF THE *SPORTS ILLUSTRATED* "SPORTSMAN OF THE YEAR" AWARD

(Year/winner(s)/sport)

1 1999 United States Women's World Cup Squad, Soccer **2** 1998 Mark McGwire and Sammy Sosa, Baseball **3** 1997 Dean Smith, Basketball coach **4** 1996 Tiger Woods, Golf **5** 1995 Cal Ripken, Jr., Baseball **6** 1994 Johan Olav Koss and Bonnie Blair, Ice skating **7** 1993 Don Shula, Football coach **8** 1992 Arthur Ashe, Tennis **9** 1991 Michael Jordan, Basketball **10** 1990 Joe Montana, Football

THE 10 LATEST WINNERS OF THE BBC "SPORTS PERSONALITY OF THE YEAR" AWARD

(Year/winner/sport)

1 1999 Lennox Lewis, Boxing **2** 1998 Michael Owen, Soccer **3** 1997 Greg Rusedski, Tennis **4** 1996 Damon Hill, Motor racing **5** 1995 Jonathan Edwards, Track and Field **6** 1994 Damon Hill, Motor racing **7** 1993 Linford Christie, Track and Field **8** 1992 Nigel Mansell, Motor racing **9** 1991 Liz McColgan, Track and Field **10** 1990 Paul Gascoigne, Soccer

This annual award is based on a poll of BBC television viewers in the UK.

ON THE BALL

In many seasons during his exceptional career, Michael Jordan achieved an average of over 30 points per game, with those listed above standing out as his highest-scoring ones.

THE 10 ★
LATEST EVANDER HOLYFIELD WINS BY KNOCKOUT

	OPPONENT	ROUND	DATE
1	Michael Moorer	8	Nov 8, 1997
2	Mike Tyson	11*	Nov 9, 1996
3	Bobby Czyz	5	May 10, 1996
4	Riddick Bowe	8*	Nov 4, 1995
5	Bert Cooper	7	Nov 23, 1991
6	Buster Douglas	3	Oct 25, 1990
7	Seamus McDonagh	4*	June 1, 1990
8	Alex Stewart	8*	Nov 4, 1989
9	Adilson Rodrigues	2	July 15, 1989
10	Michael Dokes	10*	Mar 11, 1989

* Technical knockout

Born October 19, 1962, boxer Evander Holyfield won his first undisputed heavyweight title in 1990 when he defeated Buster Douglas. His 1993 defeat of Riddick Bowe (when Holyfield won on points) and his 1996 victory over Mike Tyson established him as the only fighter, apart from Muhammad Ali, to win the heavyweight title on three occasions.

TOP 10 ★
FASTEST 100-METER RUNS BY LINFORD CHRISTIE

	STADIUM/LOCATION	DATE	TIME SECS
1	**Stuttgart**, Germany	Aug 15, 1993	9.87
2	**Victoria**, Canada	Aug 23, 1994	9.91
3	**Tokyo**, Japan	Aug 25, 1991	9.92
4	**Barcelona**, Spain	Aug 1, 1992	9.96
5	=**Seoul**, Korea	Sep 24, 1988	9.97
	=**Stuttgart**, Germany	Aug 15, 1993	9.97
	=**Johannesburg**, SA	Sep 23, 1995	9.97
8	**Victoria**, Canada	Aug 23, 1994	9.98
9	**Tokyo**, Japan	Aug 25, 1991	9.99
10	=**Barcelona**, Spain	Aug 1, 1992	10.00
	=**Stuttgart**, Germany	Aug 14, 1993	10.00

Christie made his international debut for Great Britain in 1980, became the fastest runner outside the US in 1986, and won Olympic gold in 1992.

TOP 10 ★
LONGEST LONG JUMPS BY CARL LEWIS

	STADIUM/LOCATION	DATE	DISTANCE M
1	**Tokyo**, Japan	Aug 30, 1991	8.87
2	=**Indianapolis**	June 19, 1983	8.79
	=**New York***	Jan 27, 1984	8.79
4	=**Indianapolis**	July 24, 1982	8.76
	=**Indianapolis**	July 18, 1988	8.76
6	**Indianapolis**	Aug 16, 1987	8.75
7	**Seoul**, Korea	Sep 26, 1988	8.72
8	=**Westwood**	May 13, 1984	8.71
	=**Los Angeles**	June 19, 1984	8.71
10	**Barcelona**, Spain	Aug 5, 1992	8.68

* Indoor performance

All-round athlete Lewis won four gold medals at the 1984 Olympics, two in 1988, two in 1992, and his ninth in 1996.

THE 10 ★
LATEST WINNERS OF THE JESSE OWENS INTERNATIONAL TROPHY

YEAR	WINNER	SPORT
2000	Lance Armstrong	Track and field
1999	Marion Jones	Track and field
1998	Haile Gebrselassie	Track and field
1997	Michael Johnson	Track and field
1996	Michael Johnson	Track and field
1995	Johann Olav Koss	Speed skating
1994	Wang Junxia	Track and field
1993	Vitaly Scherbo	Gymnastics
1992	Mike Powell	Track and field
1991	Greg LeMond	Cycling

The Jesse Owens International Trophy, named in honor of American Olympic athlete Jesse (James Cleveland) Owens (1913–80), has been presented by the Amateur Athletic Association since 1981, when it was won by speed skater Eric Heiden. Michael Johnson is the only sportsperson to have won on two occasions, while Marion Jones, the 1999 winner, is only the fourth woman to receive the award.

POLES APART
Ukrainian pole-vaulter Sergei Bubka (b. 1963) has ruled his sport since winning the 1983 World Championship. He has set 35 world records, which is more than any other athlete in sports history.

TOP 10 ★
HIGHEST POLE VAULTS BY SERGEI BUBKA

	STADIUM/LOCATION	DATE	HEIGHT M
1	**Donetsk**, Ukraine*	Feb 21, 1993	6.15
2	=**Lievin**, France*	Feb 13, 1993	6.14
	=**Sestriere**, Italy	July 31, 1994	6.14
4	=**Berlin**, Germany*	Feb 21, 1992	6.13
	=**Tokyo**, Japan	Sep 19, 1992	6.13
6	=**Grenoble**, France*	Mar 23, 1991	6.12
	=**Padua**, Italy	Aug 30, 1992	6.12
8	=**Donetsk**, Ukraine*	Mar 19, 1991	6.11
	=**Dijon**, France	June 13, 1992	6.11
10	=**San Sebastian**, Spain*	Mar 15, 1991	6.10
	=**Malmo**, Sweden	Aug 5, 1991	6.10

* Indoor performance

Did You Know? In little over a century, the world pole-vaulting record leaped from 3.62 m (achieved by Raymond Clapp of the US in 1898) to today's 6.14-m outdoor record.

Football Feats

LARGEST
NFL STADIUMS

STADIUM/HOME TEAM	CAPACITY
1 **Pontiac Silverdome,** Detroit Lions	80,311
2 **FedExField,** Washington Redskins	80,116
3 **Giants Stadium,** New York Giants*	79,469
4 **Arrowhead Stadium,** Kansas City Chiefs	79,409
5 **Mile High Stadium,** Denver Broncos	76,082
6 **Ralph Wilson Stadium,** Buffalo Bills	75,339
7 **Pro Player Stadium,** Miami Dolphins	74,916
8 **Sun Devil Stadium,** Arizona Cardinals	73,273
9 **Alltel Stadium,** Jacksonville Jaguars	73,000
10 **Ericsson Stadium,** Carolina Panthers	72,250

Seating reduced to 77,803 for New York Jets games

Source: *National Football League*

The roof of the octagonal Pontiac Silverdome is the world's largest air-supported structure.

BIGGEST
WINNING MARGINS
IN THE SUPER BOWL

GAME*	YEAR	MARGIN
1 **San Francisco 49ers** v Denver Broncos	1990	45
2 **Chicago Bears** v New England Patriots	1986	36
3 **Dallas Cowboys** v Buffalo Bills	1993	35
4 **Washington Redskins** v Denver Broncos	1988	32
5 **Los Angeles Raiders** v Washington Redskins	1984	29
6 **Green Bay Packers** v Kansas City Chiefs	1967	25
7 **San Francisco 49ers** v San Diego Chargers	1995	23
8 **San Francisco 49ers** v Miami Dolphins	1985	22
9 **Dallas Cowboys** v Miami Dolphins	1972	21
10 =**Green Bay Packers** v Oakland Raiders	1968	19
=**New York Giants** v Denver Broncos	1987	19

* Winners first

MOST SUCCESSFUL
TEAMS*

TEAM	WINS	LOSSES	PTS
1 **Dallas Cowboys**	5	3	13
2 **San Francisco 49ers**	5	0	10
3 **Pittsburgh Steelers**	4	1	10
4 **Washington Redskins**	3	2	8
5 **Denver Broncos**	2	4	8
6 =**Green Bay Packers**	3	1	7
=**Oakland/L.A. Raiders**	3	1	7
8 **Miami Dolphins**	2	3	7
9 **New York Giants**	2	0	4
10 =**Buffalo Bills**	0	4	4
=**Minnesota Vikings**	0	4	4

* Based on two points for a Super Bowl win and one for a loss; wins take precedence over losses in determining ranking

Source: *National Football League*

MOST SUCCESSFUL
COACHES
IN AN NFL CAREER

COACH	GAMES WON
1 **Don Shula**	347
2 **George Halas**	324
3 **Tom Landry**	270
4 **Curly Lambeau**	229
5 **Chuck Noll**	209
6 **Chuck Knox**	193
7 **Dan Reeves***	175
8 **Paul Brown**	170
9 **Bud Grant**	168
10 **Marv Levy**	154

* Still active

Source: *National Football League*

TOP COACH

Don Shula retired at the end of the 1995 season, having achieved an NFL record of coaching his team, the Miami Dolphins, to 347 wins.

Background image: **PONTIAC SILVERDOME**

PASSING GREAT

Jerry Rice, who joined the San Francisco 49ers in 1985, is one of the greatest-ever pass catchers and the player with the most career touchdowns.

TOP 10 ★
PLAYERS WITH THE MOST CAREER POINTS

	PLAYER	POINTS
1	George Blanda	2,002
2	Gary Anderson*	1,948
3	Morten Andersen*	1,840
4	Norm Johnson*	1,736
5	Nick Lowery	1,711
6	Jan Stenerud	1,699
7	Eddie Murray*	1,549
8	Pat Leahy	1,470
9	Jim Turner	1,439
10	Matt Bahr	1,422

* Still active 1999 season

Source: *National Football League*

TOP 10 ★
LONGEST CAREERS OF CURRENT NFL PLAYERS

	PLAYER	TEAM	YEARS
1	Wade Wilson	Oakland Raiders	19
2 =	Morten Andersen	Atlanta Falcons	18
=	Gary Anderson	Minnesota Vikings	18
=	Norm Johnson	Philadelphia Eagles	18
5 =	Darrell Green	Washington Redskins	17
=	Trey Junkin	Arizona Cardinals	17
=	Dan Marino	Miami Dolphins	17
=	Bruce Matthews	Tennessee Titans	17
=	Eddie Murray	Dallas Cowboys	17
=	Mike Horan	St. Louis Rams	17

Source: *National Football League*

TOP 10 ★
PLAYERS WITH THE MOST CAREER TOUCHDOWNS

	PLAYER	TOUCHDOWNS
1	Jerry Rice*	179
2	Emmitt Smith*	147
3	Marcus Allen	145
4	Jim Brown	126
5	Walter Payton	125
6	John Riggins	116
7	Lenny Moore	113
8	Don Hutson	105
9	Steve Largent	101
10	Franco Harris	100

* Still active

Source: *National Football League*

TOP 10 ★
PLAYERS WITH THE MOST PASSING YARDS IN AN NFL CAREER

	PLAYER	PASSING YARDS
1	Dan Marino*	61,243
2	John Elway	51,475
3	Warren Moon*	49,117
4	Fran Tarkenton	47,003
5	Dan Fouts	43,040
6	Joe Montana	40,551
7	Johnny Unitas	40,239
8	Dave Krieg	37,946
9	Boomer Esiason	37,920
10	Jim Kelly	35,467

* Still active 1999 season

Source: *National Football League*

TOP 10 ★
POINT SCORERS IN AN NFL SEASON

	PLAYER/TEAM/YEAR	GAMES WON
1	Paul Hornung, Green Bay Packers, 1960	176
2	Gary Anderson, Minnesota Vikings, 1998	164
3	Mark Moseley, Washington Redskins,1983	161
4	Gino Cappelletti, Boston Patriots, 1964	155*
5	Emmitt Smith, Dallas Cowboys, 1995	150
6	Chip Lohmiller, Washington Redskins, 1991	149
7	Gino Cappelletti, Boston Patriots, 1961	147
8	Paul Hornung, Green Bay Packers, 1961	146
9 =	Jim Turner, New York Jets, 1968	145
=	John Kasay, Carolina Panthers, 1996	145
=	Mike Vanderjagt, Indianapolis Colts, 1999	145

* Including a two-point conversion

Source: *National Football League*

THE 10 LATEST ATTENDANCES OF NFL TEAMS*
(Year/attendance)

❶ 1999 16,206,640   ❷ 1998 16,187,758   ❸ 1997 15,769,193   ❹ 1996 15,381,727
❺ 1995 15,834,468   ❻ 1994 14,810,173   ❼ 1993 14,781,450   ❽ 1992 14,644,797
❾ 1991 14,654,706   ❿ 1990 14,807,439

* Regular season only   Source: NFL

What sort of baskets were originally used in basketball?
see p.250 for the answer

A Fish
B Peach
C Bread

Baseball Stars

PLAYERS WITH THE MOST CAREER STRIKEOUTS

PLAYER	STRIKEOUTS
1 Nolan Ryan	5,714
2 Steve Carlton	4,136
3 Bert Blyleven	3,701
4 Tom Seaver	3,640
5 Don Sutton	3,574
6 Gaylord Perry	3,534
7 Walter Johnson	3,508
8 Phil Niekro	3,342
9 Roger Clemens*	3,316
10 Ferguson Jenkins	3,192

* Still active in 1999 season
Source: *Major League Baseball*

Nolan Ryan was known as the "Babe Ruth of strikeout pitchers," pitching faster (a record 101 mph) and longer (27 seasons – 1966 and 1968–93) than any previous player.

PLAYERS WITH THE HIGHEST CAREER BATTING AVERAGES

PLAYER	AT BAT	HITS	AVERAGE*
1 Ty Cobb	11,434	4,189	.366
2 Rogers Hornsby	8,173	2,930	.358
3 Joe Jackson	4,981	1,772	.356
4 Ed Delahanty	7,505	2,597	.346
5 Tris Speaker	10,195	3,514	.345
6 =Billy Hamilton	6,268	2,158	.344
=Ted Williams	7,706	2,654	.344
8 =Dan Brouthers	6,711	2,296	.342
=Harry Heilmann	7,787	2,660	.342
=Babe Ruth	8,399	2,873	.342

* Calculated by dividing the number of hits by the number of times a batter was at bat
Source: *Major League Baseball*

Second only to the legendary Ty Cobb, Rogers Hornsby stands as the best second-hitting baseman of all time, with an average of over .400 in a five-year period.

PLAYERS WITH THE MOST RUNS IN A CAREER*

PLAYER	RUNS
1 Ty Cobb	2,245
2 =Babe Ruth	2,174
=Hank Aaron	2,174
4 Pete Rose	2,165
5 Rickey Henderson#	2,103
6 Willie Mays	2,062
7 Stan Musial	1,949
8 Lou Gehrig	1,888
9 Tris Speaker	1,882
10 Mel Ott	1,859

* Regular season only, excluding World Series
# Still active in 1999 season
Source: *Major League Baseball*

Ty Cobb is also the only player ever to collect six hits in six at bats and hit three home runs in the same game, which he achieved on May 5, 1925, helping the Detroit Tigers to a 14–8 win over the St. Louis Browns.

PLAYERS WITH THE MOST CONSECUTIVE GAMES PLAYED

PLAYER	GAMES
1 Cal Ripken, Jr.	2,600
2 Lou Gehrig	2,130
3 Everett Scott	1,307
4 Steve Garvey	1,207
5 Billy Williams	1,117
6 Joe Sewell	1,103
7 Stan Musial	895
8 Eddie Yost	829
9 Gus Suhr	822
10 Nellie Fox	798

Source: *Major League Baseball*

Cal Ripken took himself out of the starting lineup on September 21, 1998, in a game between the Orioles and the Yankees, having played in every game since May 30, 1982.

PLAYERS WHO PLAYED THE MOST GAMES IN A CAREER

PLAYER	GAMES
1 Pete Rose	3,562
2 Carl Yastrzemski	3,308
3 Hank Aaron	3,298
4 Ty Cobb	3,034
5 =Stan Musial	3,026
=Eddie Murray	3,026
7 Willie Mays	2,992
8 Dave Winfield	2,973
9 Rusty Staub	2,951
10 Brooks Robinson	2,896

Source: *Major League Baseball*

Pete Rose is the only player to appear in over 500 games in five different positions: he was at first base in 939 games, second in 628, third in 634, left field in 671, and right field in 595.

PITCHERS WITH THE MOST CAREER WINS

PLAYER	WINS
1 Cy Young	509
2 Walter Johnson	417
3 =Grover Alexander	373
=Christy Mathewson	373
5 Warren Spahn	363
6 =Kid Nichols	361
=Pud Galvin	361
8 Tim Keefe	344
9 Steve Carlton	329
10 =Eddie Plank	326
=John Clarkson	326

Source: *Major League Baseball*

In the 1925 season, Walter Johnson became the only pitcher to win 20 games and achieve a batting average for the season of 0.433 in 97 at bats – the highest of any pitcher in baseball history.

Did You Know? The first Major League baseball player killed in a game was Raymond Chapman of the Cleveland Indians, struck by a pitch thrown by New York Yankees Carl Mays on August 16, 1920.

TOP 10 ★
HIGHEST PAID PLAYERS IN MAJOR LEAGUE BASEBALL, 1999

PLAYER	TEAM	EARNINGS ($)
1 Albert Belle	Baltimore Orioles	11,949,794
2 Pedro Martinez	Boston Red Sox	11,250,000
3 Kevin Brown	Los Angeles Dodgers	10,714,286
4 Greg Maddux	Atlanta Braves	10,600,000
5 Gary Sheffield	Los Angeles Dodgers	9,936,667
6 Bernie Williams	New York Yankees	9,857,113
7 Randy Johnson	Arizona Diamondbacks	9,650,000
8 David Cone	New York Yankees	9,500,000
9 Barry Bonds	San Francisco Giants	9,381,057
10 Mark McGwire	St. Louis Cardinals	9,308,667

The median salary for the 1999 season was $495,000, up from $427,500 in 1998.

Source: *Associated Press*

THE 10 ★
FIRST PITCHERS TO THROW PERFECT GAMES

PLAYER	MATCH	DATE
1 Lee Richmond	Worcester vs Cleveland	June 12, 1880
2 Monte Ward	Providence vs Buffalo	June 17, 1880
3 Cy Young	Boston vs Philadelphia	May 5, 1904
4 Addie Joss	Cleveland vs Chicago	Oct 2, 1908
5 Charlie Robertson	Chicago vs Detroit	Apr 30, 1922
6 Don Larsen*	New York vs Brooklyn	Oct 8, 1936
7 Jim Bunning	Philadelphia vs New York	June 21, 1964
8 Sandy Koufax	Los Angeles vs Chicago	Sept 9, 1965
9 Catfish Hunter	Oakland vs Minnesota	May 8, 1968
10 Len Barker	Cleveland vs Toronto	May 15, 1981

Larsen's perfect game was, uniquely, in the World Series

Fourteen pitchers have thrown perfect games; that is, they have pitched in all nine innings, dismissing 27 opposing batters, and without conceding a run. The last player to pitch a perfect innings was Kenny Rogers, for Texas against California, on July 28, 1994.

Source: *Major League Baseball*

TOP 10 ★
PLAYERS MOST AT BAT IN A CAREER

PLAYER	AT BAT
1 Pete Rose	14,053
2 Hank Aaron	12,364
3 Carl Yastrzemski	11,988
4 Ty Cobb	11,434
5 Eddie Murray	11,336
6 Robin Yount	11,008
7 Dave Winfield	11,003
8 Stan Musial	10,906
9 Willie Mays	10,881
10 Paul Molitor	10,835

As well as his appearance in this roll of fame, Hank Aaron collected more bases than any other hitter in baseball history, overtaking Stan Musial's previous record of 6,134 in 1972, and going on to reach 6,856 in 1976.

TOP 10 ★
LOWEST EARNED RUN AVERAGES IN A CAREER

PLAYER	EARNED RUN AVERAGES
1 Ed Walsh	1.82
2 Addie Joss	1.89
3 Three Finger Brown	2.06
4 John Ward	2.10
5 Christy Mathewson	2.13
6 Rube Waddell	2.16
7 Walter Johnson	2.17
8 Orval Overall	2.23
9 Tommy Bond	2.25
10 Ed Reulbach	2.28

Source: *Major League Baseball*

Although Addie Joss died in 1911 at the age of 31, he had gained his place in this list and also the distinction of being the only pitcher to achieve two non-hitters against the same team, playing for the Cleveland Indians against the Chicago White Sox on October 2, 1908 and April 20, 1910.

THE 10 ★
FIRST PLAYERS TO HIT FOUR HOME RUNS IN ONE GAME

PLAYER	CLUB	DATE
1 Bobby Lowe	Boston	May 30, 1884
2 Ed Delahanty	Philadelphia	July 13, 1896
3 Lou Gehrig	New York	June 3, 1932
4 Chuck Klein	Philadelphia	July 10, 1936
5 Pat Seerey	Chicago	July 18, 1948
6 Gil Hodges	Brooklyn	Aug 31, 1950
7 Joe Adcock	Milwaukee	July 31, 1954
8 Rocky Colavito	Cleveland	June 10, 1959
9 Willie Mays	San Francisco	Apr 30, 1961
10 Mike Schmidt	Philadelphia	Apr 17, 1976

The only other players to score four homers in one game are Bob Horner, who did so for Atlanta on July 6, 1986, and Mark Whitten, for St. Louis on September 7, 1993.

Soccer Stars

Pelé celebrates not only the first goal of the 1970 World Cup Final against Italy, but also his country's 100th World Cup goal.

TOP 10 ★
HIGHEST-SCORING WORLD CUP FINALS

	YEAR	GAMES	GOALS	AVERAGE PER GAME
1	1954	26	140	5.38
2	1938	18	84	4.66
3	1934	17	70	4.11
4	1950	22	88	4.00
5	1930	18	70	3.88
6	1958	35	126	3.60
7	1970	32	95	2.96
8	1982	52	146	2.81
9 =1962	32	89	2.78
=1966	32	89	2.78

TOP 10 COUNTRIES WITH THE MOST PLAYERS SENT OFF IN THE FINAL STAGES OF THE WORLD CUP

(Country/dismissals)

1 = Brazil, 8; = Argentina, 8 **3** = Uruguay, 6; = Cameroon, 6 **5** = Germany/West Germany, 5; = Hungary, 5 **7** = Czechoslovakia, 4; = Holland, 4; = Italy, 4; = Mexico, 4

A total of 97 players have received their marching orders in the final stages of the World Cup since 1930. The South American nations account for 27 of them. Brazil, Czechoslovakia, Denmark, Hungary, and South Africa have each had three players sent off in a single game – Brazil twice (1938 and 1954).

The lowest-scoring World Cup was Italia '90, which produced just 115 goals from 52 matches at an average of 2.21 per game. The 1994 final between Brazil and Italy was the first World Cup final to fail to produce a goal, with Brazil wining 3–2 on penalties.

TOP 10 ★
WORLD CUP ATTENDANCES

	MATCH (WINNERS FIRST)	VENUE	YEAR	ATTENDANCE
1	Brazil v Uruguay	Rio de Janeiro*	1950	199,854
2	Brazil v Spain	Rio de Janeiro	1950	152,772
3	Brazil v Yugoslavia	Rio de Janeiro	1950	142,409
4	Brazil v Sweden	Rio de Janeiro	1950	138,886
5	Mexico v Paraguay	Mexico City	1986	114,600
6	Argentina v West Germany	Mexico City*	1986	114,590
7 =Mexico v Bulgaria	Mexico City	1986	114,580
=Argentina v England	Mexico City	1986	114,580
9	Argentina v Belgium	Mexico City	1986	110,420
10	Mexico v Belgium	Mexico City	1986	110,000

Final tie

The biggest crowd outside Mexico or Brazil was that of 98,270 at Wembley Stadium in 1966 for England's game against France. The attendance for the Brazil–Uruguay final in 1950 is the world's highest for a soccer match.

TOP 10 ★
COUNTRIES IN THE WORLD CUP*

	COUNTRY	WIN	R/U	3RD	4TH	TOTAL
1	Brazil	4	2	2	1	27
2	Germany/West Germany	3	3	2	1	26
3	Italy	3	2	1	1	21
4	Argentina	2	2	–	–	14
5	Uruguay	2	–	–	2	10
6	France	1	–	2	1	9
7	Sweden	–	1	2	1	8
8	Holland	–	2	–	1	7
9 =Czechoslovakia	–	2	–	–	6
=Hungary	–	2	–	–	6

* *Based on 4 points for winning the tournament, 3 points for runner-up, 2 points for 3rd place, and 1 point for 4th; up to and including the 1998 World Cup*

Did You Know? When Daniel Xuereb of France played in the 1986 finals, it meant that every letter of the alphabet had been used in players' last names in the World Cup.

TOP 10 ★
EUROPEAN CUP WINNERS

COUNTRY	YEARS	WINS*
1 =England	1968–99	9
=Italy	1961–96	9
3 Spain	1956–98	8
4 Holland	1970–95	6
5 Germany	1974–97	5
6 Portugal	1961–87	3
7 =France	1993	1
=Romania	1986	1
=Scotland	1967	1
=Yugoslavia	1991	1

* Of first and last win

The European Cup, now known as the European Champions' League Cup, has been competed for annually since 1956. It was won in that year, and the next four, by Real Madrid (who also won it in 1966 and 1998) – a total of seven times. Italy's AC Milan is their only close competitor, with five wins, while Ajax and Liverpool have each won the Cup on four occasions.

TOP 10 ★
RICHEST SOCCER TEAMS

CLUB/COUNTRY	INCOME (£)
1 Manchester United, England	87,939,000
2 Barcelona, Spain	58,862,000
3 Real Madrid, Spain	55,659,000
4 Juventus, Italy	53,223,000
5 Bayern Munich, Germany	51,619,000
6 AC Milan, Italy	47,480,000
7 Borussia Dortmund, Germany	42,199,000
8 Newcastle United, England	41,134,000
9 Liverpool, England	39,153,000
10 Inter Milan, Italy	39,071,000

A survey conducted by accountants Deloitte & Touche and football magazine *FourFourTwo* compared incomes of the world's top soccer teams during the 1997/8 season. It revealed the extent to which soccer has become a major business enterprise, with many teams generating considerably more revenue from commercial activities such as the sale of merchandise and income from TV rights than they receive from admissions to matches.

TOP 10 ★
EUROPEAN TEAMS WITH THE MOST DOMESTIC LEAGUE TITLES

CLUB/COUNTRY	TITLES
1 Glasgow Rangers, Scotland	48
2 Linfield, Northern Ireland	42
3 Glasgow Celtic, Scotland	36
4 Rapid Vienna, Austria	*31
5 Benfica, Portugal	30
6 =CSKA Sofia, Bulgaria	28
=Olympiakos, Greece	28
8 =Ajax, Holland	27
=Real Madrid, Spain	27
10 =Ferencvaros, Hungary	26
=Jeunesse Esch, Luxembourg	26

* Rapid Vienna also won one German League title, in 1941

UNITED EFFORT

Manchester United confirmed their status as the world's richest team in 1999, and also captured the unique triple of League, Cup, and European Champions' League.

INTERNATIONAL STAR

Lothar Matthäus, Germany's World Cup-winning captain and European Footballer of the Year in 1990, has played for his country on 143 occasions. As a still-active player, he may yet improve on this figure.

TOP 10 ★
MOST CAPPED INTERNATIONAL PLAYERS

PLAYER/COUNTRY	YEARS	CAPS
1 =Thomas Ravelli, Sweden	1981–97	143
=Lothar Matthäus*, West Germany/Germany	1980–99	143
3 Majed Abdullah, Saudi Arabia	1978–94	140
4 Claudio Suarez*, Mexico	1982–99	131
5 Marcelo Balboa*, US	1988–98	127
6 Andoni Zubizarreta, Spain	1985–98	126
7 Peter Shilton, England	1970–90	125
8 Masami Ihara*, Japan	1988–99	123
9 =Pat Jennings, Northern Ireland	1964–86	119
=Gheorghe Hagi*, Romania	1983–99	119
=Cobi Jones*, US	1982–99	119

* Still active in 1999

TOP 10 ★ FASTEST WORLD CHAMPIONSHIP RACES OF ALL TIME

RIDER/COUNTRY	BIKE*	YEAR	AVERAGE SPEED MPH	KM/H
1 Barry Sheene, UK	Suzuki	1977	135.07	217.37
2 John Williams, UK	Suzuki	1976	133.49	214.83
3 Phil Read, UK	MV Agusta	1975	133.22	214.40
4 Wil Hartog, Holland	Suzuki	1978	132.90	213.88
5 Phil Read, UK	MV Agusta	1974	131.98	212.41
6 Giacomo Agostini, Italy	MV Agusta	1973	128.51	206.81
7 Walter Villa, Italy	Harley-Davidson	1977	127.03	204.43
8 Walter Villa, Italy	Harley-Davidson	1976	126.08	202.90
9 Giacomo Agostini, Italy	MV Agusta	1969	125.85	202.53
10 Kevin Schwartz, US	Suzuki	1991	125.34	201.72

* 500cc except for Nos. 7 and 8, which were 250cc

All races except for No. 10 were during the Belgian Grand Prix at the Spa-Francorchamps circuit. No. 10 was during the German Grand Prix at Hockenheim. The World Championships were first held in 1949, under the aegis of the Fédération Internationale Motorcycliste, when R. Leslie Graham (UK) won the 500cc class on an AJS.

TOP 10 ★ FASTEST WINNING SPEEDS OF THE DAYTONA 200

RIDER/COUNTRY*	BIKE	YEAR	AVERAGE SPEED MPH	KM/H
1 Miguel Duhamel, Canada	Honda	1999	113.46	182.61
2 Kenny Roberts	Yamaha	1984	113.14	182.08
3 Kenny Roberts	Yamaha	1983	110.93	178.52
4 Graeme Crosby, New Zealand	Yamaha	1982	109.10	175.58
5 Steve Baker	Yamaha	1977	108.85	175.18
6 Johnny Cecotto, Venezuela	Yamaha	1976	108.77	175.05
7 Dale Singleton	Yamaha	1981	108.52	174.65
8 Kenny Roberts	Yamaha	1978	108.37	174.41
9 Kevin Schwartz	Suzuki	1988	107.80	173.49
10 Dale Singleton	Yamaha	1979	107.69	173.31

* From the US unless otherwise stated

The Daytona 200, which was first held in 1937, forms a round in the AMA (American Motorcyclist Association) Grand National Dirt Track series. It is raced over 57 laps of the 3.56-mile (5.73-km) Daytona International Speedway. The other non-US winners have been: Billy Matthews (Canada), Jaarno Saarinen (Finland), Giacomo Agostini (Italy), and Patrick Pons (France).

TOP 10 ★ MOTORCYCLISTS WITH THE MOST WORLD TITLES

RIDER/COUNTRY	YEARS	TITLES
1 Giacomo Agostini, Italy	1966–75	15
2 Angel Nieto, Spain	1969–84	13
3 =Carlo Ubbiali, Italy	1951–60	9
=Mike Hailwood, UK	1961–67	9
5 =John Surtees, UK	1956–60	7
=Phil Read, UK	1964–74	7
7 =Geoff Duke, UK	1951–55	6
=Jim Redman, Southern Rhodesia	1962–65	6
=Klaus Enders, W. Germany	1967–74	6
10 Anton Mang, W. Germany	1980–87	5

THE 10 ★ LATEST WORLD CHAMPION SUPERBIKE RIDERS

YEAR	RIDER/COUNTRY	BIKE
1999	Carl Fogarty, UK	Ducati
1998	Carl Fogarty, UK	Ducati
1997	John Kocinski, US	Honda
1996	Troy Corser, Australia	Ducati
1995	Carl Fogarty, UK	Ducati
1994	Carl Fogarty, UK	Ducati
1993	Scott Russell, US	Kawasaki
1992	Doug Polen, US	Ducati
1991	Doug Polen, US	Ducati
1990	Raymond Roche, France	Ducati

SUPERBIKE CHAMPION

British motorcycle legend Carl Fogarty (b. 1966) won his first Grand Prix in 1986. Up to the 2000 season, he had won a record 59 Superbike events.

TOP 10 ★ 500CC WORLD CHAMPIONSHIPS RIDERS, 1999

(Rider/country/points)

1. Alex Criville, Spain, 267
2. Kenny Roberts, US, 220
3. Tadayuki Okada, Japan, 211
4. Max Biaggi, Italy, 194
5. Sete Gibernau, Spain, 165
6. Norick Abe, Japan, 136
7. Carlos Checa, Spain, 125
8. John Kocinski, US, 115
9. Alex Barros, Brazil, 110
10. Tetsuya Harada, Japan, 104

TOP 10 ★ TOUR DE FRANCE WINNERS

RIDER/COUNTRY	WINS
1 Jacques Anquetil, France	5
= Eddy Merckx, Belgium	5
= Bernard Hinault, France	5
= Miguel Indurain, Spain	5
5 Philippe Thys, Belgium	3
= Louison Bobet, France	3
= Greg LeMond, US	3
8 Lucien Petit-Breton, France	2
= Firmin Lambot, Belgium	2
= Ottavio Bottecchia, Italy	2
= Nicholas Frantz, Luxembourg	2
= André Leducq, France	2
= Antonin Magne, France	2
= Gino Bartali, Italy	2
= Sylvere Maës, Belgium	2
= Fausto Coppi, Italy	2
= Bernard Thevenet, France	2
= Laurent Fignon, France	2

TOUR DE FORCE

The 1999 Tour de France approaches the Eiffel Tower. The world's foremost cycle event, the Tour de France was first contested in 1903.

TOP 10 ★ RIDERS WITH THE MOST GRAND PRIX RACE WINS

RIDER/COUNTRY	YEARS	RACE WINS
1 Giacomo Agostini, Italy	1965–76	122
2 Angel Nieto, Spain	1969–85	90
3 Mike Hailwood, UK	1959–67	76
4 Rolf Biland, Switzerland	1975–90	56
5 Mick Doohan, Australia	1990–98	54
6 Phil Read, UK	1961–75	52
7 Jim Redman, Southern Rhodesia	1961–66	45
8 Anton Mang, West Germany	1976–88	42
9 Carlo Ubbiali, Italy	1950–60	39
10 John Surtees, UK	1955–60	38

TOP 10 ★ OLYMPIC CYCLING COUNTRIES

COUNTRY	MEDALS			
	GOLD	SILVER	BRONZE	TOTAL
1 France	32	19	22	73
2 Italy	32	15	6	53
3 Great Britain	9	21	16	46
4 US	11	13	16	40
5 Netherlands	10	14	7	31
6 Germany*	8	9	9	26
7 Australia	6	11	8	25
8 Soviet Union #	11	4	9	24
9 Belgium	6	6	10	22
10 Denmark	6	6	10	21

* Not including West Germany or East Germany 1968–88

Including United Team of 1992, exludes Russia since

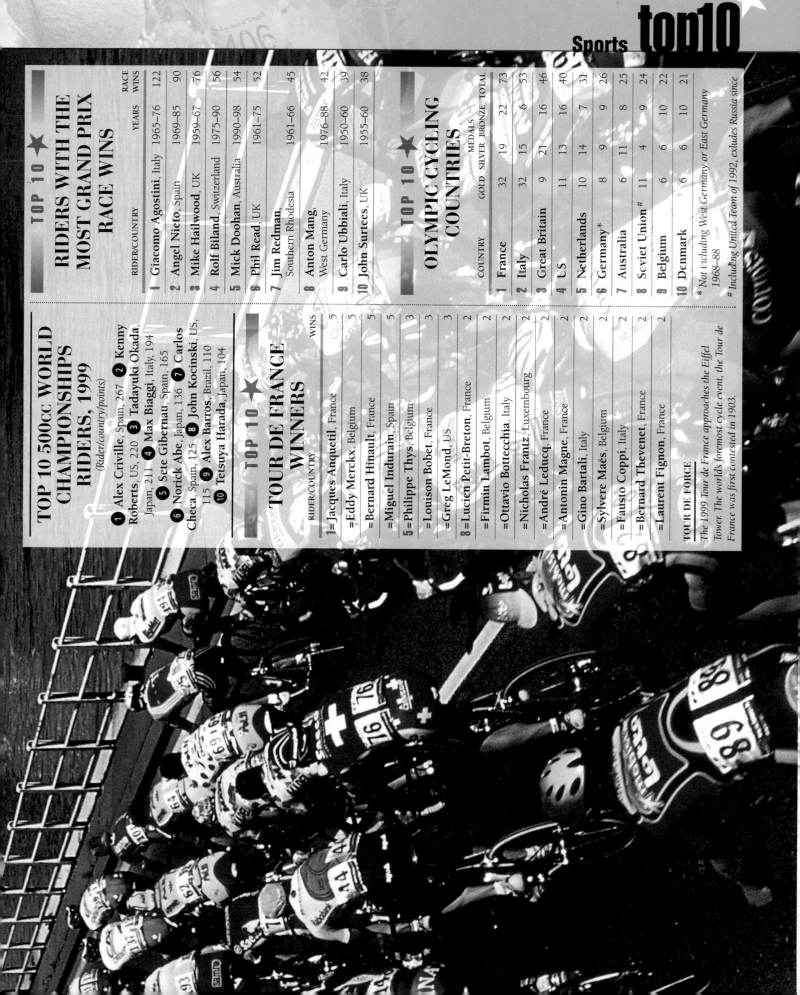

Golfing Greats

TOP 10 PLAYERS TO WIN THE MOST MAJORS IN A CAREER

	PLAYER/COUNTRY*	BRITISH OPEN	US OPEN	MASTERS	PGA	TOTAL
1	Jack Nicklaus	3	4	6	5	18
2	Walter Hagen	4	2	0	5	11
3 =	Ben Hogan	1	4	2	2	9
=	Gary Player, South Africa	3	1	3	2	9
5	Tom Watson	5	1	2	0	8
6 =	Harry Vardon, England	6	1	0	0	7
=	Gene Sarazen	1	2	1	3	7
=	Bobby Jones	3	4	0	0	7
=	Sam Snead	1	0	3	3	7
=	Arnold Palmer	2	1	4	0	7

From the US unless otherwise stated

TOP 10 ★ LOWEST FOUR-ROUND TOTALS IN THE BRITISH OPEN

	PLAYER/COUNTRY/VENUE	YEAR	TOTAL
1	Greg Norman, Australia, Sandwich	1993	267
2 =	Tom Watson, US, Turnberry	1977	268
=	Nick Price, Zimbabwe, Turnberry	1994	268
4 =	Jack Nicklaus, US, Turnberry	1977	269
=	Nick Faldo, England, Sandwich	1993	269
=	Jesper Parnevik, Sweden, Turnberry	1994	269
7 =	Nick Faldo, England, St. Andrews	1990	270
=	Bernhard Langer, Germany, Sandwich	1993	270
9 =	Tom Watson, US, Muirfield	1980	271
=	Fuzzy Zoeller, US, Turnberry	1994	271
=	Tom Lehman, US, Lytham	1996	271

TOP 10 ★ LOWEST WINNING SCORES IN THE US MASTERS

	PLAYER/COUNTRY*	YEAR	SCORE
1	Tiger Woods	1997	270
2 =	Jack Nicklaus	1965	271
=	Raymond Floyd	1976	271
4 =	Ben Hogan	1953	274
=	Ben Crenshaw	1995	274
6 =	Severiano Ballesteros, Spain	1980	275
=	Fred Couples	1992	275
8 =	Arnold Palmer	1964	276
=	Jack Nicklaus	1975	276
=	Tom Watson	1977	276
=	Nick Faldo, England	1996	276

From the US unless otherwise stated

The US Masters is the only major played on the same course each year, in Augusta, Georgia. The course was built on the site of an old nursery, and the abundance of flowers, shrubs, and plants is a reminder of its former days, with each of the holes named after the plants growing adjacent to it.

TOP 10 ★ WINNERS OF WOMEN'S MAJORS

	PLAYER*	TITLES
1	Patty Berg	16
2 =	Mickey Wright	13
=	Louise Suggs	13
4	Babe Zaharias	12
5	Betsy Rawis	8
6	JoAnne Carner	7
7 =	Kathy Whitworth	6
=	Pat Bradley	6
=	Julie Inkster	6
=	Glenna Collett Vare	6

All from the US

Women's majors once numbered six, but today consist of the US Open (first staged 1946), LPGA Championship (1955), Du Maurier Classic (1973; major status since 1979), and Dinah Shore Tournament (1972).

IRON LADY

US golfer Kathy Whitworth (b. 1939) scored a total of 88 tour wins, achieving victories in six majors, and was voted player of the year on seven occasions.

Did You Know? Mary, Queen of Scots (1542–87), is regarded as the first female golfer. In 1567, she was criticized for playing within two weeks of her husband Darnley's murder.

TOP 10 ★ LOWEST WINNING TOTALS IN THE US OPEN

PLAYER/COUNTRY*/VENUE		YEAR	SCORE
1 = **Jack Nicklaus**, Baltusrol		1980	272
= **Lee Janzen**, Baltusrol		1993	272
3 **David Graham**, Australia, Merion		1981	273
4 = **Jack Nicklaus**, Baltusrol		1967	275
= **Lee Trevino**, Oak Hill		1968	275
6 = **Ben Hogan**, Riviera		1948	276
= **Fuzzy Zoeller**, Winged Foot		1984	276
= **Ernie Els**, South Africa, Congressional		1997	276
9 = **Jerry Pate**, Atlanta		1976	277
= **Scott Simpson**, Olympic Club		1987	277

* From the US unless otherwise stated

TOP 10 ★ PLAYERS WITH THE MOST CAREER WINS ON THE US TOUR

PLAYER*	TOUR WINS
1 **Sam Snead**	81
2 **Jack Nicklaus**	71
3 **Ben Hogan**	63
4 **Arnold Palmer**	60
5 **Byron Nelson**	52
6 **Billy Casper**	51
7 = **Walter Hagen**	40
= **Cary Midlecoff**	40
9 **Gene Sarazen**	38
10 **Lloyd Mangrum**	36

* All from the US

For many years, Sam Snead's total of wins was held to be 84, but the PGA Tour amended his figure in 1990 after discrepancies had been found in their previous lists. They deducted 11 wins from his total, but added eight others that should have been included, giving a revised total of 81.

TOP 10 ★ MONEY-WINNING GOLFERS, 1999

PLAYER/COUNTRY*	WINNINGS ($)
1 **Tiger Woods**	6,981,836
2 **David Duval**	3,641,906
3 **Davis Love III**	2,475,328
4 **Vijay Singh**, Fiji	2,473,372
5 **Colin Montgomerie**, Scotland	2,281,884
6 **Ernie Els**, South Africa	2,151,574
7 **Chris Perry**	2,145,707
8 **Hal Sutton**	2,127,578
9 **Payne Stewart**	2,077,950
10 **Justin Leonard**	2,020,991

* From the US unless otherwise stated

This list is based on winnings of the world's five top tours: US PGA Tour, European PGA Tour, PGA Tour of Japan, Australasian PGA Tour, and FNB Tour of South Africa.

TOP 10 ★ GOLFERS TO PLAY MOST STROKES AT ONE HOLE*

PLAYER/COUNTRY#/YEAR/EVENT	STROKES
1 **Tommy Armour**, 1927, Shawnee Open	23
2 **Philippe Porquier**, France, 1978, French Open	21
3 **Ray Ainsley**, 1938, US Open	19
4 = **John Daly**, 1998, Bay Hill Invitational	18
= **Willie Chisolm**, 1919, US Open	18
6 = **Porky Oliver**, 1953, Bing Crosby	16
= **Ian Woosnam**, Wales, 1986, French Open	16
8 **Hermann Tissies**, Germany, 1950, British Open	15
9 = **Greg Norman**, Australia, 1982, Martini International	14
= **Orrin Vincent**, 1992, Austrian Open	14

* In a leading professional tournament
 # From the US unless otherwise stated

TOP 10 MONEY-WINNING GOLFERS OF ALL TIME

(Player/country/career winnings in $#)*

❶ **Greg Norman**, Australia, 12,507,322   ❷ **Davis Love III**, 12,487,463   ❸ **Payne Stewart**, 11,737,008   ❹ **Nick Price**, Zimbabwe, 11,386,236   ❺ **Tiger Woods**, 11,315,128   ❻ **Fred Couples**, 11,305,069   ❼ **Mark O'Meara**, 11,162,269   ❽ **Tom Kite**, 10,533,102   ❾ **Scott Hoch**, 10,308,995   ❿ **David Duval**, 10,047,947

* From the US unless otherwise stated   # As at December 6, 1999

DEATH OF A LEGEND

Payne Stewart (1957–99), one of the top professional golfers of the late 20th century, won 18 tournaments, including three major championships. In June 1999 he won his second US Open, by a single shot, with a 15-ft (4.57 m) putt. He was a leading money-winner and noted for his adherence to traditional golfing clothing of knickers and cap. On October 25, 1999, he was killed in a bizarre plane accident, when the Lear jet in which he was flying from Orlando, Florida, became depressurized and its pilots and passengers fell unconscious. The plane, shadowed by an F-16 fighter, flew on autopilot for some 1,400 miles (2,250 km) before crashing.

SNAP SHOTS

Background image: **THE CLUBHOUSE AT AUGUSTA, GEORGIA, US**

Horse Racing

MONEY-WINNING NORTH AMERICAN JOCKEYS IN A CAREER

JOCKEY	EARNINGS IN A CARER ($)
1 Chris McCarron	234,274,989
2 Pat Day	224,401,759
3 Laffit Pincay Jr.	207,472,414
4 Gary Stevens	187,176,371
5 Jerry Bailey	182,070,303
6 Eddie Delahoussaye	175,279,854
7 Angel Cordero Jr.	164,561,227
8 Jose Santos	134,527,287
9 Kent Desormeauc	128,148,779
10 Mike Smith	128,080,626

Source: *NTRA Communications*

US JOCKEYS WITH THE MOST WINS IN A CAREER

JOCKEY	YEARS RIDING	WINS
1 Laffit Pincay Jr.	36	8,851
2 Willie Shoemaker	42	8,833
3 Pat Day	27	7,625
4 David Gall	42	7,396
5 Angel Cordero Jr.	35	7,057
6 Chris McCarron	26	6,853
7 Russell Baze	26	6,822
8 Jorge Velasquez	35	6,795
9 Sandy Hawley	31	6,449
10 Larry Snyder	37	6,388

Source: *NTRA Communications*

JOCKEYS IN THE BREEDERS CUP

JOCKEY	YEARS	WINS
1 Pat Day	1984–99	11
2 =Mike Smith	1992–97	8
=Jerry Bailey	1991–99	8
4 =Eddie Delahoussaye	1984–93	7
=Laffit Pincay Jr.	1985–93	7
=Chris McCarron	1985–96	7
=Gary Stevens	1990–99	7
8 =Pat Valenzuela	1986–92	6
=Jose Santos	1986–97	6
10 Corey Nakatani	1996–99	5

Source: *The Breeders Cup*

Held at a different venue each year, the Breeders Cup is an end-of-season gathering with seven races run during the day, and with the season's best thoroughbreds competing in each category. Staged in October or November, there is $10 million prize money available, with $3 million going to the winner of the day's senior race, the Classic.

MONEY-WINNING HORSES ALL TIME

HORSE/STARTS/WINS	WINNINGS ($)
1 Cigar, 33, 19	9,999,815
2 Skip Away, 38, 18	9,616,360
3 Silver Charm, 24, 12	6,944,369
4 Alysheba, 26, 11	6,679,242
5 John Henry, 83, 39	6,597,947
6 Singspiel, 20, 9	5,950,217
7 Best Pal, 47, 18	5,668,245
8 Taiki Blizzard, 22, 6	5,544,484
9 Sunday Silence, 14, 9	4,968,554
10 Easy Goer, 20, 14	4,873,770

Source: *National Thoroughbred Racing Association*

OLYMPIC EQUESTRIAN COUNTRIES

COUNTRY	MEDALS			
	GOLD	SILVER	BRONZE	TOTAL
1 West Germany/ Germany	31	17	20	68
2 Sweden	17	8	14	39
3 US	8	17	13	38
4 France	11	12	11	34
5 Italy	7	9	7	23
6 Great Britain	5	7	9	21
7 Switzerland	4	9	7	20
8 =Holland	6	7	2	15
=USSR	6	5	4	15
10 Belgium	4	2	5	11

FASTEST WINNING TIMES OF THE KENTUCKY DERBY

HORSE	YEAR	TIME MINS	SECS
1 Secretariat	1973	1	59.2
2 Northern Dancer	1964	2	00.0
3 Spend A Buck	1985	2	00.2
4 Decidedly	1962	2	00.4
5 Proud Clarion	1967	2	00.6
6 Grindstone	1996	2	01.0
7 =Lucky Debonair	1965	2	01.2
=Affirmed	1978	2	01.2
=Thunder Gulch	1995	2	01.2
10 Whirlaway	1941	2	01.4

Source: *The Jockey Club*

The Kentucky Derby is held on the first Saturday in May at Churchill Downs, Louisville, Kentucky. The first leg of the Triple Crown, it was first raced in 1875 over a distance of 1 mile 4 furlongs, but after 1896 it was reduced to 1 mile 2 furlongs.

TOP 10 MONEY-WINNING HORSES, 1999

(Horse/winnings in $)

1 Almutawakel, 3,290,000　2 Cat Thief, 3,020,500　3 Daylami, 2,190,000
4 Charismatic, 2,007,404　5 Budroyale, 1,735,640　6 Behrens, 1,735,000
7 Beautiful Pleasure, 1,716,404　8 Silverbulletday, 1,707,640　9 Menifee, 1,695,400
10 General Pleasure, 1,658,100

Source: *National Thoroughbred Racing Association*

THE 10 LAST TRIPLE CROWN-WINNING HORSES*

(Horse/year)

1 Affirmed, 1978 **2** Seattle Slew, 1977
3 Secretariat, 1973 **4** Citation, 1948
5 Assault, 1946 **6** Count Fleet, 1943
7 Whirlaway, 1941 **8** War Admiral, 1937 **9** Omaha, 1935
10 Gallant Fox, 1930

* Horses that have won the Kentucky Derby, the Preakness Stakes, and the Belmont Stakes in the same season

---

TOP 10 ★
STEEPLECHASE TRAINERS IN NORTH AMERICA

	TRAINER	WINNINGS ($)	WINS
1	Jonathan Sheppard	866,389	26
2	Jack Fisher	509,695	19
3	Bruce Miller	539,946	14
4	Tom Voss	240,978	12
5	Sanna Neilson	306,220	11
6 =	Janet Elliot	382,720	10
=	Charlie Fenwick	225,453	10
8 =	Ricky Hendriks	117,990	9
=	Neil Morris	114,250	9
10	Toby Edwards	111,540	6

Source: Steeplechase Times/*National Steeplechase Association*

TOP 10 JOCKEYS IN THE PRIX DE L'ARC DE TRIOMPHE

(Jockey/wins)

1 = Jacko Doyasbère, 4; = Pat Eddery, 4;
= Freddy Head, 4; = Yves Saint-Martin, 4
5 = Enrico Camici, 3; = Charlie Elliott, 3; = Olivier Peslier, 3;
= Lester Piggot, 3; = Roger Poincelet, 3; = Charles Semblat, 3

TOP 10 ★
JOCKEYS IN THE TRIPLE CROWN RACES

	JOCKEY	KENTUCKY	PREAKNESS	BELMONT	TOTAL
1	Eddie Arcaro	5	6	6	17
2	Bill Shoemaker	4	2	5	11
3 =	Bill Hartack	5	3	1	9
=	Earle Sande	3	1	5	9
5 =	Pat Day	1	5	2	8
=	Jimmy McLaughlin	1	1	6	8
7 =	Angel Cordero Jr.	3	2	1	6
=	Chas Kurtsinger	2	2	2	6
=	Ron Turcotte	2	2	2	6
=	Gary Stevens	3	1	2	6

The US Triple Crown consists of the Kentucky Derby, the Preakness Stakes, and the Belmont Stakes. Since 1875, only 11 horses have won all three races in one season. The only jockey to complete the Triple Crown twice is Eddie Arcaro, on Whirlaway in 1941 and Citation in 1948.

TOP 10 ★
MONEY-WINNING TROTTERS IN A HARNESS-RACING CAREER*

	HORSE	WINNINGS ($)
1	Moni Maker	4,175,503
2	Peace Corps	4,137,737
3	Ourasi	4,010,105
4	Mack Lobell	3,917,594
5	Reve d'Udon	3,611,351
6	Zoogin	3,428,311
7	Sea Cove	3,138,986
8	Ina Scot	2,897,044
9	Ideal du Gazeau	2,744,777
10	Vrai Lutin	2,612,429

* A trotter is a horse whose diagonally opposite legs move forward together.

Harness racing is one of the oldest sports in the US; its origins go back to the Colonial period, when many races were held along the turnpikes of New York and the New England colonies. After growing in popularity in the nineteenth century, the exotically titled governing body, the National Association for the Promotion of the Interests of the Trotting Turf (now the National Trotting Association), was founded in 1870.

TOP 10 ★
MONEY-WINNING PACERS IN A HARNESS-RACING CAREER*

	HORSE	WINNINGS ($)
1	Nihilator	3,225,653
2	Artsplace	3,085,083
3	Presidential Ball	3,021,363
4	Matt's Scooter	2,944,591
5	On the Road Again	2,819,102
6	Riyadh	2,793,527
7	Beach Towel	2,570,357
8	Western Hanover	2,541,647
9	Cam's Card Shark	2,498,204
10	Pacific Rocket	2,333,401

* A pacer's legs are extended laterally and with a "swinging motion"; pacers usually travel faster than trotters.

Unlike thoroughbred racehorses, standardbred harness-racing horses are trained to trot and pace, but do not gallop. While widespread in the United States, harness racing is also popular in Australia and New Zealand, and, increasingly, elsewhere in the globe.

Which sport was originally called "sphairistike"?

see p.271 for the answer

A Lawn tennis
B Polo
C Croquet

Hockey Headlines

GOAL SCORERS
IN AN NHL SEASON

	PLAYER/TEAM	SEASON	GOALS
1	**Wayne Gretzky**, Edmonton Oilers	1981–82	92
2	**Wayne Gretzky**, Edmonton Oilers	1983–84	87
3	**Brett Hull**, St. Louis Blues	1990–91	86
4	**Mario Lemieux**, Pittsburgh Penguins	1988–89	85
5	=**Phil Esposito**, Boston Bruins	1970–71	76
	=**Alexander Mogilny**, Buffalo Sabres	1992–93	76
	=**Teemu Selanne**, Winnipeg Jets	1992–93	76
8	**Wayne Gretzky**, Edmonton Oilers	1984–85	73
9	**Brett Hull**, St. Louis Blues	1989–90	72
10	=**Wayne Gretzky**, Edmonton Oilers	1982–83	71
	=**Jari Kurri**, Edmonton Oilers	1984–85	71

TOP 10 ★

BIGGEST NHL ARENAS

	STADIUM/LOCATION	HOME TEAM	CAPACITY
1	**Molson Center**, Montreal	Montreal Canadiens	21,273
2	=**United Center**, Chicago	Chicago Blackhawks	20,500
	=**Raleigh Entertainment & Sports Arena**, Raleigh	Carolina Hurricanes	20,500
4	=**Canadian Airlines Saddledrome**, Calgary	Calgary Flames	20,000
	=**Staples Center**, Los Angeles	Los Angeles Kings	20,000
6	**Joe Louis Arena**, Detroit	Detroit Red Wings	19,983
7	**MCI Center**, Washington	Washington Capitals	19,740
8	**First Union Center**, Philadelphia	Philadelphia Flyers	19,511
9	**Ice Palace**, Tampa	Tampa Bay Lightning	19,500
10	**Kiel Center**, St. Louis	St. Louis Blues	19,260

TOP 10 TEAM SALARIES
IN THE NHL, 1999–2000

(Team/salary in $)

1 **New York Rangers**, 64,509,011 2 **Philadelphia Flyers**, 52,233,976 3 **Detroit Red Wings**, 48,545,849 4 **Dallas Stars**, 43,659,500 5 **Colorado Avalanche**, 41,130,000 6 **Florida Panthers**, 41,032,423 7 **Chicago Blackhawks**, 39,999,500 8 **St. Louis Blues**, 39,032,072 9 **San Jose Sharks**, 38,276,806 10 **Los Angeles Kings**, 36,958,000

Source: *National Hockey League Players Association*

TOP 10 GOAL SCORERS
IN 1998-99

(Player/team/goals)

1 **Teemu Selanne**, Mighty Ducks of Anaheim, 47 2 = **Jaromir Jagr**, Pittsburgh Penguins, 44; = **Alexei Yashin**, Ottawa Senators, 44; = **Tony Amonte**, Chicago Blackhawks, 44 5 **John LeClair**, Philadelphia Flyers, 43 6 **Joe Sakic**, Colorado Avalanche, 41 7 = **Eric Lindros**, Philadelphia Flyers, 40; = **Theoren Fleury**, Colorado Avalanche, 40; = **Miroslave Satan**, Buffalo Sabres, 40 10 = **Paul Kariya**, Mighty Ducks of Anaheim, 39; = **Luc Robitaille**, Los Angeles Kings, 39

Source: *National Hockey League*

TOP 10 ★

GOAL TENDERS IN AN NHL CAREER*

	PLAYER	SEASONS	GAMES WON
1	**Terry Sawchuk**	21	447
2	**Jacques Plante**	18	434
3	**Tony Esposito**	16	423
4	**Patrick Roy** #	14	412
5	**Glenn Hall**	18	407
6	**Grant Fuhr** #	18	398
7	**Andy Moog**	18	372
8	**Rogie Vachon**	16	355
9	**Mike Vernon** #	16	347
10	**Tom Barrasso** #	16	345

* Regular season only　　*# Still active at start of 1999–2000 season*

TOP 10 ★

BEST-PAID PLAYERS IN THE NHL,
1999-2000

	PLAYER	TEAM	SALARY ($)
1	**Jaromir Jagr**	Pittsburgh Penguins	10,359,852
2	**Paul Kariya**	Anaheim Mighty Ducks	10,000,000
3	**Peter Forsberg**	Colorado Avalanche	9,000,000
4	=**Theoren Fleury**	New York Rangers	8,500,000
	=**Eric Lindros**	Philadelphia Flyers	8,500,000
6	**Pavel Bure**	Florida Panthers	8,000,000
7	**Patrick Roy**	Colorado Avalanche	7,500,000
8	=**Dominik Hasek**	Buffalo Sabres	7,000,000
	=**Mats Sundin**	Toronto Maple Leafs	7,000,000
10	**Brian Leetch**	New York Rangers	6,680,000

Source: *National Hockey League Players Association*

TOP 10 ★
WINNERS OF THE HART TROPHY

	PLAYER	YEARS	WINS
1	Wayne Gretzky	1980–89	9
2	Gordie Howe	1952–63	6
3	Eddie Shore	1933–38	4
4=	Bobby Clarke	1973–76	3
=	Howie Morenz	1928–32	3
=	Bobby Orr	1970–72	3
=	Mario Lemieux	1988–96	3
8=	Jean Beliveau	1956–64	2
=	Bill Cowley	1941–43	2
=	Phil Esposito	1969–74	2
=	Dominic Hasek	1997-98	2
=	Bobby Hull	1965–66	2
=	Guy Lafleur	1977–78	2
=	Mark Messier	1990–92	2
=	Stan Mikita	1967–68	2
=	Nels Stewart	1926–30	2

Source: *National Hockey League*

The Hart Trophy, named after Cecil Hart, former manager/coach of the Montreal Canadiens, has been awarded annually since 1924 to the player considered the most valuable to his team.

TOP 10 ★
TEAMS WITH THE MOST STANLEY CUP WINS

	TEAM	WINS
1	Montreal Canadiens	23
2	Toronto Maple Leafs	13
3	Detroit Red Wings	9
4=	Boston Bruins	5
=	Edmonton Oilers	5
6=	New York Islanders	4
=	New York Rangers	4
=	Ottawa Senators	4
9	Chicago Black Hawks	3
10=	Philadelphia Flyers	2
=	Pittsburgh Penguins	2
=	Montreal Maroons	2

Source: *National Hockey League*

During his time as Governor General of Canada from 1888 to 1893, Sir Frederick Arthur Stanley (Lord Stanley of Preston and 16th Earl of Derby) became interested in ice hockey, and in 1893 presented a trophy to be contested by the best amateur teams in Canada. The first trophy went to the Montreal Amateur Athletic Association, who won it without a challenge from any other team.

TOP 10 ★
POINT SCORERS IN STANLEY CUP PLAY-OFF MATCHES

	PLAYER	TOTAL POINTS
1	Wayne Gretzky	382
2	Mark Messier*	295
3	Jari Kurri	233
4	Glenn Anderson	214
5	Paul Coffey*	196
6	Bryan Trottier	184
7	Jean Beliveau	176
8	Denis Savard	175
9	Doug Gilmour*	171
10	Denis Potvin	164

* Still active at start of 1999–2000 season

In his 20 playing seasons, Wayne Gretzky, who heads virtually every ice hockey league table, achieved some 61 NHL records, leading Edmonton to four Stanley Cups (1984–85 and 1987–88). In addition to scoring the most points, he leads for most goals and most assists in Stanley Cup matches. The Stanley Cup itself is a silver bowl. Each winning team has its club name and year engraved on a silver ring that is fitted to the Cup, and is obliged to return it in good condition.

TOP 10 ★
GOAL SCORERS IN AN NHL CAREER*

	PLAYER	SEASONS	GOALS
1	Wayne Gretzky	20	894
2	Gordie Howe	26	801
3	Marcel Dionne	18	731
4	Phil Esposito	18	717
5	Mike Gartner	19	708
6	Mario Lemieux	12	613
7=	Bobby Hull	16	610
=	Mark Messier#	20	610
9	Dino Ciccarelli	19	608
10	Jari Kurri	17	601

* Regular season only

Still active at start of 1999–2000 season

TOP 10 ★
NHL GAMES TO PRODUCE THE MOST GOALS

	GAME	SCORE	DATE	TOTAL GOALS
1=	Montreal Canadiens v Toronto St. Patricks	14—7	Jan 10, 1920	21
=	Edmonton Oilers v Chicago Black Hawks	12—9	Dec 11, 1985	21
3=	Edmonton Oilers v Minnesota North Stars	12—8	Jan 4, 1984	20
=	Toronto Maple Leafs v Edmonton Oilers	11—9	Jan 8, 1986	20
5=	Montreal Wanderers v Toronto Arenas	10—9	Dec 19, 1917	19
=	Montreal Canadiens v Quebec Bulldogs	16—3	Mar 3, 1920	19
=	Montreal Canadiens v Hamilton Tigers	13—3	Feb 26, 1921	19
=	Boston Bruins v New York Rangers	10—9	Mar 4, 1944	19
=	Boston Bruins v Detroit Red Wings	10—9	Mar 16, 1944	19
=	Vancouver Canucks v Minnesota North Stars	10—9	Oct 7, 1983	19

What were once used as targets in Olympic archery events?
see p.273 for the answer

A Rabbits
B Birds
C Goats

Tennis Triumphs

MEN WITH THE MOST WIMBLEDON TITLES

	PLAYER/COUNTRY	YEARS	TITLES S	D	M	TOTAL
1	William Renshaw, UK	1880–89	7	7	0	14
2	Lawrence Doherty, UK	1897–1905	5	8	0	13
3	Reginald Doherty, UK	1897–1905	4	8	0	12
4	John Newcombe, Australia	1965–74	3	6	0	9
5=	Ernest Renshaw, UK	1880–89	1	7	0	8
=	Tony Wilding, New Zealand	1907–14	4	4	0	8
7=	Wilfred Baddeley, UK	1891–96	3	4	0	7
=	Bob Hewitt, Australia/S. Africa	1962–79	0	5	2	7
=	Rod Laver, Australia	1959–69	4	1	2	7
=	John McEnroe, US	1979–84	3	4	0	7

S – singles; D – doubles; M – mixed

TOP 10 TOURNAMENT WINNERS, MALE*
(Player/country/tournament wins)

1 Jimmy Connors, US, 109 **2** Ivan Lendl, Czechoslovakia, 94 **3** John McEnroe, US, 77 **4** = Bjorn Borg, Sweden, 62; = Guillermo Vilas, Argentina, 62 **6** Ilie Nastase, Romania, 57 **7** Pete Sampras, US, 56 **8** Boris Becker, Germany, 49 **9** Rod Laver, Australia, 47 **10** Thomas Muster, Austria, 44

* Tournament leaders since Open Tennis introduced in 1968. Totals include ATP tour, Grand Prix, and WCT tournaments.

WINNERS OF MEN'S GRAND SLAM SINGLES TITLES

	PLAYER/COUNTRY	TITLES A	F	W	US	TOTAL
1	Roy Emerson, Australia	6	2	2	2	12
2=	Björn Borg, Sweden	0	6	5	0	11
=	Rod Laver, Australia	3	2	4	2	11
=	Pete Sampras, US	2	0	5	4	11
5	Bill Tilden, US	0	0	3	7	10
6=	Jimmy Connors, US	1	0	2	5	8
=	Ivan Lendl, Czechoslovakia	2	3	0	3	8
=	Fred Perry, UK	1	1	3	3	8
=	Ken Rosewall, Australia	4	2	0	2	8
10=	Henri Cochet, France	0	4	2	1	7
=	René Lacoste, France	0	3	2	2	7
=	William Larned, US	0	0	0	7	7
=	John McEnroe, US	0	0	3	4	7
=	John Newcombe, Australia	2	0	3	2	7
=	William Renshaw, UK	0	0	7	0	7
=	Richard Sears, US	0	0	0	7	7
=	Mats Wilander, Sweden	3	3	0	1	7

A – Australian Open; F – French Open; W – Wimbledon; US – US Open

THE 10 LAST WINNERS OF THE US OPEN MEN'S CHAMPIONSHIP
(Year/winner/country)

1 1999, Andre Agassi, US **2** 1998, Patrick Rafter, Australia **3** 1997, Patrick Rafter, Australia **4** 1996, Pete Sampras, US **5** 1995, Pete Sampras, US **6** 1994, Andre Agassi, US **7** 1993, Pete Sampras, US **8** 1992, Stefan Edberg, Sweden **9** 1991, Stefan Edberg, Sweden **10** 1990, Pete Sampras, US

TOP 10 MALE PLAYERS*
(Player/country/weeks at No. 1)

1 Pete Sampras, US, 276 **2** Ivan Lendl, Czechoslovakia, 270 **3** Jimmy Connors, US, 268 **4** John McEnroe, US, 170 **5** Bjorn Borg, Sweden, 109 **6** Stefan Edberg, Sweden, 72 **7** Jim Courier, US, 58 **8** Andre Agassi, US, 47 **9** Ilie Nastase, Romania, 40 **10** Mats Wilander, Sweden, 20

* Based on weeks at No. 1 in ATP rankings (1973 to 1999)

TOP 10 ★
WINNERS OF WOMEN'S GRAND SLAM SINGLES TITLES

PLAYER/COUNTRY	TITLES				
	A	F	W	US	TOTAL
1 **Margaret Court**, Australia	11	5	3	5	24
2 **Steffi Graf**, Germany	4	5	7	5	21
3 **Helen Wills-Moody**, US	0	4	8	7	19
4 = **Chris Evert-Lloyd**, US	2	7	3	6	18
= **Martina Navratilova**, US	3	2	9	4	18
6 = **Billie Jean King**, US	1	1	6	4	12
= **Suzanne Lenglen**, France	0	6	6	0	12
8 = **Maureen Connolly**, US	1	2	3	3	9
= **Monica Seles**, US	4	3	0	2	9
10 **Molla Mallory**, US	0	0	0	8	8

A – Australian Open; F – French Open; W – Wimbledon; US – US Open

TOP 10 ★
TOURNAMENT WINNERS, FEMALE*

PLAYER/COUNTRY	TOURNAMENT WINS
1 **Martina Navratilova**, US	167
2 **Chris Evert-Lloyd**, US	154
3 **Steffi Graf**, Germany	106
4 **Margaret Court**, Australia	92
5 **Billie Jean King**, US	67
6 **Evonne Goolagong Cawley**, Australia	65
7 **Virginia Wade**, UK	55
8 **Monica Seles**, US	43
9 **Conchita Martinez**, Spain	30
10 **Tracy Austin**, US	29

* Tournament leaders since Open Tennis introduced in 1968

TOP 10 ★
DAVIS CUP WINNING TEAMS

COUNTRY	WINS
1 United States	31
2 Australia	21
3 France	8
4 Sweden	7
5 Australasia	6
6 British Isles	5
7 Great Britain	4
8 West Germany	2
9 = Germany	1
= Czechoslovakia	1
= Italy	1
= South Africa	1

South Africa's sole win was gained when, for political reasons, India refused to meet them in the 1974 final.

BRILLIANT CAREER

In 1995, Andre Agassi was the 12th player to be ranked world No. 1. In 1999, he became only the fifth male player to complete a Grand Slam.

TOP 10 CAREER MONEY-WINNING WOMEN*

(Player/country/winnings in $)

1 Steffi Graf, Germany, 20,646,410 **2** Martina Navratilova, US, 20,344,061 **3** Arantxa Sanchez-Vicario, Spain, 14,119,642 **4** Monica Seles, US, 10,928,640 **5** Jana Novotna, Czech Republic, 10,507,680 **6** Chris Evert-Lloyd, US, 8,896,195 **7** Gabriela Sabatini, Argentina, 8,785,850 **8** Martina Hingis, Switzerland, 8,331,496 **9** Conchita Martinez, Spain, 7,780,941 **10** Natasha Zvereva, Belarus, 7,036,143

* To end of 1999 season

GOLDEN GIRL

German-born Steffi Graf was one of the youngest players ever ranked, aged just 13 in 1982. As her career progressed, she was first ranked No. 1 in 1987, and held the No. 1 ranking for a record 374 weeks. Aged just 19 in 1988, she became the youngest-ever winner of the Grand Slam, and also won Olympic gold at Seoul. She continued to win at least one Grand Slam title a year for the next 10 years, until knee injuries prevented her from competing. In 1999, after winning her sixth French Open championship, and her 22nd Grand Slam title, Steffi Graf announced her decision to retire. In 2000, her romantic involvement with Andre Agassi made press headlines.

SNAP SHOTS ★

Did You Know? Lawn tennis was patented in 1874 by Major Walter Clopton Wingfield, who originally called it "sphairistike" (from *sphaira*, Greek for ball).

Team Games

WINNERS OF THE TABLE TENNIS WORLD CHAMPIONSHIP

	COUNTRY	MEN'S	WOMEN'S	TOTAL
1	China	13	13	26
2	Japan	7	8	15
3	Hungary	12	–	12
4	Czechoslovakia	6	3	9
5	Romania	–	5	5
6	Sweden	4	–	4
7	=England	1	2	3
	=US	1	2	3
9	Germany	–	2	2
10	=Austria	1	–	1
	=North Korea	–	1	1
	=South Korea	–	1	1
	=USSR	–	1	1

Originally a European event, it was later extended to a world championship.

TOP 10 POLO TEAMS WITH THE MOST BRITISH OPEN CHAMPIONSHIP WINS

(Team/wins)

1 = Stowell Park, 5; = Tramontana, 5
3 = Ellerston, 3; = Cowdray Park, 3;
= Pimms, 3; = Windsor Park, 3
7 = Casarejo, 2; = Jersey Lillies, 2;
= Woolmer's Park, 2; = Falcons, 2;
= Southfield, 2

TOP 10 COUNTIES WITH THE MOST WINS IN THE ALL-IRELAND HURLING CHAMPIONSHIPS

(County/wins)

1 Cork, 28 **2** Kilkenny, 25
3 Tipperary, 24 **4** Limerick, 7
5 = Dublin, 6; = Wexford, 6
7 = Galway, 4; = Offaly, 4 **9** Clare, 3
10 Waterford, 2

EYE ON THE BALL

Table tennis is believed to have originated in England in the 1880s, with cigar box lids used as paddles and books as nets. Now a world sport, it is dominated by Chinese players like Song Ding, 1997 World Champion.

LAST WINNERS OF THE ROLLER HOCKEY WORLD CHAMPIONSHIP

YEAR	WINNER
1999	Argentina
1997	Italy
1995	Argentina
1993	Portugal
1991	Portugal
1989	Spain
1988	Spain
1986	Spain
1984	Argentina
1982	Portugal

Roller hockey, a five-a-side game formerly called rink hockey, has been played for more than 100 years. The first international tournament was held in Paris in 1910, the first European Championships in Britain in 1926, and the men's World Championship biennially since 1936 (odd-numbered years since 1989). Portugal is the overall winner, with 14 titles to its credit.

OLYMPIC FIELD HOCKEY COUNTRIES

COUNTRY	GOLD	MEDALS SILVER	BRONZE	TOTAL
1 India	8	1	2	11
2 Great Britain*	3	2	5	10
3 Netherlands	2	2	5	9
4 Pakistan	3	3	2	8
5 Australia	2	3	2	7
6 Germany #	1	2	2	5
7 =Spain	1	2	1	4
=West Germany	1	3	–	4
9 =South Korea	–	2	–	2
=US	–	–	2	2
=Soviet Union	–	–	2	2

* Including England, Ireland, Scotland, and Wales, which competed separately in the 1908 Olympics

Not including West Germany or East Germany 1968–88

OLYMPIC ARCHERY COUNTRIES

COUNTRY	GOLD	MEDALS SILVER	BRONZE	TOTAL
1 US	13	7	7	27
2 France	6	10	6	22
3 South Korea	10	6	3	19
4 Soviet Union	1	3	5	9
5 Great Britain	2	2	4	8
6 Finland	1	1	2	4
7 =China	0	3	0	3
=Italy	0	0	3	3
9 =Sweden	0	2	0	2
=Japan	0	1	1	2
=Poland	0	1	1	2

Archery was introduced as an Olympic sport at the second modern Olympics, held in Paris in 1900. The format has changed considerably over succeeding Games, with events such as shooting live birds being discontinued in favor of target shooting. Individual and team events for men and women are now included in the program.

OLYMPIC VOLLEYBALL COUNTRIES

COUNTRY	GOLD	MEDALS SILVER	BRONZE	TOTAL
1 Soviet Union*	7	5	1	13
2 Japan	3	3	2	8
3 US	2	1	2	5
4 =Cuba	2	–	1	3
=Brazil	1	1	1	3
=China	1	1	1	3
=Poland	1	–	2	3
8 =Netherlands	1	1	–	2
=East Germany	–	2	–	2
=Bulgaria	–	1	1	2
=Czechoslovakia	–	1	1	2
=Italy	–	1	1	2

* Includes United Team of 1992; excludes Russia since this date

UP AND OVER DOWN UNDER

Matther Allan (Carlton) and Steven King (Geelong) battle for possession in an Australian football match.

TOP 10 AUSTRALIAN FOOTBALL LEAGUE TEAMS

(Team/Grand Final wins)

1 Carlton Blues, 16 **2** Essendon Bombers, 15 **3** Collingwood Magpies, 14 **4** Melbourne Demons, 12 **5** Richmond Tigers, 10 **6** Hawthorn Hawks, 9 **7** Fitzroy Lions, 8 **8** Geelong Cats, 6 **9** Kangaroos (North Melbourne), 4 **10** South Melbourne, 3

OLYMPIC SHOOTING COUNTRIES

COUNTRY	GOLD	MEDALS SILVER	BRONZE	TOTAL
1 US	45	26	21	92
2 Soviet Union	22	17	81	57
3 Sweden	13	23	19	55
4 Great Britain	13	14	18	45
5 France	13	16	13	42
6 Norway	16	9	11	36
7 Switzerland	11	11	12	34
8 Italy	8	5	10	23
9 Greece	5	7	7	19
10 =China	7	5	5	17
=Finland	3	5	9	17

Did You Know? At the 1932 Los Angeles Olympics, India's field hockey team beat the US by a record 24–1 (with 12 of the goals scored by one player, Roop Singh), and Japan by 11–1.

Water Sports

TOP 10 ★
WINNERS OF MEN'S WORLD WATER-SKIING TITLES

SKIER/COUNTRY	OVERALL	SLALOM	TRICKS	JUMP	TOTAL
1 Patrice Martin, France	6	0	4	0	10
2 Sammy Duvall, US	4	0	0	2	6
3 =Alfredo Mendoza, US	2	1	0	2	5
=Mike Suyderhoud, US	2	1	0	2	5
=Bob La Point, US	0	4	1	0	5
=Andy Mapple, UK	0	5	0	0	5
7 =George Athans, Canada	2	1	0	0	3
=Guy de Clercq, Belgium	1	0	0	2	3
=Wayne Grimditch, US	0	0	2	1	3
=Mike Hazelwood, UK	1	0	0	2	3
=Ricky McCormick, US	0	0	1	2	3
=Billy Spencer, US	1	1	1	0	3

TOP 10 ★
WINNERS OF WOMEN'S WORLD WATER-SKIING TITLES

SKIER/COUNTRY	OVERALL	SLALOM	TRICKS	JUMP	TOTAL
1 Liz Shetter, US	3	3	1	4	11
2 Willa McGuire, US	3	2	1	2	8
3 Cindy Todd, US	2	3	0	2	7
4 Deena Mapple, US	2	0	0	4	6
5 =Marina Doria, Switzerland	1	1	2	0	4
=Tawn Hahn, US	0	0	4	0	4
=Helena Kjellander, Sweden	0	4	0	0	4
=Natalya Ponomaryeva, USSR	1	0	3	0	4
9 =Maria Victoria Carrasco, Venezuela	0	0	3	0	3
=Yelena Milakova, Russia	2	0	0	1	3

TOP 10 POWERBOAT DRIVERS WITH MOST RACE WINS
(Owner/country/wins)

1 **Bill Seebold**, US, 912 2 **Jumbo McConnell**, US, 217 3 **Chip Hanuer**, US, 203 4 **Steve Curtis**, UK, 184 5 **Mikeal Frode**, Sweden, 152 6 **Neil Holmes**, UK, 147 7 **Peter Bloomfield**, UK, 126 8 **Renato Molinari**, Italy, 113 9 **Cees Van der Valden**, Netherlands, 98 10 **Bill Muney**, US, 96

Source: Raceboat International

TOP 10 COLLEGES IN THE INTERCOLLEGIATE ROWING ASSOCIATION REGATTA*
(College/first and last winning years/wins)

1 **Cornell**, 1896–1982, 24 2 **Navy**, 1921–84, 13 3 = **Washington**, 1923–97, 11; = **California**, 1928–99, 11 5 **Pennsylvania**, 1898–1989, 9 6 = **Wisconsin**, 1951–90, 7; = **Brown**, 1979–95, 7 8 **Syracuse**, 1904–78, 6 9 **Columbia**, 1895–1929, 4 10 **Princeton**, 1985–98, 3 * Men's varsity eight-oared shells event

TOP 10 ★
OLYMPIC YACHTING COUNTRIES

COUNTRY	MEDALS			
	GOLD	SILVER	BRONZE	TOTAL
1 US	16	19	16	51
2 Great Britain	14	12	9	35
3 Sweden	9	12	9	30
4 Norway	16	11	2	29
5 France	12	6	9	27
6 Denmark	10	8	4	22
7 Germany/West Germany	6	5	6	17
8 Netherlands	4	5	6	15
9 New Zealand	6	4	3	13
10 =Australia	3	2	7	12
=Soviet Union*	4	5	3	12
=Spain	9	2	1	12

* Includes United Team of 1992; excludes Russia since this date

TOP 10 ★
OLYMPIC ROWING COUNTRIES

COUNTRY	MEDALS			
	GOLD	SILVER	BRONZE	TOTAL
1 US	29	28	19	76
2 East Germany	33	7	8	48
3 Soviet Union*	12	20	11	43
4 Germany#	19	12	11	42
5 Great Britain	19	15	7	41
6 =Italy	12	11	9	32
=Canada	8	12	12	32
8 France	4	14	12	30
9 Romania	12	10	7	29
10 Switzerland	6	7	9	22

* Includes United Team of 1992; excludes Russia since this date

Not including West Germany or East Germany 1968–88

Did You Know? John B. Kelly (1891–1960), father of actress Grace Kelly, later Princess Grace of Monaco, won three rowing gold medals at the 1920 and 1924 Olympics.

TOP 10 ★

OLYMPIC SWIMMING COUNTRIES

COUNTRY	MEDALS			
	GOLD	SILVER	BRONZE	TOTAL
1 US	230	176	137	543
2 Australia	41	37	47	125
3 East Germany	40	34	25	99
4 Soviet Union*	24	32	38	94
5 Germany#	19	33	34	86
6 =Great Britain	18	23	30	71
=Hungary	29	23	19	71
8 Sweden	13	21	21	55
9 Japan	15	18	19	52
10 Canada	11	17	20	48

* *Includes United Team of 1992; excludes Russia since this date*

Not including West Germany or East Germany 1968–88

The medal table includes medals for the synchronized swimming, diving, and water polo events that form part of the Olympic swimming program. Swimming has been part of the Olympics since the first modern games in 1896, at which only members of the Greek navy were eligible for one event – the 100-m (328-ft) swimming race for sailors. Events were held in the open water until 1908, when specially built pools were introduced.

TOP 10 ★

OLYMPIC CANOEING COUNTRIES

COUNTRY	MEDALS			
	GOLD	SILVER	BRONZE	TOTAL
1 =Hungary	10	23	20	53
=Soviet Union*	30	13	10	53
3 Germany#	18	15	12	45
4 Romania	9	10	12	31
5 East Germany	14	7	9	30
6 Sweden	14	10	4	28
7 France	2	6	14	22
8 =Bulgaria	4	3	8	15
=US	5	4	6	15
10 Canada	3	7	4	14

* *Includes United Team of 1992; excludes Russia since this date*

Not including West Germany or East Germany 1968–88

PADDLE POWER

Canoeing has been an Olympic sport since 1936. Six of Sweden's golds were won by one contestant, Gert Fredriksson, who also gained a silver and a bronze, in Games from 1948–60.

Winter Sports

SWISS ROLL
The bobsled event has been part of the Winter Olympics since 1924. Switzerland has won more medals than any other country.

MEN'S WORLD AND OLYMPIC FIGURE SKATING TITLES

	SKATER/COUNTRY	YEARS	TITLES
1	**Ulrich Salchow**, Sweden	1901–11	11
2	**Karl Schäfer**, Austria	1930–36	9
3	**Richard Button**, US	1948–52	7
4	**Gillis Grafstrom**, Sweden	1920–29	6
5=	**Hayes Jenkins**, US	1953–56	5
=	**Scott Hamilton**, US	1981–84	5
7=	**Willy Bockl**, Austria	1925–28	4
=	**David Jenkins**, US	1957–60	4
=	**Ondrej Nepela**, Czechoslovakia	1971–73	4
=	**Kurt Browning**, Canada	1989–93	4

TOP 10 OLYMPIC BOBSLEDDING COUNTRIES

(Country/medals)

1 Switzerland, 26 **2** US, 14 **3** East Germany, 13
4 = Germany*, 11; = Italy, 11 **6** West Germany, 6 **7** UK, 4
8 = Austria, 3; = Soviet Union#, 3 **10** = Canada, 2; = Belgium, 2

* Not including West or East Germany 1968–88
 # Includes United Team of 1992; excludes Russia since then

TOP 10 ★
SKIERS WITH THE MOST ALPINE SKIING WORLD CUP TITLES (MALE)

	SKIER/COUNTRY	YEARS	TOTAL
1	**Ingemar Stenmark**, Sweden	1976–84	18
2	**Pirmin Zurbriggen**, Switzerland	1984–90	15
3	**Marc Girardelli**, Luxembourg	1984–94	11
4=	**Gustavo Thoeni**, Italy	1971–74	9
=	**Alberto Tomba**, Italy	1988–95	9
6	**Hermann Maier**, Austria	1998–2000	8
7=	**Jean-Claude Killy**, France	1967–68	6
=	**Phil Mahre**, US	1981–83	6
9=	**Luc Alphand**, France	1997	5
=	**Franz Klammer**, Austria	1975–83	5

TOP 10 ★
SKIERS WITH THE MOST ALPINE SKIING WORLD CUP TITLES (FEMALE)

	SKIER/COUNTRY	YEARS	TOTAL
1	**Annemarie Moser-Pröll**, Austria	1971–79	16
2	**Vreni Schneider**, Switzerland	1986–95	14
3	**Katia Seizinger**, Germany	1992–98	11
4	**Erika Hess**, Switzerland	1981–84	8
5	**Michela Figini**, Switzerland	1985–89	7
6	**Lise-Marie Morerod**, Switzerland	1975–78	6
7=	**Maria Walliser**, Switzerland	1986–87	5
=	**Hanni Wenzel**, Liechtenstein	1974–80	5
9=	**Renate Goetschl**, Germany	1997–2000	4
=	**Nancy Greene**, Canada	1967–68	4
=	**Petra Kronberger**, Austria	1990–92	4
=	**Tamara McKinney**, USA	1981–84	4
=	**Carole Merle**, France	1989–92	4

The Alpine Skiing World Cup was launched as an annual event in 1967, with the addition of the super-giant slalom in 1986. Points are awarded for performances over a series of selected races during the winter months at meetings worldwide. In addition to her 16 titles, Annemarie Moser-Pröll won a record 62 individual events in the period 1970–79, and went on to win gold for the Downhill event in the 1980 Olympic Games.

Did You Know? At the Third Winter Olympics, in Lake Placid, New York, in 1932, an early thaw meant that snow had to be taken to the venue from Canada by a fleet of trucks.

TOP 10 ★
WOMEN'S WORLD AND OLYMPIC FIGURE SKATING TITLES

SKATER/COUNTRY/YEARS	TITLES
1 Sonja Henie, Norway, 1927–36	13
2= Carol Heiss, US, 1956–60	6
=Herma Planck Szabo, Austria, 1922–26	6
=Katarina Witt, E. Germany, 1984–88	6
5=Lily Kronberger, Hungary, 1908–11	4
=Sjoukje Dijkstra, Holland, 1962–64	4
=Peggy Fleming, US, 1966–68	4
8=Meray Horvath, Hungary, 1912–14	3
=Tenley Albright, US, 1953–56	3
=Michelle Kwan, US, 1996–2000	3
=Annett Poetzsch, E. Gemany, 1978–80	3
=Beatrix Schuba, Austria, 1971–72	3
=Barbara Ann Scott, Canada, 1947–48	3
=Kristi Yamaguchi, US, 1991–92	3
=Madge Syers, GB, 1906–08	3

TOP 10 ★
OLYMPIC FIGURE SKATING COUNTRIES

COUNTRY	GOLD	SILVER	BRONZE	TOTAL
1 US	12	13	14	39
2 Soviet Union*	13	10	6	29
3 Austria	7	9	4	20
4 Canada	2	7	9	18
5 Great Britain	5	3	7	15
6 France	2	2	7	11
7=Sweden	5	3	2	10
=East Germany	3	3	4	10
9 Germany#	4	4	1	9
10=Norway	3	2	1	6
=Hungary	0	2	4	6

* *Includes United Team of 1992; excludes Russia since then*

Not including West Germany or East Germany 1968–88

Figure skating was part of the Summer Olympics in 1908 and 1920, becoming part of the Winter program in 1924.

TOP 10 ★
WINTER OLYMPIC MEDAL-WINNING COUNTRIES, 1908–98

COUNTRY	GOLD	SILVER	BRONZE	TOTAL
1 Norway	83	87	69	239
2 Soviet Union*	87	63	67	217
3 US	59	59	41	159
4 Austria	39	53	53	145
5 Finland	38	49	48	135
6 Germany#	66	38	32	116
7 East Germany	39	36	35	110
8 Sweden	39	28	35	102
9 Switzerland	29	31	32	92
10 Canada	25	25	28	79

* *Includes United Team of 1992; excludes Russia since then*

Not including West or East Germany 1968–88

Only skating and ice hockey were featured in the 1908 and 1920 Summer Olympics. The first Winter Olympics was held at Chamonix, France, in 1924.

TOP 10 ★
FASTEST WINNING TIMES OF THE IDITAROD DOG SLED RACE

WINNER	YEAR	DAY	HR	MIN	SEC
1 Doug Swingley	2000	9	0	58	6
2 Doug Swingley	1995	9	2	42	19
3 Jeff King	1996	9	5	43	19
4 Jeff King	1998	9	5	52	26
5 Martin Buser	1997	9	8	30	45
6 Doug Swingley	1999	9	14	31	7
7 Martin Buser	1994	10	13	2	39
8 Jeff King	1993	10	15	38	15
9 Martin Buser	1992	10	19	17	15
10 Susan Butcher	1990	11	1	53	28

Source: *Iditarod Trail Committee*

TOP DOUG

Doug Swingley from Simms, Montana, is one of the few non-Alaskans to win the grueling 1,158-mile (1,864-km) Anchorage-to-Nome Iditarod dog sled race.

Background image: **IDITAROD DOG SLED RACE, 1999**

Sports Trivia

PARTICIPATION SPORTS, GAMES, AND PHYSICAL ACTIVITIES IN THE US

	ACTIVITY	NUMBER PARTICIPATING
1	Exercise walking	77,600,000
2	Swimming	58,200,000
3	Camping	46,500,000
4	Exercising with equipment	46,100,000
5	Fishing	43,600,000
6	Bicycle riding	43,500,000
7	Bowling	40,100,000
8	Billiards/pool	32,300,000
9	Basketball	29,400,000
10	Golf	27,500,000

* Participated more than once during the year

Source: *National Sporting Goods Association*

MOST COMMON SPORTS INJURIES

	COMMON NAME	MEDICAL TERM
1	Bruise	A soft tissue contusion
2	Sprained ankle	Sprain of the lateral ligament
3	Sprained knee	Sprain of the medial collateral ligament
4	Low back strain	Lumbar joint dysfunction
5	Hamstring tear	Muscle tear of the hamstrings
6	Jumper's knee	Patella tendinitis
7	Achilles tendinitis	Tendinitis of the Achilles tendon
8	Shin splints	Medial periostitis of the tibia
9	Tennis elbow	Lateral epicondylitis
10	Shoulder strain	Rotator cuff tendinitis

WINGS WINNER

Soviet-born Detroit Red Wings star Sergei Federov is one of the highest scoring and highest earning of all sports personalities.

SPORTING EVENTS WITH THE LARGEST TV AUDIENCES IN THE US

	EVENT	DATE	RATING
1	Super Bowl XVI	Jan 24, 1982	49.1
2	Super Bowl XVII	Jan 30, 1983	48.6
3	XVII Winter Olympics	Feb 23, 1994	48.5
4	Super Bowl XX	Jan 26, 1986	48.3
5	Super Bowl XII	Jan 15, 1978	47.2
6	Super Bowl XIII	Jan 21, 1979	47.1
7=	Super Bowl XVIII	Jan 22, 1984	46.4
=	Super Bowl XIX	Jan 20, 1985	46.4
9	Super Bowl XIV	Jan 20, 1980	46.3
10	Super Bowl XXX	Jan 28, 1996	46.0

Source: *Nielsen Media Research*

Those listed here, along with ten further Super Bowls, back to VI in 1972, are among the Top 50 networked programs of all time in the US. In this extended list, the XVII Lillehammer, Norway, Winter Olympics makes two showings, on Feb 23 and Feb 25 1994 (the latter achieving a rating of 44.2). Despite the national enthusiasm (fueled by media interest in figure skater Nancy Kerrigan, who had been physically attacked before the Games), the US finished a disappointing 5th in the overall medals table.

HIGHEST-EARNING SPORTSMEN

	SPORTSMAN*	SPORT	1999 INCOME ($)
1	Michael Shumacher, Germany	Motor racing	49,000,000
2	Tiger Woods	Golf	47,000,000
3	Oscar De La Hoya	Boxing	43,500,000
4	Michael Jordan	Basketball	40,000,000
5	Evander Holyfield	Boxing	35,500,000
6	Mike Tyson	Boxing	33,000,000
7	Shaquille O'Neal	Basketball	31,000,000
8	Lennox Lewis, UK	Boxing	29,000,000
9	Dale Earnhardt	Stock car racing	26,500,000
10	Grant Hill	Basketball	23,000,000

* From the US unless otherwise stated   Source: Forbes *magazine*

TOP 10 COLLEGE SPORTS IN THE US

(Sport/participants in NCAA sports*)

1 Football, 54,793   **2** Outdoor track, 35,308

3 Soccer, 33,191   **4** Indoor track, 29,638   **5** Basketball, 28,829

6 Baseball, 24,806   **7** Cross-country, 21,000   **8** Swimming/diving, 16,737   **9** Tennis, 15,741   **10** Softball, 13,750

* In latest year for which figures available   Source: *NCAA*

Did You Know? The Tour de France bicycle race is believed to be watched by more spectators than any other sport, with some 10 million people lining the route during the three-week event.

THE 10 ★
LATEST TRIATHLON WORLD CHAMPIONS

MAN/COUNTRY	TIME	YEAR	TIME	WOMAN/COUNTRY
Dimitry Gaag, Kazahkstan	1:45:25	**1999**	1:55:28	**Loretta Harrop**, Australia
Simon Lessing, UK	1:55:31	**1998**	2:07:25	**Joanne King**, Australia
Chris McCormack, Australia	1:48:29	**1997**	1:59:22	**Emma Carney**, Australia
Simon Lessing, UK	1:39:50	**1996**	1:50:52	**Jackie Gallagher**, Australia
Simon Lessing, UK	1:48:29	**1995**	2:04:58	**Karen Smyers**, US
Spencer Smith, UK	1:51:04	**1994**	2:03:19	**Emma Carney**, Australia
Spencer Smith, UK	1:51:20	**1993**	2:07:41	**Michellie Jones**, Australia
Simon Lessing, UK	1:49:04	**1992**	2:02:08	**Michellie Jones**, Australia
Miles Stewart, Australia	1:48:20	**1991**	2:02:04	**Joanne Ritchie**, Canada
Greg Welch, Australia	1:51:37	**1990**	2:03:33	**Karen Smyers**, US

The Triathlon World Championship has been contested since 1989 and consists of a 1-mile (1.5-km) swim, a 25-mile (40-km) bike ride, and a 6¼-mile (10-km) run.

TOP 10 ★
ALL-AROUND CHAMPION COWBOYS

	COWBOY	YEARS	WINS
1	Ty Murray	1989–98	7
2	=Tom Ferguson	1974–79	6
	=Larry Mahan	1966–73	6
4	Jim Shoulders	1949–59	5
5	=Lewis Feild	1985–87	3
	=Dean Oliver	1963–65	3
7	=Joe Beaver	1995–96	2
	=Everett Bowman	1935–37	2
	=Louis Brooks	1943–44	2
	=Clay Carr	1930–33	2
	=Bill Linderman	1950–53	2
	=Phil Lyne	1971–72	2
	=Gerald Roberts	1942–48	2
	=Casey Tibbs	1951–55	2
	=Harry Tompkins	1952–60	2

The All-Around World Champion Cowboy title is presented by the Professional Rodeo Cowboys Association (PRCA) each year. The winner is the rodeo athlete who wins the most prize money in a single year in two or more events, with minimum earnings of $2,000 per event. During the 1990s, several winners earned more than $250,000 a year.

TOP 10 ★
FASTEST WINNING TIMES FOR THE HAWAII IRONMAN

	WINNER/COUNTRY*	YEAR	TIME HR:MIN:SEC
1	Luc Van Lierde, Belgium	1996	8:04:08
2	Mark Allen	1993	8:07:45
3	Mark Allen	1992	8:09:08
4	Mark Allen	1989	8:09:16
5	Luc Van Lierde	1999	8:17:17
6	Mark Allen	1991	8:18:32
7	Greg Welch, Australia	1994	8:20:27
8	Mark Allen	1995	8:20:34
9	Peter Reid, Canada	1998	8:24:20
10	Mark Allen	1990	8:28:17

From the US unless otherwise stated

In perhaps one of the most grueling sporting contests, competitors engage in a 2½-mile (3.86-km) swim, a 112-mile (180-km) cycle race, and a 26¼-mile (42.195-km) run.

DANGER BELOW

The risk of injury or becoming trapped underground has resulted in spelunking being ranked among the world's most hazardous sports.

TOP 10 ★
MOST DANGEROUS AMATEUR SPORTS

	SPORT	RISK FACTOR*
1	Powerboat racing	15
2	Ocean yacht racing	10
3	Cave diving	7
4	Spelunking	6
5	=Drag racing	5
	=Karting	5
7	Microlyte	4
8	=Hang gliding	3
	=Motor racing	3
	=Mountaineering	3

Risk factor refers to the premium that insurance companies place on insuring someone for that activity – the higher the risk factor, the higher the premium

Source: *General Accident*

Index

Acknowledgments

Special US research:
Dafydd Rees

UK research assistants: Harriet Hart, Lucy Hemming

Thanks to the individuals, organizations, and publications listed below who kindly supplied information to enable me to prepare many of the lists.

Caroline Ash, Mark Atterton, John Bardsley, Richard Braddish, Lesley Coldham, Pete Compton, Stanley Coren, Luke Crampton, François Curiel, Sidney S. Culbert, Bonnie Fantasia, Christopher Forbes, Professor Ken Fox, Darryl Francis, Simon Gilbert, Russell E. Gough, Monica Grady, Stan Greenberg, Duncan Hislop, Andreas Hoerstemeier, Tony Hutson, Alan Jeffreys, Robert Lamb, Dr. Jaquie Lavin, Dr. Benjamin Lucas, John Malam, Ian Morrison, Vincent Nasso, Christiaan Rees, Linda Rees, Adrian Room, Bill Rudman, Joanne Schioppi, Robert Senior, Lisa E. Smith, Mitchell Symons, Tony Waltham, Professor Edward O. Wilson

Academy of Motion Picture Arts and Sciences, *Advertising Age,* American Athletic Association, American Film Institute, American Forestry Association, American Kennel Club, American Library Association, American Music Conference, American Pet Classics, American Theater Wing, *Amusement Business, Art Newspaper,* Art Institute of Chicago, Art Sales Index, Associated Press, Association of Tennis Professionals (ATP), Audit Bureau of Circulations, Beverage Marketing Corporation, *Billboard,* Boston Athletics Association, BPI, *BP Statistical Review of World Energy,* Breeders Cup, British Cave Research Association, British Columbia Vital Statistics Agency, British Library, Bureau of Federal Prisons, Bureau of Justice Statistics, Cannes Film Festival, Carbon Dioxide Information Analysis Center, Cat Fancier's Association, Center for Disease Control, Central Intelligence Agency, Central Statistics Office/An Príomh-Oifig Staidrimh, Ireland, Champagne Bureau, Championship Auto Racing Teams (CART), Channel Swimming Association, Christian Research, Christie's, *Classical Music,* Coca-Cola, Columbia University/ Pulitzer Prizes, Computer Industry Almanac, Inc., Country Music Association, *Crime in the United States, Criminal Statistics England & Wales,* Dateline International, Death Penalty Information Center, De Beers, Duncan's

American Radio, *Economist, Editor & Publisher Year Book,* Electoral Reform Society, Energy Information Administration, Environmental Protection Agency, Euromonitor, *FBI Uniform Crime Reports,* Feste Catalogue Index Database/ Alan Somerset, *Financial Times,* Fine Arts Museum, Boston, *Flight International,* Food and Agriculture Organization of the United Nations, Food Marketing Institute, *Forbes, Fortune,* Gemstone Publishing, Inc., General Accident, Generation AB, Gold Fields Mineral Services Ltd., H. J. Heinz, Hollywood Foreign Press Association (Golden Globe Awards), Home Office, UK, Indianapolis Motor Speedway, Iditarod Trail Committee, Interbrand, International Associatiion of Ports and Harbors, International Atomic Energy Agency, International Civil Aviation Organization, International Cocoa Organization, International Coffee Organization, International Commission on Large Dams, International Dairy Foods Association, International Game Fish Association, International Union for the Conservation of Nature, Inter-Parliamentary Union, Interpol, Jockey Club, Kellogg's, Korbel Champagne Cellars, League of American Theaters and Producers, Lloyds Register of Shipping/ MIPG/PPMS, Magazine Publishers of America, Major League Baseball, Mansell Color Company Inc., Mars, Inc., Meat and Livestock Commission, Metropolitan Opera House, New York, Modern Language Association of America, MRIB, M Street, MTV, NASA, National Academy of Recording Arts and Sciences (NARAS), National Academy of Television Arts and Sciences (Emmy Awards), National Ambulatory Medical Care Survey, National Association of Broadcasters, National Association of Stock Car Auto Racing, Inc (NASCAR), National Basketball Association (NBA), National Center for Health Statistics, National Climatic Data Center, National Collegiate Athletic Association (NCAA), National Dairy Council, National Fire Protection Association, National Football League (NFL), National Highway Traffic Safety Administration, National Hockey League (NHL), National Hockey League Players Association, National Hurricane Center, National Public Radio, National Safety Council, National Sporting Goods Association, National Steeplechase Association, National Thoroughbred Racing Association, National Trotting Association, New South Wales Registry of Births, Deaths and Marriages, New York City Transit Authority, New York Road Runners Club, Niagara Falls Museum,

ACNielsen MMS, Nielsen Media Research, Nobel Foundation, *NonProfit Times,* NOP, Northern Ireland Statistics and Research Agency, NPD TRSTS, Toy Tracking Service, Nua Ltd., Office for National Statistics, UK, Peabody Awards, PC Data Online, Pet Industry Joint Advisory Council, Phillips Group, Phobics Society, Popular Music Database, Produktschap voor Gedistilleerde Dranken, Professional Rodeo Cowboys Association (PRCA), Project Feeder Watch/Cornell Lab of Ornithology, Public Broadcasting System (PBS), *Publishers' Weekly, Raceboat International, Railway Gazette International,* Recording Industry Association of America (RIAA), Rock 'n' Roll Hall of Fame, Royal Aeronautical Society, *Screen Digest,* Shakespeare Birthplace Trust, Siemens AG, *Slimming World,* Songwriters Hall of Fame, Sotheby's, *Spaceflight, Sporting News, Sports Illustrated, Statistical Abstract of the United States,* Statistics Norway, STATS Inc., *Steeplechase Times,* Stockholm International Peace Research Institute, *Time,* Tourism Industries, International Trade Administration, Ty Inc., UNESCO, United Nations, Universal Postal Union, US Board on Geographic Names, US Bureau of Labor Statistics, US Bureau of Engraving and Printing, US Bureau of the Census, US Consumer Product Safety Commission, US Department of Agriculture/ Economic Research Service, US Department of Justice, US Department of the Interior, US Fish and Wildlife Service, US Geological Survey, US Mint, US Patent Office, US Social Security Administration, *Variety,* VideoScan, Inc., *Video Store,* Ward's Automotive, Whitbread Literary Awards, Women's National Basketball Association (WNBA), World Association of Newspapers, World Bank, World Health Organization, World Meteorological Organization, World Resources Institute, World Science Fiction Society, World Tourism Organization, Zenith International

Index
Patrica Coward

DK Picture Librarians
Denise O'Brien, Melanie Simmonds

Packager's acknowledgments:
Cooling Brown would like to thank the following: Pauline Clarke for design assistance; Peter Cooling for technical support; Carolyn MacKenzie for proof reading; Chris and Eleanor Bolus for the loan of the Beanie Babies.